What UNIONS No Longer Do

What UNIONS No Longer Do

Jake Rosenfeld

Harvard University Press

Cambridge, Massachusetts
London, England
2014

Printed in the United States of America

Library of Congress Cataloging-in-Publication Data

Rosenfeld, Jake, 1978–
What unions no longer do / Jake Rosenfeld. — First Edition.
pages cm
Includes bibliographical references and index.
ISBN 978-0-674-72511-9
1. Labor movement—United States. 2. Income distribution—United States.
3. Labor unions—Political activity—United States.
4. Minorities—United States—Social conditions. I. Title.
HD8072.5.R67 2014
331.880973—dc23
2013021124

For Frances Hoffmann

Her courage and dignity are a daily inspiration,
and her generous efforts shaped this book.

Contents

Introduction

Today the only thing big about "Big Labor" is its problems. By the early 1970s, organized labor had already begun its decades-long decline, but still nearly a quarter of all private-sector employees belonged to a union. The late 1970s and 1980s proved especially brutal for Big Labor, with unionization rates halving during the period. The nation's journalists and intellectuals covered this phenomenon extensively, linking union decline to the transition to a postindustrial economy increasingly open to global trade. Recent trends have garnered less press attention, yet private-sector unionization rates nearly halved again between 1990 and 2009, settling firmly in the single digits.[1] The country's unionization rate is lower than at any point since the early decades of the twentieth century. And the contemporary American labor movement stands alone in its smallness. As labor activist Richard Yeselson recently recounted, "There has never been an advanced capitalist country with as weakened and small a union movement as today's United States."[2]

But back during its post-World War II peak, Big Labor was positively enormous. Over a third of the non-agricultural workforce belonged to a labor union during the mid-1940s through the 1950s, and millions more Americans resided in households reliant on a union wage. During the heyday of collective bargaining in this country, unions helped pattern pay and benefit packages among union *and* nonunion workers, as employers often matched union contracts to forestall organizing drives and maintain a competitive workforce. Politicians—Democrats especially—depended on organized labor's support during elections, and consulted closely with labor leaders when devising policy in office. As President Richard Nixon once put it, "No program works without Labor cooperation."[3]

The importance of Big Labor to the polity and economy in the mid-twentieth century helped launch a rich and extensive literature investigating the *causes* of labor's decline. No comparable effort exists to explain the broad *consequences* of labor's loss in the United States. This book fills that gap. Three interlocking arguments underlie the empirical chapters. First, the collapse of the labor movement in the United States isn't simply a story of one hidebound institution unable to weather the storms convulsing capitalist development in the second half of the twentieth century. There is something to that narrative. But organized labor wasn't simply a minor bit player in the "golden age" of welfare capitalism in the United States. It was *the* core equalizing institution.

During the prosperous decades of the mid-twentieth century, the tripartite arrangement of a robust labor movement, an active state, and large employers helped shape the earnings distribution of the nation's fast-growing economy. Simultaneously, unions' political power helped elect lawmakers beholden to the labor movement for financial and organizational support. Unions leveraged this economic and political influence to counterbalance corporate interests at the bargaining table, while acting as a powerful normative voice for the welfare of non-elites. As a result, for decades productivity increases led to rising economic fortunes for the vast middle of the income distribution. The collapse of organized labor dismantled this governing arrangement, and with it the tight coupling of economic growth with the economic fortunes of average American workers. In recent decades, government has retreated, content to leave wage determination to employers and to a labor movement that has been devastated. As I demonstrate throughout the book, the ramifications of this institutional shift for American workers are much broader and transformative than have previously been known.

The scope of the problem for labor today is on display in Figure I.1. Union decline in the United States is entirely a private-sector phenomenon. The series in the figure begins in 1973, as do many of the analyses in the book, because that is when the Current Population Survey—a major data resource for research on organized labor—began asking

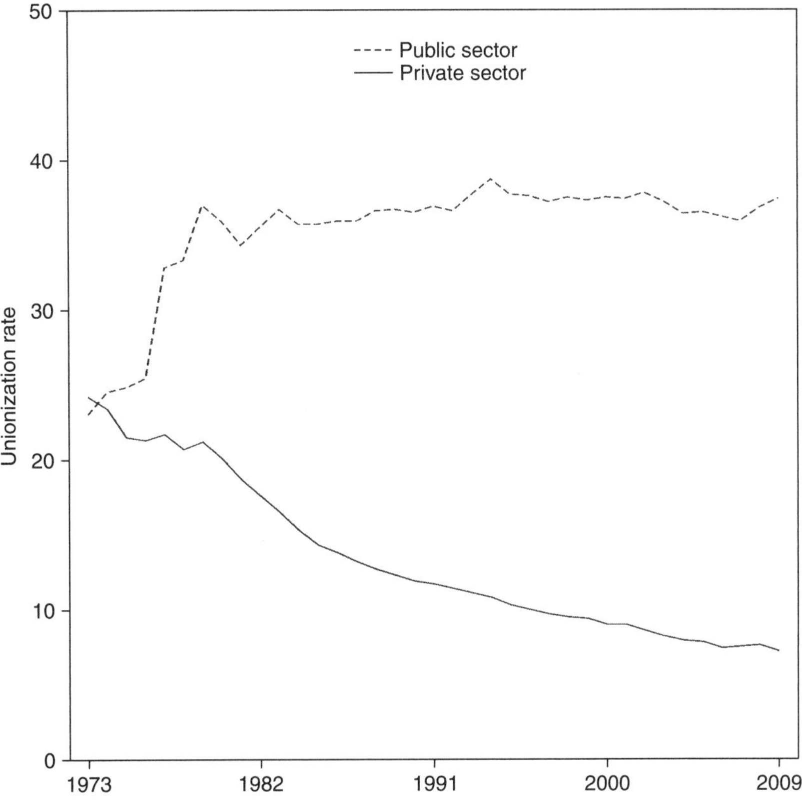

Figure I.1. Unionization rates in the United States, 1973–2009. *Note:* Sample restricted to employed wage and salary workers, ages sixteen and over. *Source:* Hirsch and Macpherson's Unionstats database, based on the CPS-May and CPS-MORG files. See www.unionstats.com.

survey respondents whether or not they belong to a labor union. As noted above, private-sector union membership in this country peaked in the 1940s and 1950s, and thus this picture begins after organized labor had already begun its long decline.[4] By the early years of the 1970s, the fraction of the private sector belonging to a union had fallen below a fourth. The decline gained speed throughout the 1970s and 1980s and continues to this day. Between 1973 and 2009, the private-sector organization rate fell by over two-thirds, down to just 7 percent.

After a burst of organizing activity in the 1970s, the portion of the public sector belonging to a union settled at just over a third, where it currently remains. As I establish in Chapter 2, organized labor's collapse in the private sector has shifted much of the power and remaining resources of the labor movement to public-sector unions and their members, given robust organization rates among governmental employees. Yet compared to their private-sector counterparts, public-sector unions' influence on pay and key benefits such as pensions is constrained. And given the higher education and income levels of public-sector workers, a labor movement dominated by governmental employees further erodes unions' equalizing effect.

Thus organized labor has nearly disappeared in the very sector where it once had the greatest impact on workers' livelihoods. Part of this impact rested on the frequent deployment of labor's most powerful weapon in its once-formidable arsenal: the strike. Once upon a time, union members struck, and struck often. As Yeselson maintained, while millions of Americans "supported these strikes, millions despised them—but nobody could ignore them."[5] And among those who had to pay attention to the labor movement's power to disrupt commerce were the nation's business and political leaders, who were often eager to avoid confrontation during contract negotiations or when devising domestic policy. As I show in Chapter 3, strikes hardly occur anymore, and the ones that do rarely result in a victory for workers.

The decline of the strike, along with steady membership losses, reduces the effectiveness of existing unions in narrowing economic inequality and raising wages for the entire private sector, as I show in Chapter 4. While those segments of the private-sector workforce that remain organized continue to have comparatively high wages, these segments are now so few and far between that labor's ability to prevent widespread wage stagnation among men and inequality among men and women has virtually disappeared. Private-sector unions' role today consists largely of forestalling wage declines among organized workers only. It wasn't always so. For decades, unions helped bond productivity levels with average wages for both union *and* nonunion workers. That connection has been severed.

Being the core equalizing institution certainly doesn't mean that all labor unions throughout the twentieth century stood strong against the inequities many American workers faced in their daily lives. Racist and sexist treatment was ubiquitous throughout organized labor through the middle of the century. Union connections to organized crime were legion in certain industries. And many locals to this day remain stubbornly wed to their role as protectors of a fast-eroding model of labor relations often incompatible with the realities many employers face in an increasingly dynamic and open economy. These and other critiques of the American labor movement have received prominent attention in the nation's press and among academics.[6] But all the focus on labor's flaws can distract us from the bigger picture. On the whole, for generations now the labor movement has stood as the most prominent and effective voice for economic justice in the United States. It used this voice to shape cultural understandings of what is considered fair in the workplace, to move policy in directions more hospitable to the needs of average workers, and its bargaining clout to deliver tangible rewards to nonmanagerial, nonsupervisory employees.

And being the core equalizing institution does not simply mean that organized labor's reach was wide, although it was, or that its effects on a range of economic, political, and cultural outcomes were substantial, although they surely were. Stereotypical images of union members include the burly white male Teamster clocking out early for a full day's pay. More recently, we hear of cosseted public-sector employees such as teachers jealously guarding their tenure protections and free summers. But as I demonstrate throughout the second half of the book, unions' equalizing effect was strongest for society's most vulnerable and historically disadvantaged workers, and today unions have nearly disappeared within the sector and among the subgroups where they once had their strongest impact. That is the second argument I advance: Stereotypical images of unions notwithstanding, for decades the labor movement was vital in supporting the economic and civic advancement of historically disadvantaged populations. The near disappearance of labor unions in the private sector, especially within manufacturing industries and transportation and construction, is felt most acutely by those workers already facing a number of challenges navigating these turbulent economic times.

Take African Americans. Among women, after almost closing by 1980, the gap between blacks' and whites' private-sector wages nearly tripled during the 1980s and 1990s. Existing research on the topic has identified higher levels of employment instability among African Americans and lower economic payoffs from education as possible explanations for the phenomenon. But a sizable portion of the gap remains unexplained. Largely overlooked in existing accounts of the decline and subsequent rise in female racial inequality is differential access to pay-setting institutions, chief among them labor unions. Soul singer Joe Tex crooned back in 1969 that "A woman's hands just weren't made to work hard all the time."[7] He would be disappointed to witness women, African Americans especially, rushing into the labor market—and into labor unions—throughout the 1970s.[8] And these women were not simply entering white-collar public-sector jobs. They also flooded into traditionally male manual labor occupations and organized in blue-collar unions. But their timing coincided with the convergence of potent political, economic, and institutional forces buffeting private-sector unions, precipitating the dramatic decline in membership rates displayed previously. As I explore in Chapter 5, African American overrepresentation in a fast-crumbling institution contributed greatly both to black-white economic inequality among women, and to stagnating wage levels among black men.

Or take the economic incorporation of immigrants and their offspring. Many debates in immigration research today focus on how patterns of economic incorporation of contemporary migrants and their offspring—especially those migrants from Mexico and the rest of Latin America—mirror or diverge from those of the European immigrant populations of generations past. The successful economic incorporation of Italians, Poles, Russians, and others rested on a context of reception here in the United States that included a rapidly growing labor movement. Indeed, some of this rapid growth was due to the energies and organizational capacities of European migrants. The labor movement provided millions of low-skill immigrants and their children with jobs that paid comparatively well, thus helping to propel whole populations into the expanding middle class by mid-century.

The context of reception has changed dramatically since that period. One of the major transformations has been the near disappearance of private-sector unions. As I argue in Chapter 6, what this means is that low-skill newcomers today face a labor market lacking the once-common pathway upward, with a result being a "segmented" assimilation pattern in which many well-educated immigrants and their offspring move up the class ladder, while less-educated populations languish in jobs providing low pay and little opportunity for advancement.

Or take Americans without a college education. In the contemporary political landscape, a rare issue that both sides of the ideological divide agree on is the importance of higher education for combating inequality. The chairman of the Federal Reserve, Ben Bernanke, recently remarked that rising inequality was "creating two societies. And it's based very much . . . on educational differences,"[9] a statement that would find agreement among Republicans and Democrats alike, including President Barack Obama. Often overlooked in these discussions about the growing importance of higher education is the role unions once played in supporting Americans without college experience. Unions supported them economically, by boosting non-college-educated workers' pay. But unions supported them politically as well, by providing them with resources and training to engage in politics, and translating their political activity into support for policies that benefited average workers. As I investigate in Chapter 7, the political consequences of massive deunionization include widening gaps in civic participation. And here too the sectoral shift in organized labor has reshaped the relationship between the labor movement and average workers—especially workers without a college education. Political participation rises with education. Public-sector workers, on average, have higher schooling levels than workers in the private sector. As I demonstrate, unions' abilities to influence their members to vote are much more potent in the private sector, especially among workers without a college education. Here again we see that unions are vanishing in exactly the sector and among the subgroups where they once served as a powerful equalizing force—in both the economy and the polity.

> We like driving the car and we're not going to give the steering wheel to anyone but us.
>
> —Former Walmart CEO H. Lee Scott[10]

Third, and finally, this is a story about power. The ability to get one's way even in the face of opposition—that is the essence of power, as the sociologist Max Weber defined it generations ago.[11] The concluding argument of the book is that the collapse of private-sector unions results in a profound power shift throughout American workplaces. Walmart is now the largest private-sector employer in the country, a company whose reach extends into numerous industries across every state in the nation. And as Walmart's ex-CEO made clear, major employers today enjoy the power they have gained, and they do not intend to give any of it back.

The strike is labor's most visible and dramatic exercise in power. Shutting down production in the face of employer opposition in order to leverage its position at the bargaining table is the essence of a strike. Through striking, unions historically increased their members' share of economic rewards while instilling fear in employers about the consequences of crossing unions in the future. As mentioned, unions rarely strike nowadays, and the few strikes that occur usually signal little more than labor's desperation.

But the pacification of the labor movement through the breaking of the strike represents just one avenue through which power has shifted to the employer in contemporary American labor relations. All the upcoming chapters touch on the various ways in which labor unions have receded from American workers' livelihoods, leaving workers increasingly exposed to the vagaries of the market. This exposure benefits certain types of workers, especially the highly skilled, whose relative scarceness provides them with negotiating power over their employers. It hurts others, especially the less-educated working in occupations facing severe competition in our increasingly open and dynamic economy.

The book is organized as follows: In Chapter 1 I provide synopses of the dominant set of explanations for deunionization in the United States, and end the chapter with a discussion of what I feel to be the most compelling factors that account for the collapse of private-sector unions in this country. This overview of the causes of deunionization helps provide the context to understand the consequences of union decline. The empirical chapters—Chapters 2–7—are divided into two parts. Chapters 2–4 advance the first argument of the book by focusing on the consequences of union decline for broad segments of the labor force, including public- and private-sector union members (Chapters 2 and 3), as well as the vast majority of the private sector that is no longer organized in unions (Chapter 4). Many of the issues covered in the first part of the book—strikes, wages, and growing inequality—will be familiar to many readers, but the findings won't be. Chapters 5–7 advance the second argument by zeroing in on some of the country's most vulnerable workers: racial and ethnic minorities (Chapters 5 and 6) and Americans who lack a college education (Chapter 7). I conclude the book in Chapter 8 by discussing the major implications for average Americans who now toil in a largely unorganized economy in which their employers have amassed exceptional power to define nearly everything about their working lives.

1

The Collapse of Organized Labor in the United States

> Why should we worry about organizing groups of people who do not appear to want to be organized? I used to worry about . . . the size of the membership. But quite a few years ago I stopped worrying about it, because to me it doesn't make any difference.
>
> —Former AFL-CIO president George Meany[1]

Speaking in 1972, the long-standing leader of the American Federation of Labor and Congress of Industrial Organizations (AFL-CIO) couldn't see what was right around the corner for his organization. The "size of the membership" shrank at an accelerating pace throughout the 1970s and 1980s. And what Meany said mattered. Even late into his nearly three-decade reign, a rival labor leader admitted, "Meany is the boss . . . he has achieved centralization of authority," a feat previous labor leaders failed to accomplish.[2] Meany's opinion of and attitude toward organizing set the tone for much of the labor movement. This complacency about organizing exemplified the postwar era of "business unionism" in the United States. During this period, many unions grew into enormous bureaucracies, overseeing millions of members, millions of dollars, and large staffs charged with handling workplace matters. The organizing arms of these unions, meanwhile, "tended to enter a state of atrophy," according to the sociologists Rick Fantasia and Kim Voss.[3] At the same time, battles over collective bargaining became routinized and scripted, sapping much of the grassroots militancy that had characterized earlier upsurges in unionization. Instead, members began to view their union as a service provider: In exchange for a fee (or dues), the union delivered certain predictable benefits. Lost in the transformation was the sense of rank-and-file ownership of the union—and with it the capacity for collective mobilization that could reenergize labor's organizing muscles, or fend off employer onslaughts on existing unions.

In recent years many labor scholars suggested that organized labor's transformation from a broad-based social movement to a narrow service provider was a primary factor explaining unions' present malaise.[4] This perspective argued that during the decades spent contentedly servicing existing memberships, many unions lost touch with their rank and file, and were caught unawares by brewing economic transformations and growing employer backlash. Much of this work is dedicated to identifying the organizing blueprints that have proven successful in the contemporary antiunion climate—blueprints that had nearly disappeared during the 1970s and 1980s.[5] And indeed, those unions that have embraced the repertoire of tactics and strategies encompassing "social movement unionism" have scored some remarkable victories of late, including the widely-heralded "Justice for Janitors" campaign devised by the Service Employees International Union (SEIU). From this perspective, then, organized labor's decline in the United States was due in no small part to organized labor itself.

Two countervailing arguments call this conclusion into question: the relative failure of recent unionization drives to reverse membership declines, and parallel unionization trends in other major industrialized nations. First, even the most innovative and energetic unions in the United States have learned that organizing in the present economic and institutional environment is exceedingly difficult. These unions have learned the lesson through bitter experience. It is not only labor scholars who have argued that unions' current predicament stems from labor's own complacency; after all, many labor leaders also rallied around this view. Over the past two decades schisms have roiled the labor movement, including the 1995 leadership transition within the AFL-CIO and the 2005 split between the AFL-CIO and the newly formed Change to Win coalition of unions. Frustration with a lack of organizing played a major role in both developments. During the early 1990s many unions saw the AFL-CIO, then headed by Lane Kirkland, as unresponsive to the urgent needs of the movement and complacent in the face of the economic and political challenges facing American workers. John Sweeney emerged as the consensus candidate of the insurgents and assumed the presidency of the federation in 1995, promising to inject new energy into the movement in part by redoubling organizing efforts. Just ten years later, unions such as SEIU had grown frustrated with Sweeney's lack of progress and broke off to form the rival Change to Win federation—once again promising to focus heavily on organizing. But neither the leadership transition at the AFL-CIO nor the new competition between Change to Win and the AFL-CIO has stemmed membership losses.

Second, for those who emphasize lethargic (or nonexistent) organizing as the primary cause of labor's woes in the United States, a complicating factor is the international picture. Falling membership rates are by no means a distinctively American phenomenon. Indeed, in some countries unions underwent steeper declines than in the United States. Figure 1.1 displays unionization trends for eight advanced industrial democracies from 1973 to the present. All these countries—dissimilar in so many other ways—experienced at least some union membership erosion. The exact timing and pattern of the declines differ, with countries like the United States and France experiencing steady, linear losses throughout the years covered, while other countries like Sweden show a more curvilinear pattern, peaking in the middle of the series before declining again during the early years of the twenty-first century. The sizes of the membership losses vary as well. Canada's unionization rate in 2009 stood 21 percent lower than its peak in the early 1980s, a minor drop-off compared to other nations. Between 1973 and 2009, unionization rates in the United States halved. In Australia, membership peaked in 1976, when unions had successfully organized over half the workforce. By 2009, union rolls had fallen by 60 percent relative to their highest level. In France, they fell by more than two-thirds.[6]

Now it could be that labor unions in all these countries, to one degree or another, simply lost their organizing initiative over the period covered by the figure. Some variant of "business unionism" may have existed beyond the U.S. border, draining other labor movements' energy, creativity, and drive to reach out and organize new members. And perhaps unions in those countries that were able to limit losses,

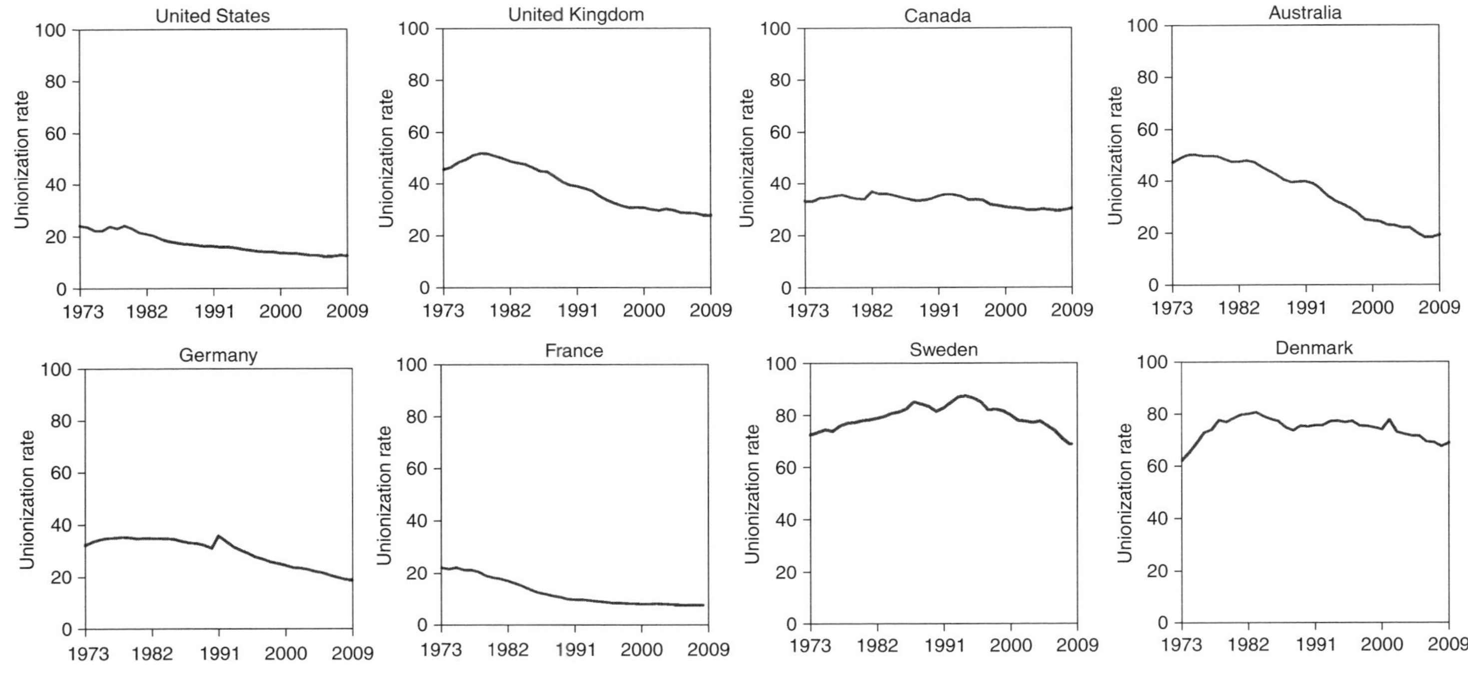

Figure 1.1. Unionization rates by country, 1973–2009. *Note:* Samples restricted to employed wage and salary earners. *Source:* Visser 2009.

like in Canada, remained more attentive to organizing in the postindustrial period. There certainly may be some merit to that argument. But a more comprehensive explanation of union decline likely lies outside of the relative zeal with which contemporary unions are seeking to expand their memberships.

Public Approval

Organizing is impossible if there is no demand for unionization. Declining popularity rates constitute another potential explanation for labor's collapse. Gallup has surveyed Americans on their opinion of organized labor for seventy-five years. In 2009, for the first time ever, union approval rates fell below 50 percent—although they rebounded slightly in more recent years. Disapproval rates, meanwhile, doubled from their low point in the 1950s. Could it be that "resentment has replaced solidarity," as the *New Yorker*'s financial writer James Surowiecki recently asked?[7] And could this growing resentment by many Americans help explain labor's contemporary plight?

In a word, no. Unions in the United States are not now nor have they ever been all that unpopular. Figure 1.2 charts trends in unionization as well as responses to the Gallup poll question asking Americans whether they "approve or disapprove of labor unions." As shown, union disapproval rates in the United States never reach 50 percent. Approval rates have declined in recent years, and they remain well below their 1953 peak of 75 percent. Yet despite 2009's dip, today a majority of the American public approves of unions.

It is important to highlight the unionization trend during these years. From the mid-1950s onward, organization rates fell, and with them the fraction of the Gallup samples who were union members. Assuming these samples were roughly representative of the U.S. workforce, the portion of interviewees who belonged to a labor union declined by about two-thirds between 1953 and 2011. We know that union members approve of unions by overwhelming majorities—upward of 90 percent.[8] The fact that union approval has not fallen further speaks to unions' popularity among unorganized Americans. A recent poll of nonmanagerial, nonunion workers found that over half would vote for a union if given the opportunity.[9] The fraction of the U.S. workforce that is nonunion and desires union representation is

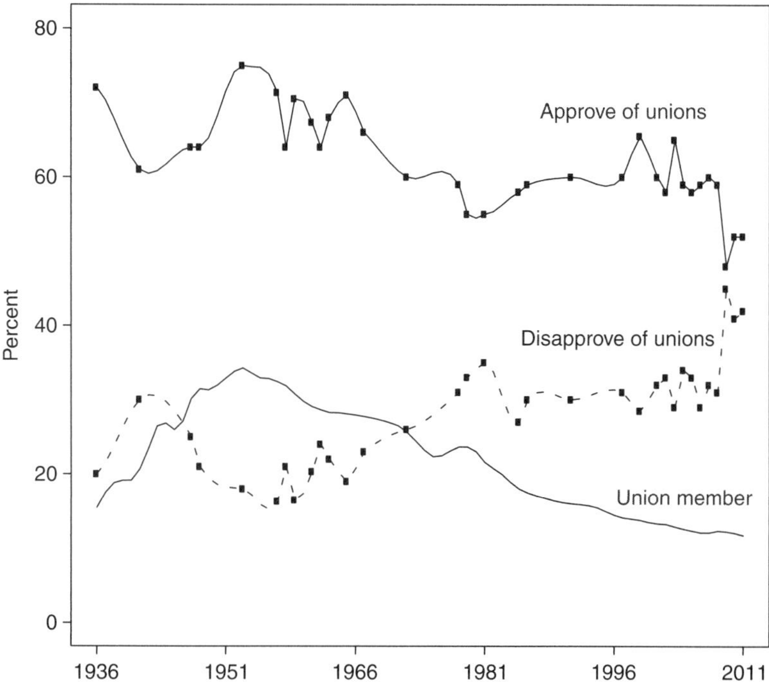

Figure 1.2. Union approval and unionization rates, 1936–2011. *Notes:* Gallup data are not available for all years. Approval and disapproval trend lines are two-period moving averages. For years with more than one Gallup survey, estimates represent the average rating for the year. Unionization rates for 1948–2011 are for all wage and salary workers; for 1936–1947, unionization rates are for all employed workers. *Source:* Approval and disapproval ratings are from Gallup. Unionization data for 1973–2011 are from Hirsch and Macpherson's Unionstats database, based on the CPS-May and CPS-MORG files. See www.unionstats.com. Unionization rates before 1973 are from Mayer (2004) and are based on data from the Bureau of Labor Statistics.

higher in the United States than in peer nations such as Canada, Britain, and Australia.[10] If the unionization rate in the United States was simply a function of unfilled demand for unions, then the rate would stand at roughly 50 percent.[11]

The relationship between approval of unions and the overall unionization rate is weak not just in the United States, it is also weak in Europe. Figure 1.3 plots the fraction of the population that supports unions and the overall unionization rate for twenty European nations in 2002. As shown, there is little correlation between approval and organization rates.

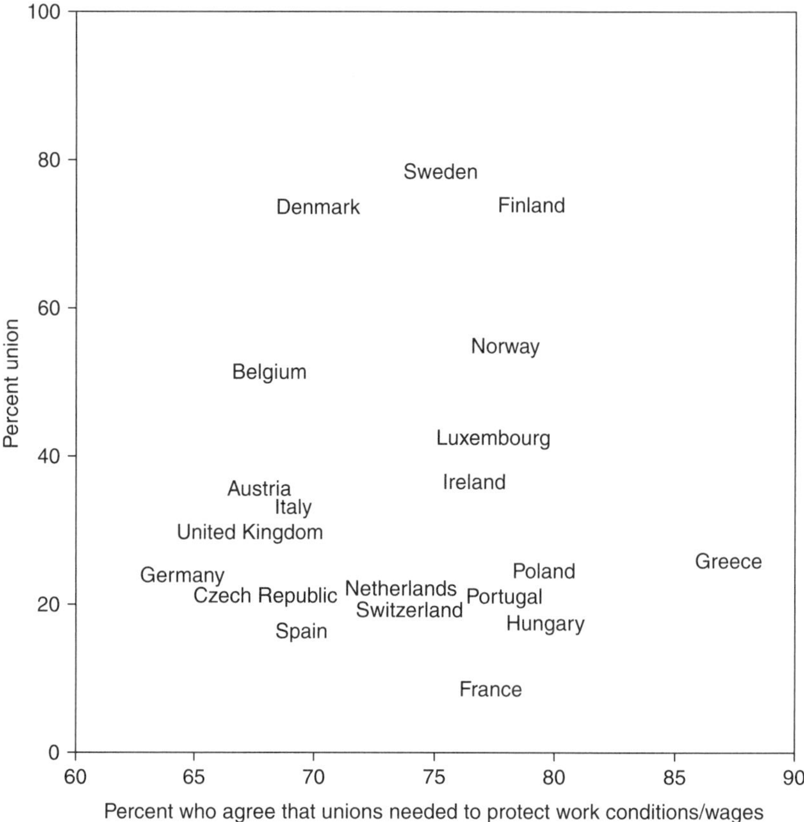

Figure 1.3. Union approval and unionization rates in Europe, 2002. *Source:* Union opinion data come from the European Social Survey (percent agree or strongly agree). Unionization rates are from the Organisation for Economic Co-operation and Development.

In the recent state skirmishes over collective bargaining rights of public employees, polls consistently found that one group in particular supports greater restrictions on public-sector unions: Republicans.[12] Republican—and conservative—disapproval of unions extends beyond the public sector. In recent years, the partisan gap in union approval has exceeded 50 percentage points. In 2011, for example, only a quarter of Republicans expressed support for organized labor, versus nearly 80 percent of Democrats.[13] Why do right-wing Americans oppose unions? Similar to many American employers (and there is substantial overlap between the groups), conservatives often believe unions interfere with the workings of the free market, and therefore are bad for the economy. For others, the very notion of a union challenges the values of individualism and self-reliance.

This conservative disapproval of labor unions is not new. The *Wall Street Journal*'s editorial page has long reflected the perspectives of economic conservatives in the United States. And its decidedly antiunion slant extends back over half a century. Typical editorials include "Stooges Unwanted" (1951), about union influence in politics, "Hoodwinking Consumers" (1974), about the costs of unionization to customers, and "American Federation of Lemmings" (1983), about the AFL-CIO's policy prescriptions.

Employers' opposition to organized labor also has a long lineage, although a unified business stance against labor took some time to coalesce. The historian Elizabeth Fones-Wolf, for example, suggests that division within the business community existed during the early decades of the twentieth century, with some employers not adamantly opposed to the nation's fast-growing labor unions.[14] The political scientist Peter Swenson echoes Fones-Wolf's contention that certain employers did not initially resist labor, even showing that in various sectors "employer organizations welcomed well-organized unions" who helped prevent competitors from undercutting existing businesses.[15] However, by the late 1930s, "a partial mobilization" by the business community began to oppose pro-union policies.[16] The National Association of Manufacturers, for example, lobbied furiously against the National Labor Relations Act (NLRA), the 1935 law that enshrined collective bargaining rights in the country. Labor historian Nelson Lichtenstein describes the 1940s and 1950s as decades marked by "corporate inspired ideological warfare" against organized labor.[17]

In sum, the relationship between public approval and unionization rates is weak in the United States and abroad. If it were not, the nation's unionization rate would be four times its current size. It is certainly the case that conservative Americans—especially those most concerned with corporate interests—largely oppose unions. This opposition has been with us for some time; according to labor activist Richard Yeselson, "there is no more consistent trope of conservative ideology stretching back over a century than a nearly pathological hatred of unions."[18] What has changed, then? In part, the ability of employers to accomplish their long-standing antiunion agenda. This ability has three core antecedents: one, economic changes; two, the interaction between those economic developments and collective bargaining institutions; and three, political developments, which helped reinforce the employers' agenda.

Economics

Paramount among the major economic transformations occurring over the past decades was the global recession of the late 1970s and early 1980s, and the increasing openness of previously protected industries to competition at home and abroad. In the United States, stagnant growth combined with rising prices motivated the Federal Reserve to sharply increase borrowing costs, sparking unemployment. Unemployment lowered workers' bargaining leverage, as employers could substitute labor more easily, and could weather reduced output during strikes or other industrial actions when demand for their products was low. For workers, the stakes of involvement in a unionization effort during a slack labor market were high: Employer retaliation might land the pro-union worker at the back of the hiring queue.

In the United States, the tough economic climate coincided with the deregulation of previously protected industries, such as trucking and telecommunications, and the rising threat of overseas competition, most notably from Japan and other fast-rising Asian economies. Growing competition from within and abroad raised the costs of unionization for many U.S. firms. Some of these companies responded by mounting a concerted and disciplined attack on unions that would prove incredibly effective (more on that below). Others, meanwhile, found themselves less profitable than their peers, and less able to adapt to rapidly changing economic conditions.[19] And the opening of previously protected industries helped shift employment patterns in the United States—also to the detriment of the labor movement. Union penetration in the United States and other countries was concentrated in core manufacturing industries, along with transportation, telecommunications, and construction. Growing competition in these industries had two major effects on their heavily unionized workforces in the United States. First, they spurred labor-saving technological innovations, reducing employment levels at surviving firms, and second, they forced the closure of thousands of firms unable to compete in the new terrain. Take Cleveland, once a manufacturing redoubt and once one of the ten most populous cities in the nation. Cleveland's population at the middle of the twentieth century stood at over nine hundred thousand. By 2010, it had more than halved, to under four hundred thousand. Thousands upon thousands of union jobs disappeared with the city's shrinkage.

As the traditional labor strongholds hemorrhaged employment, job growth shifted to service and high-tech industries, sectors that unions had little experience in organizing. It also shifted south, to a region where unions had been largely unsuccessful in organizing. Given the differential growth rates between the union and nonunion sectors, even an enormous organizing push within existing union strongholds was unlikely to arrest membership losses—employment gains outside of unionized industries were just too high. And absent a radical recalculation of the costs of unionization by employers in the nonunion sectors, it was unlikely that organization alone could reverse labor's fortunes. As economist Henry Farber and sociologist Bruce Western concluded in their investigation of the causes of labor decline, "The quantity of organizing activity required to make a substantial difference in the steady-state unionization rate is simply staggering."[20]

Institutions

Collective bargaining institutions filter the effects of economic transformations. As the economist John Godard has argued, "Market pressures are inexorable only to the extent that the broader institutional environment fosters them."[21] Given vast differences in the ways in which labor movements are institutionalized throughout the developed world, this filtering process has weakened organized labor in certain institutional contexts such as in the United States, while leaving membership rates robust in others. Two institutional designs seem most relevant to this discussion: the degree of centralization, and union control of unemployment insurance systems. The centralization of collective bargaining institutions varies widely across the industrialized democracies. In some nations, such as Norway, wage bargaining occurs at the national level, involving representatives from government and from labor and employer federations. In other countries, bargaining is decentralized to the industry level, where wage agreements are decided between representatives of, say, transportation unions, alongside representatives from major transportation companies. In the United States and countries such as Great Britain with similar arrangements, bargaining typically occurs at a level even lower than industry. Here, with a few notable exceptions, bargaining occurs at the enterprise level, where individual employers square off against individual locals, locals that are sometimes—but not always—supported by the controlling international union.

Why does the degree of centralization matter for labor's fortunes? Comparative research has offered multiple reasons. First, in highly centralized systems, the negotiated wage frameworks often extend to nonmembers, reducing employers' resistance to unionization.[22] Why bother fighting off an organizing drive if the pay and benefit scales are likely similar regardless of whether your firm is unionized or not? Second, centralized labor movements coordinate better, preventing the type of bitter interunion battles so common in the United States. Third, in highly centralized systems, organized labor often plays a large role in devising macroeconomic policy. This influence helps steer policymakers away from decisions harmful to unions.[23]

Despite huge variation in the degree of centralization across countries, in the 1980s union membership declined in the vast majority of the developed nations. Economic shocks put organized labor on the defensive, and many countries responded to the shocks in part by dissolving existing bargaining structures, disadvantaging organized labor. But some countries' labor movements were able to withstand the shocks better than others, especially those in which unions controlled unemployment assistance systems. These so-called Ghent systems (named after the city in Belgium where the scheme was first adopted) helped cushion the effect of economic downturns on labor's fortunes: Unemployed workers gained familiarity with and tangible benefits from unions as they sought new employment. Union control of unemployment insurance systems helps explain both the generally high rates of organization in countries like Sweden and Denmark, and the lack of substantial decline in representation rates during the 1980s.[24]

In the United States, the unemployment insurance system is administered by the Department of Labor—a government agency—together with each state. That has been true since congressional passage of the

Social Security Act in 1935. Thus while the lack of union-disbursed unemployment benefits helps explain the United States' generally low organization rate compared to other nations, it can't explain why membership losses were so steep from the 1970s forward.

But just as institutions matter, institutional change matters as well. Industry-level bargaining once predominated in core unionized sectors in the United States. Agreements hashed out between a union and a key firm in an industry—say, Ford in auto manufacturing—would serve as the basis for contracts among the other major firms in that industry. Beginning in the 1980s, however, employers successfully broke so-called pattern bargaining, preferring instead to handle wage and benefit negotiations at the level of the individual enterprise. Highly decentralized, enterprise-level bargaining has typified labor-management relations in the United States for the last few decades. And this level of bargaining places labor at a severe disadvantage. For one, it encourages jurisdictional disputes among various unions who expend resources fighting over the most fertile terrain. Employers, meanwhile, can claim to their workers that unionization will reduce the company's ability to compete with the neighboring nonunion firm, dampening rank-and-file support for the drive. Or they can simply shift operations to nonunion enterprises. Employers in core union industries like aerospace, auto, steel, and mining perfected these tactics and others, putting unions on the defensive during tough economic times. These tough economic times, meanwhile, helped foment a political climate that turned sharply against organized labor.

Politics

In early August 2011 many Americans—not to mention international holders of U.S. Treasury securities—exhaled in relief after Congress narrowly avoided a default on the nation's debt obligations. But relief would have to wait a bit for over seventy thousand idled workers caught up in an ongoing congressional battle over reauthorizing the Federal Aviation Administration (FAA). Negotiations concerning the lifting of the country's debt ceiling had consumed congressional activity for months, leaving little time for policymakers to address other pressing items. Paramount among these items was the impasse at the FAA, resulting in the postponement of all ongoing airport construction projects, which in turn triggered the immediate furloughing of tens of thousands of construction workers on July 22. The dispute had other tangible costs, including hundreds of millions of dollars in uncollected airline taxes as the imbroglio kept thousands of FAA staff at home without pay. The nation's politicians emptied the capital for their summer recess without solving the issue.

President Barack Obama summarized the impasse as a "lose, lose, lose situation."[25] It certainly was a loss to all the workers without paychecks at a time when the nation's unemployment rate neared double digits. Growing pressure from the public and key politicians—including the president—led to a temporary solution as the Senate majority leader, Harry Reid, along with House Republicans and Secretary of Transportation Ray LaHood, devised a short-term measure that returned workers to their jobs in return for promises to end certain government subsidies to rural airports. All sides agreed to reenter the battle over a longer-term reauthorization bill later.

Why the impasse in the first place? On the surface, the dispute appeared to be another in a long line of standard partisan battles, with the two parties agreeing to disagree simply for the sake of disagreeing. Underneath, though, was a bitter power struggle over unionization rules. In April 2010 the National Mediation Board (NMB) handed down a regulation concerning union election procedures in the airline and railway industries. Congress established the NMB in 1934, and its jurisdictional bounds extend no further than those two transportation industries. The National Labor Relations Board (NLRB) governs collective bargaining procedures in most other areas of the economy outside the public sector. And in contrast to the union election process in industries overseen by the NLRB, since the NMB's birth it has specified that a successful unionization election in airlines and railways requires that the union secure the votes of over half of all *eligible* voters. Take, for example, flight attendants at Delta. Should they desire union representation, 50 percent plus one of all Delta flight attendants must vote for the union. Abstentions, spoiled ballots—and all of those Delta flight attendants who for one reason or another did not participate in the election—these all count as "no" votes under the prevailing NMB rules. The labor scholar Kate Bronfenbrenner has argued that this system creates an incentive for companies to suppress turnout, since every vote not cast counts in the firm's favor.[26] Two unionization battles involving

Delta Airlines in 2000 and 2002 certainly support her testimony, as the airline blanketed work sites with "Give a Rip" posters urging workers to shred their ballots.[27]

The 2010 decision by the three-member NMB board altered the election procedure, bringing it in line with how union elections are conducted elsewhere in the private sector—and how every election for political office is conducted in the United States.[28] Certain Republican congressmen objected to the move and inserted language reversing the board's ruling in the FAA reauthorization bill. In response, Democratic senators rejected the House's bill, demanding a clean one stripped of any union-related language. The House then sent the Senate a temporary reauthorization bill without the union provision, but this time demanded the end of federal subsidies to certain rural airports, with the likely effect of forcing the closure of a few airports that happened to be located in the home states of key Democratic senators. The senators weren't amused, and the FAA limped on without proper authorization until the temporary deal was reached weeks later.

As noted above, institutions are not fixed, and the NMB example highlights one way in which the blueprints that guide collective bargaining can change over time. It also highlights how these institutional changes often stem from bitter political fights. The NMB ruling was instituted only after President Obama tipped the ideological scales of the agency by appointing a past president of a flight attendants' union to the board. As we have seen, the rule change was not greeted neutrally by policymakers. It incensed congressional Republicans, and temporarily led to a partial shutdown of a major government agency. And while the change to the NMB was significant, it was limited to just two industries. The NLRA, and the NLRB—the act's ruling board—provide the guidelines for collective bargaining in the rest of the private sector. One institution that *has* been fixed in stone is the NLRA. It hasn't been significantly altered for over half a century. Yet this lack of change to the nation's labor laws is itself a direct result of multiple political fights, with one clear winner.

Organized labor has mounted repeated efforts to alter the NLRA, and has lost on every occasion. This resistance to change, in turn, has political roots. A massive influx of corporate donations helped persuade many policymakers to vote against efforts to alter the existing laws governing employers and labor unions. And scholars have argued that a cumulative result of all these failed efforts has been private-sector union decline. How can a lack of a change contribute to declining unionization rates? After all, unions in this country thrived in the past when the collective bargaining framework looked little different from how it looks today.

Answering this question requires an examination of what happens when one side begins to break the formal rules established by the NLRA. Beginning in the 1960s, employers started to test the law's limits. While business opposition to labor unions was not new, scholars agree that by the late 1960s and into the 1970s and 1980s, organized business had really begun to perfect its antiunion tactics.[29] Instead of playing by a mutually agreed-upon set of rules that had governed what was deemed permissible in collective bargaining disputes, employers began skirting the law, pricing in the resulting penalties as simply one of the costs involved in fighting unions.[30] As the political scientists Jacob Hacker and Paul Pierson have argued, this recalculation proved fruitful, as companies quickly discovered that "defying the law was far cheaper than risking any prospect of unionization."[31] Unions responded predictably, by filing an increasing number of unfair labor practice (ULP) charges against companies and demanding back-pay and the reinstatement of workers unlawfully terminated during election drives. They won a lot of these legal battles, but would lose the war. This period corresponded first with a decline in union win rates, and subsequently with a dramatic decrease in union election drives.[32]

How come? To take one example, the union UNITE HERE embarked on a organizing drive of Goya warehouse workers in 1998. Goya is a food manufacturer whose reach extends throughout the Western Hemisphere and parts of Europe, but the site of this particular labor strife was in Miami, Florida—a lightly unionized city in a lightly unionized state. During the course of the campaign, the NLRB found that the company had committed over twenty infractions. Yet the penalties for these infractions did nothing to deter the company from delaying the unionization process. After over seven years of legal wrangling, the NLRB issued a final ruling ordering Goya to resume bargaining with UNITE HERE, although under existing laws the board cannot force the company to agree to a contract. As the former president of the union remarked, "If this is winning, it's hard to imagine what losing looks like."[33]

While companies increasingly stepped over the breach separating permissible from impermissible behavior during union elections, many of the tactics perfected by firms against unions were perfectly legal: captive-audience meetings, distribution of antiunion literature, delays in the establishment of a first contract following a union win—these were all allowed under the law. What changed was employers' willingness to deploy these and other weapons. Over time, they simply became automatic responses to a unionization drive—their use was institutionalized. Combining legal stratagems with tactics clearly impermissible under the law, employers enjoyed great success at stifling organization. And this is why unions in recent decades have expended so many resources in the political arena trying to change the NLRA. Unfortunately for them, the political environment has turned decisively against organized labor.

As it became clear to unions that the game—if not the formal rules—had changed, the labor movement pressed politicians in Washington to update the NLRA to reflect the new challenges labor faced when confronting employers. A major legislative push began in the late 1970s. First unions hoped to dismantle the section of the Taft-Hartley Act of 1947 authorizing states to pass "right-to-work" statutes. In a state with a right-to-work law, employees in unionized workplaces are allowed to opt out of union membership and, by extension, paying dues. Recognizing that it lacked the votes in Congress for such a reversal, organized labor then concentrated its efforts on updating union election procedures: increasing fines levied on corporations found in violation of the law during unionization drives, and shortening the deadline by which companies had to pay for their violations. The changes passed the House of Representatives by a large margin, and the showdown turned to the Senate. There, intense lobbying by U.S. businesses against the update—antiunion companies and their allies outspent organized labor by a three-to-one margin—paid off when a successful filibuster by Senate Republicans ultimately torpedoed the bill.[34] The labor historian Jefferson Cowie concluded that "one could hear the death rattle of American working-class political power" in this legislative defeat.[35]

Other major reform initiatives bubbled up over time, only to fizzle out in the face of political realities. Unions simply did not have the votes in Congress or enough presidential support to remake labor law to a degree that could counteract steady membership declines. For example, early in President Bill Clinton's first term, unions' political allies reintroduced a "strikers' rights" bill that would bar the (increasing) use of permanent replacement workers by employers during work stoppages. Once again, the bill stalled over a successful Republican filibuster in the Senate.[36]

Establishing a filibuster-proof majority in the Senate appeared to be a necessary—if not sufficient—precondition to any major change in labor law. That opening arrived nearly two decades after the strikers' rights bill went down, when for a very brief period Democratic control of the White House, House of Representatives, and a filibuster-proof majority in the Senate provided organized labor with a narrow window to push through their latest proposal, the Employee Free Choice Act (EFCA). Initial drafts of the legislation would have radically recast how union elections are held in the United States, bypassing the traditional election campaign in favor of a "card check" policy whereby a union is recognized after over half of workers sign up in support of collective bargaining. A compromise version of the bill would have retained the "secret ballot" election procedure but would have reduced election times, granted organizers greater access to employees on the work site, and instituted binding arbitration if a contract has not been agreed upon after a specified period. During the presidential primary campaign of 2007–2008, unions urged the leading Democratic candidates to support their signature measure, and all obliged, including the eventual nominee and president, Barack Obama. Predictably, business united in opposition to the law, with the vice president of the Chamber of Commerce announcing that the battle over EFCA amounted to "a firestorm bordering on Armageddon."[37]

In the end, there was no firestorm; there was no Armageddon. Since taking the oath of office Obama has "presented virtually no prepared remarks on EFCA," according to the law professor Anne Marie Lofaso.[38] And key Democratic defections in the Senate delayed the party's leadership from proceeding with the legislation. Shortly thereafter, the narrow window for action slammed shut following the 2010 midterm elections that returned the speakership of the House to the Republicans. Over two decades ago, the labor lawyer Thomas Geoghegan doubted "if any group of workers can form a union if their employer is truly determined to resist."[39] No major political progress on labor's behalf in the intervening decades has altered the state of collective bargaining in this country. In order to update the labor laws that have helped depress membership rates, unions will have to wait for the perfect political alignment, yet again. Private-sector unionization rates, meanwhile, have settled in the single digits, down 40 percent since Geoghegan's conclusion.

And that is what makes the NMB airline and railway election ruling so anomalous in today's era. It was an unambiguous win for unions. Its reach is too circumscribed to affect the overall private-sector unionization rate significantly, and its hold is tenuous—the ruling can always be overturned with a change in the board's makeup, or nullified by persistent congressional pressure. But for unions it stands as a rare victory in what has been a decades-long essentially futile battle to shift organizing rules in a direction that benefits them and not companies.

The preceding set of explanations for union decline in the United States is by no means exhaustive. Other scholars have advanced alternative arguments, some of which are variants of the ones I present above, and others of which creatively combine elements of the list to produce novel accounts of labor's demise. For example, the political scientist Paul Frymer has suggested that desegregation played a role in exhausting labor's strength. During the 1970s many unions, "besieged by litigation costs," reluctantly implemented court-ordered affirmative action programs.[40] These messy battles would produce an exceptionally diverse labor movement, but one with a battered reputation and a shrunken financial base. In this explanation we see the intertwining of institutional change and politics. Frymer's fellow political scientist Peter Swenson suggests that in certain U.S. industries employer backlash against unions was necessitated by labor's overreach. He argues that many unions' insistence on managerial control helped spark companies' decisive turn against organized labor in the political arena.[41] In this explanation we see the creative combining of a variant of the self-inflicted-damage explanation with politics. The sociologist David Brady's analysis of cross-national patterns of union membership suggests an important role for conservative party control, along with more standard institutional explanations.[42] These various accounts should not be seen as mutually exclusive. In the messy social world we inhabit, it is exceedingly rare that a single, tidy argument can fully explain such a major change as the collapse of organized labor.

What these accounts do offer is a synthesis of the dominant set of explanations for the decline of private-sector unions in the United States. More than three decades of research on this topic provide the outlines of a fairly comprehensive account of labor's demise. A small part may have been self-inflicted. Certainly labor's inability or unwillingness to reach out to new sectors as their strongholds began to crumble did not help arrest membership declines. But it is important to note that organizing the sectors that have experienced rapid employment growth in recent years, sectors like retail and high-tech, has proven exceptionally difficult *nearly everywhere*. And here is where the international picture is so illustrative. Comparative political economy scholars group together the United States with Great Britain, Canada, Australia, and New Zealand as countries sharing a common political economic framework in which coordination between firms is driven primarily by competitive market arrangements.[43] Comparative welfare state scholars likewise pinpoint a similar group of nations as sharing a common approach to redistribution and, with it, tax policies.[44] These countries' collective bargaining arrangements—especially recently—are typified by localized bargaining between individual unions and establishments. It is not so surprising, then, that their union membership rates rank consistently lower than those of other groups of countries, and that their recent membership trends have all tilted downward.

A combination of the institutional and economic explanations for labor's declining fortunes can seem a bit mechanistic: Economic shocks were filtered through the existing institutional architecture, which, in the U.S. case, disadvantaged organized labor. But underlying these developments, it is crucial to remember, was a bitter power struggle between firms and unions—a struggle often waged on the political battlefield. And here is where politics played such a prominent role. After all, the economic developments of the 1970s and 1980s did not have to affect labor as adversely as they did. Policymakers, in concert with union leaders, could have radically changed the rules governing collective bargaining. Or, barring something so transformative, they could have increased penalties on employers eager to exploit loopholes or otherwise take advantage of existing labor law. Such moves are unlikely to have reversed labor's decline completely, as other countries with collective bargaining rules much more advantageous to unions also experienced eroding memberships. But they may have helped to limit the damage to unions.

In the United States and, to a significant extent, Great Britain and Australia, the exact opposite happened. Political developments reinforced employer offensives against organized labor. In Great Britain, over a decade of uninterrupted Conservative rule produced a range of policies aimed at restricting unions' power.[45] In Australia, legislation introduced in the 1990s abetted the rapid devolution of the collective bargaining system.[46] In the United States, Congress did not pass and therefore the president did not sign any major piece of legislation altering the basic framework governing collective bargaining. This very inaction had tangible consequences. It left labor largely powerless to combat employers' legal and illegal tactics during organizing campaigns and decertification drives. Employers exploited this power mismatch, simultaneously lobbying lawmakers to refrain from altering labor law while taking advantage of the law's reach and its limits to fight existing unions and fend off unionization attempts. And political leaders set the tone, no more so than in August of 1981 when President Ronald Reagan issued an ultimatum to striking air traffic control workers demanding they return to their jobs within forty-eight hours or he would fire them all and permanently replace them with nonunion workers. The striking workers, members of the Professional Air Traffic Controllers Organization, did not back down, and Reagan followed through on his promise, decertified the union, and barred the fired employees from working as air traffic controllers in the future.

All of this unfolded in a highly fragmented, firm-centered collective bargaining system during a period of rapid deregulation, increasing competition, and major employment shifts in the industries in which Americans worked. General Motors was once the nation's largest private employer. Back when organized labor was at its peak, agreements between the company and its highly unionized workforce set the pattern for wage and benefit negotiations within the auto industry and many other firms in the manufacturing sector. Today, the retailing giant Walmart is the nation's largest employer in the private sector, with approximately one and a half million U.S. employees.[47] Nearly one in one hundred workers in the country today is employed by Walmart, a union-free company in a sector with very little union presence. And today, Walmart is the company whose reach extends well beyond its stores' walls, affecting the working conditions in its thousands of suppliers and among its competitors in various industries. As Lichtenstein has remarked, the company has become a "world transforming economic institution."[48] It is also a union-free institution, and the leaders of the company plan on keeping it that way, as former CEO H. Lee Scott has made abundantly clear.

The private sector in this country is now also nearly union-free, to a degree not seen in a century. The causes of this transformation have been thoroughly discussed and debated, both within the academy and among the nation's press and opinion leaders. It is time we explore the consequences.

2

Government Is Not the Answer

Why Public-Sector Unionism Won't Rescue the Labor Movement

On February 18, 2005, Illinois governor Rod Blagojevich signed an executive order granting collective bargaining rights to nearly fifty thousand child-care workers. The order represented the culmination of a multiyear lobbying campaign by the Service Employees International Union (SEIU). The union had backed Blagojevich's 2002 gubernatorial bid early, contributing valuable manpower and financial resources to the then-congressman's primary effort in the crowded Democratic field. Blagojevich eked out a narrow victory and, once ensconced in the governor's mansion, granted one of SEIU's long-standing wishes: the ability to unionize child-care workers. Previously categorized as independent contractors, those workers whose clients received state funds were reclassified under Blagojevich's order as de facto public employees. With the stroke of a pen, Blagojevich opened the door to one of the largest unionization drives in the nation's history. After winning a bruising jurisdictional battle with the American Federation of State, County, and Municipal Employees (AFSCME) over which union had the right to organize the state's child-care workers, SEIU triumphed in the actual union election, gaining an overwhelming majority of the votes cast. With that, the union had succeeded on a scale nearly unheard of in modern America.

Nearly, but not totally unheard of: In California during the 1990s, the same union spent years pressuring legislators and donating generously to Governor Gray Davis's campaign coffers. SEIU's efforts paid off when the state agreed to create an agency to bargain with home-care employees over wages and benefits. Now that the state served as the home-care workers' employer, unions were free to begin organizing the disproportionately female, disproportionately minority employee base of the fast-growing industry. In the ensuing union election, workers voted by a margin of over eight to one to have SEIU represent them in bargaining with the state, and the union gained seventy-four thousand new dues-paying members. This organizing drive was the single largest in the United States since 1937, a "home run for labor amidst a lot of strike outs," according to labor relations expert Harley Shaiken.[1] Today, home-care workers constitute a quarter of SEIU's total membership base.[2]

A similar effort spearheaded by other unions succeeded in New York in 2007, when Governor Eliot Spitzer issued an executive order granting collective bargaining rights to home-based day-care workers. During the same period, the chief executives of other states, including Oregon, Iowa, New Jersey, and Wisconsin, would follow Blagojevich's precedent and reclassify thousands of child-care providers as public employees entitled to bargain collectively with the state. While few of these efforts matched the sheer magnitude of SEIU's successes in Illinois and California, they stood as bright spots for the labor movement in an otherwise bleak organizing landscape. George Meany, the legendary labor leader who headed the American Federal of Labor (AFL) and then the American Federation of Labor and Congress of Industrial Organizations (AFL-CIO) until 1979, once declared that it was "impossible to bargain collectively with the government."[3] Meany was clearly wrong.

The preceding examples point to crucial sectoral differences in labor organizing in modern America. In so doing they help illuminate why it is that public-sector unionization rates have remained relatively constant over the last three and a half decades. Aside from the rather ignoble political endings suffered by the governors mentioned above, what unites them and other elected officials who recently opened up collective bargaining rights to new classes of employees is that they are Democrats.[4]

The rise of public-sector unionization in this country, which began nearly a half century ago, was initially a bipartisan affair. For example, as governor of California, Ronald Reagan—rarely remembered for his fondness for organized labor—signed an act allowing collective bargaining between local governments and their workers.[5] And, in certain regions—most notably the South—opposition to the rapid expansion of collective bargaining was bipartisan as well, contributing to the uneven spread of laws granting collective bargaining rights to government employees. However, as the Republican Party coalesced around an anti-union agenda in the 1970s and 1980s, public-sector unions and their members became a core Democratic constituency. Democratic office-holders fought to expand and protect governmental employees' unions; Republicans were increasingly united against them. In recent years, with Democratic backing in statehouses and state legislatures, proactive unions have succeeded through direct political pressure in extending collective bargaining rights to millions of government employees, and in broadening the legal definition of public-sector work to encompass occupations previously off-limits to labor organizing. They have done so on a scale and through a process unimaginable in the private sector.

First, consider the sheer size. The SEIU efforts in California and Illinois combined to add over one hundred thousand workers to unions. In the private sector, the long-standing legal model of organizing requires unions to win an election of a defined "bargaining unit": a group of employees performing similar jobs who share the same work conditions and employer. In practice, the narrow scope of the bargaining unit generally works against the coordinated bargaining that occurs in many European countries. Instead, working through the National Labor Relations Board process largely limits unions to organizing individual establishments. To unionize a huge company like McDonald's, for example, would require organizing individual McDonald's stores. In many states, on the other hand, "the state" counts as the employer and all state workers performing similar jobs count as the bargaining unit—allowing for the type of enormous, occupation-based organizing drives described above.

Second, consider the process. In the private sector, once the parties agree on the bargaining unit, the election period commences—a period in which the employer is free to contest the union's case for representation. And contest they do, with increasing regularity and effectiveness, as I explored in Chapter 1.[6] Public-sector unionism works somewhat similarly, with one clear difference. States with high rates of public-sector union membership tend to have union-friendly legislation on their books. And the passage of these laws is a pretty clear signal of an employer—in this case the state—amenable to labor unions, and thus unlikely to fight unionization drives. The result, as labor economist Richard Freeman has concluded, is that "in the public sector, once workers choose union representation, they get what they choose."[7]

So why can't the public sector lead the march to a revitalized labor movement? And what are the consequences of a labor movement dominated—as the labor movement in the United States increasingly is—by public-sector unionists? In what follows I argue that there are limits to what unions can accomplish through public-sector representation. Past successes in public-sector organization have appeared to plateau, with more-recent battles between Republican governors and public-sector unions threatening to undo labor's gains. And even if these recent setbacks for labor prove temporary, and unions are able to expand the portion of the public sector that is organized, a labor movement tilted toward the government sector looks and acts quite differently from the one that predominated in this country during the post–World War II decades.

The Limits of Growth

North Carolina law expressly forbids collective bargaining between state workers and government agencies. General statute 95–98, passed over fifty years ago, nullified labor agreements between the state and unions representing public employees, removing one of the most vital purposes of unionization. As a result, public-sector unionization rates in North Carolina rank among the lowest in the nation. Virginia has passed similar legislation. The extension of collective bargaining rights to public workers throughout the nation during the 1960s and 1970s spread fast and wide. But it did not spread everywhere. States and jurisdictions unfriendly to unions, such as North Carolina, took the opposite approach, enacting statutes making it more difficult to organize their public-sector workforce. Other states simply took no action at all, leaving no formal procedures through which public-sector unions can bargain with state and local government agencies.[8] These states appear in no hurry to undo the impediments to organization. For example, the current governor of South Carolina—a state with one of the lowest public-sector unionization rates in the country—recently announced that "unions are not needed, not wanted and not welcome" in her state.[9]

The discretion that states and other governmental jurisdictions have over their employees' bargaining rights has produced tremendous variation in unionization laws. The pattern of this variation is relatively predictable. As mentioned, the initial legislation that allowed for state- and local-level collective bargaining found sympathetic sponsors in both parties, but Republican support for public-sector unions quickly dissipated. Today, where Republicans rule, unions generally don't. Conservative states have proven particularly unfriendly terrain not only for private-sector unions, but for public ones too.

A consequence of these differences in collective bargaining laws is considerable variation among states in public-sector unionization. Figure 2.1 ranks states according to their 2009 public-sector unionization rates, displaying the states with the ten highest and ten lowest rates. As shown, the highest-ranking state—New York—has a rate of public-sector organization fully twelve times that of Mississippi, the lowest-ranking state. Mississippi's rate of public-sector unionization ranks below the level of union representation in the nation's private sector, a pretty exceptional feat, given all the troubles currently plaguing private-sector organizing. The states at the top end and the bottom end of the rankings cluster politically and geographically. The top five states are all in the Northeast, have historically been Democratic-leaning in their politics, and have above-average private-sector unionization rates. With the exception of Wyoming, all the bottom-ranking states are located in the South, a region comparatively antiunion and Republican-friendly.

Thus there are political realities that govern the extent of public-sector unionization. These political forces exert a cross-sectional limit on unions' growth possibilities in the public sector. At any given point in time, stark differences among states in political attitudes toward organized labor and the relevant legislation governing public-sector unions restrict where and how deeply organized labor can penetrate the public

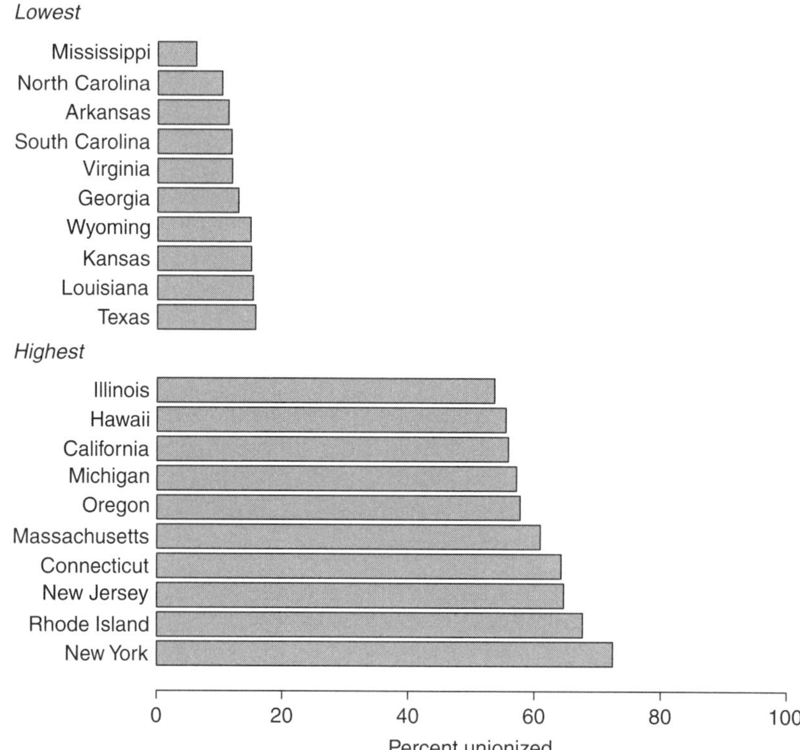

Figure 2.1. Public-sector unionization rates by state, 2009. *Note:* Sample restricted to employed wage and salary workers, ages sixteen and over. *Source:* Hirsch and Macpherson's Unionstats database, based on the 2009 CPS-MORG file. See www.unionstats.com.

sector. While it is plausible that areas unfriendly to organized labor will shift and take action to allow greater union representation of public workers, the opposite could happen as well.

The initial flurry of activity surrounding collective bargaining in the public sector erupted nearly a half century ago. For decades, the few skirmishes that occurred tended to revolve around expanding or restricting the classes of workers subject to existing rules and regulations, such as the successful fights in Illinois and California spearheaded by SEIU. But among those workers classified as working for state or local governments, the question of whether they had the right to bargain collectively seemed settled, establishing a rough equilibrium in public-sector unionization laws, and the resulting unionization rate among government workers.

* * *

> We can no longer live in a society where the public employees are the haves and the taxpayers who foot the bills are the have-nots.
>
> —Wisconsin governor Scott Walker[10]

This would change. Today there seems to be a growing sentiment about government unions that has opened space for state and local officeholders to step in and take action, and it is not action that public-sector unions welcome. Traditionally, Wisconsin has been a labor-friendly state, evidenced by its above average unionization rates, especially among public employees. As of 2009, over half of all governmental workers in Wisconsin were organized.[11] Just over half a century ago, Wisconsin became the first state to enact legislation regulating collective bargaining with local government workers. Yet governor Scott Walker initiated his 2011 term by investigating ways to undo the collective bargaining rights of Wisconsin's public servants—nearly all of them. Walker's proposal elicited a storm of criticism both for its wide scope and for the process by which he shepherded it through the state legislature. It also sparked a revolt among Democratic state senators, who fled Wisconsin to camp out in Illinois for weeks to protest what they saw as the radical nature of the governor's plan. Their absconding was tactical. Without the ability to form a quorum, the Republicans were unable to move forward on a vote on the governor's proposal—at least temporarily. The Democratic lawmakers would eventually return, following legislative maneuvering that rendered their absence ineffectual. Republicans in the State Senate reworked the legislation to avoid the quorum requirement and passed Walker's bill on March 9, 2011. The State Assembly passed the antiunion legislation the next day, and Walker quickly signed it.[12]

Walker's political troubles did not end with the law's eventual passage. A campaign to recall the governor gained momentum in the aftermath of the bruising battle in the Capitol and culminated in a special election pitting the governor against Milwaukee mayor Tom Barrett in the spring of 2012. Walker survived, defeating his Democratic challenger by 7 percentage points. Thus, despite all the controversy, as of now Governor Walker's efforts appear to be successful. Except for protective services, public-sector unions in Wisconsin no longer have the right to bargain over any issue except wages. And even the wage bargaining allowed in the legislation is highly circumscribed. Raises cannot exceed cost-of-living adjustments unless voters agree to the increase in a referendum. Aside from police and firefighter unions, then, public-sector unions in Wisconsin are now largely limited to bargaining over whether their annual wages will keep up with inflation.[13]

Unions are understandably concerned about what this radical reduction in their bargaining rights means for memberships in the state. After court delays, the Walker administration began implementing the law in June 2011. The most recent publicly available data stem from 2011 and capture about six months of post-implementation information. The data reveal that public-sector rolls remained essentially unchanged from 2010 to 2011, but it is likely too soon to tell what the longer-term implications of the Walker legislation mean for collective bargaining in the state.[14] A more recent *Wall Street Journal* article from the spring of 2012 suggested that unions such as the American Federation of Teachers and AFSCME suffered tremendous membership losses throughout the end of 2011 and first half of 2012.[15]

Walker's move was not entirely unprecedented. In 2005, in just his second day in office, Republican governor Mitch Daniels of Indiana rescinded an executive order granting bargaining rights to Indiana's public-sector employees. With the stroke of a pen, tens of thousands of unionized teachers and cops and other public servants lost their ability to bargain over pay and benefits.[16] So in the same year in which the governor in the neighboring state of Illinois expanded the classes of workers eligible for public-sector union membership, Daniels stripped the right to bargain with the state from all classes of public-sector employees. Daniels's move—and Walker's some six years later—demonstrated that just as a labor-friendly state executive can expand union eligibility at a pace and on a scale nearly impossible in the private sector, an antiunion executive can remove eligibility equally quickly and substantially.

Daniels's executive order did not seem to hurt him politically. In 2008, despite the Democratic wave that swept away Republican rule from the executive branch, the Senate, and statehouses across the country, Daniels won reelection by 18 percentage points.[17] Since his reelection, he has maintained pressure on public-sector workers, labeling them "a new privileged class in America."[18] This spirit would be taken up by Walker and other politicians throughout the land.

In neighboring Ohio, for example, Republican governor John Kasich took advantage of large Republican majorities in the House and Senate to pass a bill similar to Walker's, except Ohio's included protective workers under its purview. Unlike in Wisconsin, this effort proved too audacious for Ohio voters. Instead of trying to unseat Kasich, opponents submitted the bill itself to a citizens' referendum, along with a handful of other ballot initiatives. In November 2011, Ohioans overwhelmingly rejected the legislation, forcing the chastened governor to admit that the result "requires me to take a deep breath and to spend some time to reflect on what happened here."[19]

The Ohio referendum represents a rare recent victory for public-sector unions that are otherwise facing serious challenges. The combination of Republican victories in statehouses across the country in 2010 and the fiscal crisis of 2008 has spurred Republican-led efforts to rein in public-sector unions not only in Indiana, Wisconsin, and Ohio, but even in what was once arguably the center of the American labor movement, Michigan. Many conservatives have coalesced around the view that public-sector unions represent "the single biggest problem" standing in the way of economic growth and a balanced budget, as a 2010 editorial from the *Wall Street Journal* argued.[20] The fact that neutering public-sector unions carries the promise of removing a vital source of Democratic campaign contributions may also underlie the recent actions.

The growing animus toward public-sector unions and the government workers they represent is not limited to Republicans and right-wing publications, however. States struggling to balance their books have zeroed in on union-negotiated health and pension benefits for public employees as potential areas to cut. And many of these states, such as California and New York, are governed by Democrats. Referring to state government efforts to forestall or altogether avoid the costs associated with public-employee pension and benefit plans, the then-president of AFSCME recently declared: "They are readying a massive assault on us."[21]

Take teachers' unions. Of the nearly five million local government workers who belonged to a union in 2008, over 40 percent were teachers.[22] At the national level, the current administration's educational initiatives have emphasized greater school competition, including the opening of charter schools, and pegging teacher pay to student test scores.[23] These developments have often (although not always) met with stiff union opposition. At the more local level, recent contract negotiations in such cities as Baltimore and Washington, D.C., introduced reforms that weakened teacher tenure, replaced seniority with merit pay, and gave central administration greater leeway over hiring and firing decisions. These developments aligned union contracts more closely with those that govern nonunion teachers. In the private sector, concessions such as these are commonly referred to as "givebacks" and have characterized much private-sector bargaining over the preceding decades. In many cases, givebacks served as a harbinger of eventual union dissolution.

That has not happened in the public sector on a large scale—yet. Instead, after the initial run-up in public-sector organizing during the 1960s and 1970s, levels of organization have stabilized. Figure 2.2 spotlights trends in public-sector union representation from 1973 to 2009. After a steep increase in public-sector organizing during the 1970s, overall unionization rates have flattened, averaging in the mid-30s for the past three decades. It is too soon to tell whether recent developments represent temporary setbacks for public-sector unions, or are early signs of a permanent realignment. All those who suggest that Governor Walker's survival and other recent events herald the death of public-sector unions would do well to remember the enormous organizing victories in California, Illinois, and elsewhere just a few years earlier. Moreover, unless union opponents can make inroads in dismantling the power of public-sector unions in places like New York and California—huge states with public-sector unionization rates well over 50 percent—the unionization rate in the public sector will remain high, and certainly higher than in the private sector.

The overall rate obscures real differences in organization by class of government worker. Postal workers lead the group with an average unionization rate of over 70 percent across the series, although in more recent years the level among postal employees has declined slightly. Local public employees have the second-highest levels of representation, followed by state and federal workers. Fewer than one in five federal

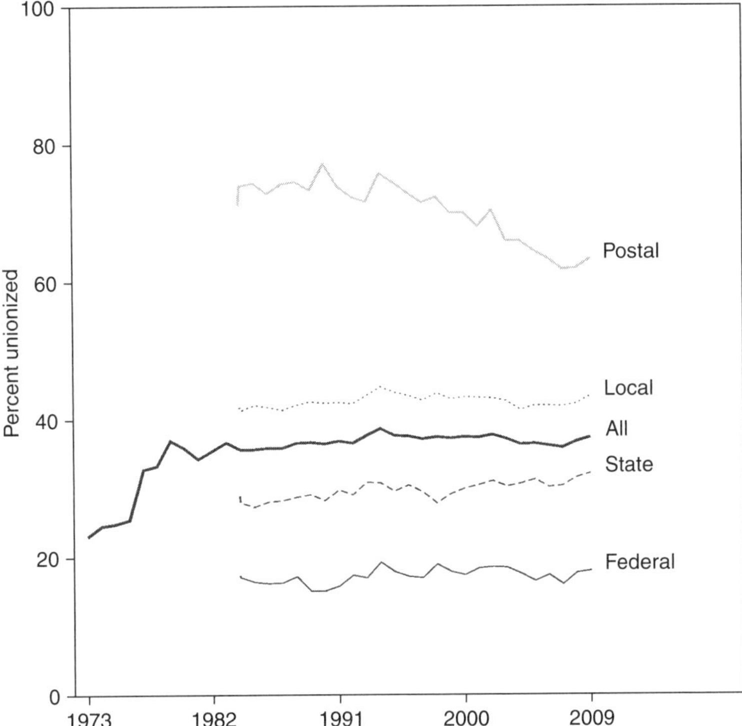

Figure 2.2. Public-sector union memberships, 1973–2009. *Note:* Sample restricted to employed wage and salary workers, ages sixteen and over. *Source:* Hirsch and Macpherson's Unionstats database, based on the 2009 CPS-MORG file. See www.unionstats.com.

employees are unionized. This low level reflects in part the restricted scope federal unions have in contract negotiations. By law, unions representing federal workers cannot bargain over wage rates, which are instead set by Congress. I will return to this issue shortly.

In sum, over a third of the public-sector workforce is unionized, and has been for thirty-five years. If we assume this trend holds—obviously a big "if"—then the other avenue through which public-sector unions can increase their presence in the United States is through growth of the government sector itself.

Invoking the specter of "big government" has proven a potent political campaign tactic for centuries in the United States. The past fifty years are no exception. President Reagan famously proclaimed government "the problem," even (humorously) hinting that government overreach went beyond dollars and cents: "When you get in bed with government, you're going to get something more than a good night's sleep."[24] A decade and a half earlier, in a speech announcing his bid for the presidency, Barry Goldwater referred to government growth as "cancerous," proclaiming that "government has been absorbing or controlling more and more of our resources, our energy, and our ambition." Accepting his party's vice-presidential nomination in 1976, Senator Robert Dole warned of the government's growing grip on the private sector, calling on lawmakers to "free the free enterprise system."[25] Antigovernment rhetoric has not been the sole province of the Republican Party. Seeking to neutralize the politically toxic issue of government growth, President Bill Clinton famously remarked in his 1996 State of the Union address that "the era of big government is over."[26]

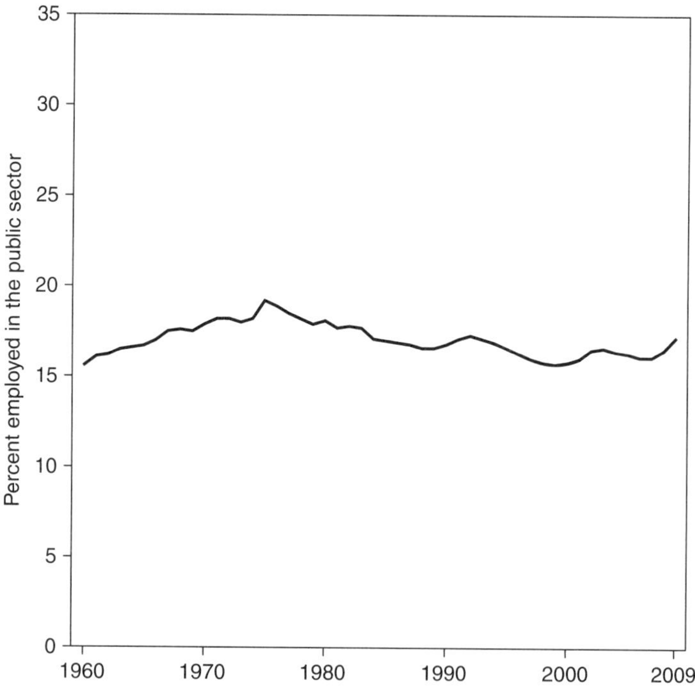

Figure 2.3. Percentage of workforce employed in the public sector, 1960–2009. *Note:* Sample restricted to nonfarm employees. *Source:* Bureau of Labor Statistics Employment, Hours, and Earnings historical data.

Yet at least as measured by its total share of employment, government—big or otherwise—has not gone anywhere. In Figure 2.3, I present the public sector's share of nonfarm employment from 1960 to 2009, based on data provided by the Bureau of Labor Statistics. Aside from public-sector unionization rates, if there is another economic area in which stability reigns, it is the public sector's share of the workforce. Despite repeated campaign promises by politicians to shrink the size of government by cutting public-sector programs, the fraction of workers employed by the government has not budged in half a century. And regardless of the overheated discourse that often dominates the airwaves during election seasons, that portion is not and has not been very large, totaling less than a fifth of the nonfarm workforce. The public-sector contribution to employment rolls stood just 1 percentage point higher in 2009 than it did fifty years prior.

What does this mean for public-sector unions? Hemmed in by political forces that threaten their power within the public sector, they are also limited by the government's small share of total employment—a share that has remained remarkably consistent across major transformations in the nation's political economy. Thus it is hard to imagine a future in which public-sector unionization is able to expand dramatically as a result of sharp growth in the government's share of the workforce. Indeed, over the preceding decades many industries once heavily regulated or outright controlled by the government have been turned over to the private sector. While the resulting losses in public-sector employment rolls have been offset by gains elsewhere, there is little indication of a coming structural transformation that would see the wholesale government takeover of major employment sectors in the United States.[27]

As private-sector unions suffer declines in nearly all advanced economies, the ability of labor movements to maintain their membership numbers depends more and more on the relative size and union penetration of the public sector. Government's employment share in the United States trails that of many other developed countries, contributing to the low overall unionization ranking of the United States.[28] And the small U.S. public sector carries a troubling implication for the future of the labor movement in this country. Let us assume for a moment that public-sector unions were somehow able to increase their organization rates by a third, from 35 percent to 47 percent. This would represent a pretty monumental feat for labor unions, especially given the current political climate, although the resulting public-sector organization rate would still lag the rates in Canada and Great Britain.[29] Yet given the public sector's small share of the total workforce, it would only boost the U.S. labor movement's overall unionization rate 2 percentage points—from 12 percent to 14 percent.

The Limits of Government Representation

Whether unions in the United States can make further inroads in the public sector concerns the labor movement's future. How unions representing government workers actually operate concerns labor's present. It turns out that some of the key functions of union representation, including bargaining over wages and benefits, differ between sectors. In many examinations of union effects in the United States, if public-sector unions are considered at all, scholars commonly assume that unions operate similarly in both the private and public sectors. This assumption is misguided. Given that the majority of union members in the United States today work for the government, inter-sectoral differences in union outcomes mean that we need to adjust our understandings of what unions do—and what unions once did—to include the growing role of those unions that represent government workers.

Wages

Labor economists refer to the impact of union membership on wages as the union wage premium. The union wage premium is the wage benefit a worker receives as a result of his or her union membership, and membership alone. While many factors influence both the likelihood of belonging to a union and one's wages, the premium is the wage effect of union membership adjusted for the impact of other confounding factors. Ideal laboratory conditions where a social scientist could assign union membership to half of a homogeneous group of employees are hard to replicate in the messy workings of modern labor markets. Instead, we try to match workers statistically, using data sets containing many of the factors found to affect wages and unionization.[30]

Does the union wage premium differ between public-sector and private-sector workers? Past research suggests that in the United States the average wage advantage attributable to union membership is lower in the public sector compared with the private sector, although the gap appears to have narrowed.[31] Below I update and extend this work by estimating union wage premiums for public- and private-sector workers between 1973 and 2009, using various series of the Current Population Survey (CPS).[32] Uncovering public-sector union wage effects is not as straightforward as analyses of those effects in the private sector, given important differences in wage-setting practices within the public sector itself. Unlike past scholarly work on the topic, my analyses account for variation in state-level public-sector bargaining laws, as well as differences in bargaining practices between the various classes of government workers in order to estimate a range of public-sector wage premiums.

As a first step, I follow precedent and estimate annual union wage premiums for public- and private-sector members across all states and types of public-sector employment. The analyses predict weekly wages (logged) for each survey year, and control for a range of demographic, geographic, and labor-market characteristics that influence one's pay rate, such as education, race/ethnicity, occupation, and industry. Figure 2.4 displays the results from these analyses.[33]

As shown, union wage premiums in the private sector are substantial, maxing out at around a 30 percent wage advantage in the mid-1980s. Since then the private-sector union wage advantage has declined, and by 2009 had settled at a weekly premium of 22 percent above the wages of otherwise similar nonunion workers. Union wage premiums for public-sector workers never approach such levels. They peaked in 1999 at 19 percent, before declining to a more typical public-sector union wage advantage of 14 percent by the early years of the twenty-first century. Over the nearly four decades covered by these data, the highest public-sector wage premium on record is smaller than the lowest private-sector premium. And similar to the private sector, public-sector premiums have remained relatively constant over time. At the beginning of the series, public-sector union members enjoyed a 14 percent wage advantage over otherwise similar nonunion government employees; by the end of the series, the advantage was roughly comparable. While the swelling state government coffers of the late-1990s' economic boom seemed to have benefited public-sector unions, once the economy slowed, the public-sector unionization advantage returned to more standard levels.

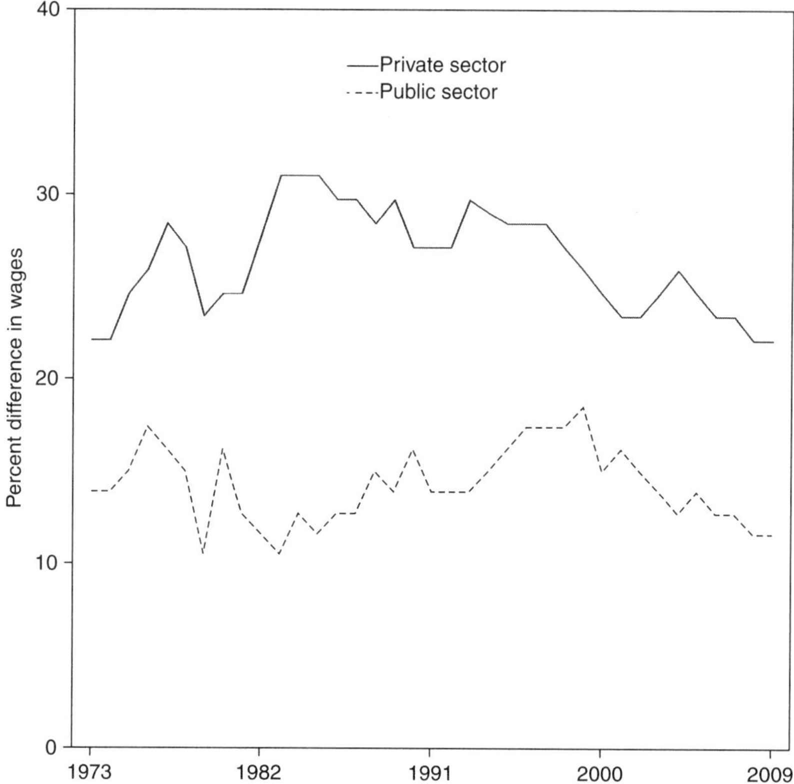

Figure 2.4. Union wage premiums, 1973–2009. *Note:* Sample restricted to employed workers, ages sixteen to sixty-four, with positive wages. *Source:* Author's compilations. Data for 1973–1981 come from the CPS-May files; data for 1983–2009 come from the CPS-MORG files.

The results shown in Figure 2.4 largely conform to prior investigations of public-sector union wage effects. For example, the labor economists David Blanchflower and Alex Bryson found substantially higher union wage premiums for private-sector workers than for public-sector workers in the early years of their investigation (1983–1988).[34] By the late 1990s, the gap had narrowed—although, as Figure 2.4 demonstrates, that period appears to be a historically anomalous time of relatively high public-sector union wage advantages. The authors also find that public-sector union wage premiums differ dramatically by the type of government work. Since federal workers are barred from negotiating over wages and benefits, union premiums among federal workers are quite low. In Blanchflower and Bryson's estimates, union wage premiums for federal employees range between 2 percent and 8 percent, although the authors caution that even these small differences "may not be very meaningful," given difficulties in accurately surveying union members who work for the federal government.[35] While premiums among state employees lag those among local government workers, they still average about 10 percent in Blanchflower and Bryson's investigation—significantly higher than those enjoyed by federal workers.

Thus it is worth reestimating public-sector union wage premiums with federal workers excluded. These results provide an indication of the wage gains public-sector unions are able to secure for their members among classes of unions—local and state—legally entitled to bargain over wages and benefits. In addition to what is displayed in Figure 2.4, I estimated a series of public-sector premiums in which I limited the public-sector worker samples to state and local government employees. This series begins in 1983 because of difficulties in dividing the public sector by level of employment (local, state, or federal) prior to that survey year.[36] The results reveal a slightly elevated public-sector premium. The state and local public-sector union wage premium peaks at 20 percent in 1999, before falling back to 15 percent a decade later. Yet that peak of 20 percent matches the lowest private-sector premium on record. On average, then, even among the classes of public-sector workers entitled to bargain over pay, the wage advantages attributable to union membership lag those found in the private sector.

As we have seen, the rules governing collective bargaining in the public sector differ not only between class of worker (federal, state, and local) but between states. So it is also worth investigating whether public-sector unions in states with the most comprehensive bargaining laws deliver wage gains commensurate with their private-sector counterparts. After all, the National Labor Relations Act applies to nearly all private-sector unions across the land, granting bargaining rights to unions in every state. Lacking a similar law in the public sector, the lower average wage premiums shown in Figure 2.4 and found in other research may be weighed down by those states like North Carolina and Virginia in which collective bargaining with the state is not recognized. And thus it could be that in states in which public-sector unions *are* recognized *and* legally entitled to bargain over wages, the wage premiums approximate those found in the private sector.

Table 2.1 presents the results from a series of analyses in which I first include all public-sector workers, then limit the public-sector samples to state and local government workers only, and then to state and local public-sector workers who reside in states with comprehensive bargaining laws. According to political scientist Richard Kearney, twenty-seven states have existing legislation that can be classified as "comprehensive": basically, statutes that grant state and local public-sector unions the right to collectively bargain with the state.[37] Other states ban all collective bargaining with the state, as discussed previously, while still other states, like Kentucky, Texas, and now Wisconsin, have adopted a hybrid approach that confers bargaining rights only to certain public-sector occupations, such as police and firefighters. Unlike the annual estimates shown in Figure 2.4, Table 2.1 displays the results of analyses that average across all years of available data.[38]

The results reveal an overall public-sector premium of 14 percent averaged across the 1983–2009 period. Eliminating federal workers, who have their pay set by Congress, results in a public-sector premium 2 percentage points higher. In the final analysis, I further restricted the data to states in which public-sector unions are recognized and all major public-sector occupations are granted bargaining rights. In other words, this final estimate represents what public-sector unions are able to deliver for their members in terms of wages in union-friendly states. This further constraint raises the public-sector premium only an additional 2 percentage points, to 18 percent—substantially below the wage gains secured by private-sector unionists.

Table 2.1 Public-sector premiums, 1983–2009

	Premium	Percent wage advantage
1. All public-sector workers	0.13	14%
2. Excluding fed workers	0.15	16%
3. Excluding fed workers, comp. bargaining laws only	0.17	18%

Source: Author's compilations. Data come from the CPS-MORG files, 1983–2009.
Note: Sample restricted to employed wage and salary workers, ages 16 to 64.

Not displayed in the table are the results of two more analyses: one limited to federal workers only and another limited to governmental workers in states without comprehensive collective bargaining laws. These results indicate that public-sector unions' ability to raise the wages among the class of workers—federal employees—unable to bargain collectively over wages is negligible. Unionized federal workers earn approximately 4 percent higher wages than their nonunion counterparts. As mentioned above, even that small advantage is likely overstated.

Organized state and local public employees in states without comprehensive collective bargaining legislation outearn nonunion workers by 11 percent, lower than the 18 percent differential we saw among those workers in states with comprehensive laws, but certainly not insubstantial. This premium likely derives in part from the various classes of workers in some of these states that are granted collective bargaining rights. But even among those classes of workers without collective bargaining abilities, unionized workers may outearn the unorganized. How so? Public-sector unions often lobby legislators to raise members' wages not only through collective bargaining but also through the legislative process. During the 1980s, home-based care workers in Illinois were not entitled to bargain with the state. Nonetheless, some were unionized—and the union delivered results. As an organizer explained to the labor scholars Eileen Boris and Jennifer Klein, "Legislators recognized us as a union even if the state did not."[39] Thus public-sector unions can deliver tangible results even in the absence of comprehensive collective bargaining laws, although this type of "political unionism" is much more insecure and unstable, reliant as it is on political relationships rather than being encoded in a set of predictable rules and procedures.[40]

The public-versus-private-sector premium comparisons may actually understate how effective public-sector unions are in shaping wage patterns within the government sector. Labor unions often support measures to *lower* the union wage premium, if those measures raise the wages of nonunion workers to approximate union pay rates. For example, unions have repeatedly lobbied states and the federal government first to establish and then to raise minimum wages across the country.[41] And in countries with strong labor movements, the wage gains achieved by collective bargaining often extend well beyond the class of unionized workers. Some of this can be attributed to threat effects: Nonunion employers worried about the potential of a unionization drive may raise wages to match union levels in order to forestall an organizing campaign. Threat effects, however, are less likely to operate in the public sector, where the employer is the government. Typically, if a state government grants bargaining rights to a certain public-sector occupation, that very action signals an employer amenable to working with labor unions. Yet the extension of union wage gains to nonunion workers can occur in the absence of a unionization threat. In certain countries where organized labor has achieved substantial political and economic power, the higher wages earned by union members are automatically extended to nonunion workers in similar industries and occupations, as I discuss in Chapter 1. These extensions lead to lower union wage premiums in countries with deeply institutionalized labor movements.[42] And organized labor often fights hard for these extensions, hoping to increase labor's aggregate share of total income.

Why would unions work to extend their hard-won gains to workers outside the labor movement? In the United States, organized labor has often stood as a political voice for a broad-based egalitarianism, supporting a range of policies that buttress the social and material well-being of average Americans. For example, organized labor lobbied the government to expand Medicare during the program's early years, and to keep the food stamp program solvent during the 1970s and 1980s. Referring to unions' role as an advocate for fairer employment and living conditions for all workers, a former secretary-treasurer of the AFL-CIO once put it: "We are the people's lobby."[43] But there are more self-interested reasons for such stances as well. Growing union-nonunion wage differentials, all else equal, raise the operating costs of union firms, reducing their competitiveness. As a result, union workers could lose their jobs. Moreover, the establishment of an industry-wide wage base provides unions with a floor from which to bargain during the next round of negotiations.

Whether operating from an egalitarian spirit or naked self-interest, public-sector unions may be successful in extending their gains to otherwise similar workers. In the context of the contemporary United States, with decentralized bargaining and a greatly weakened labor movement, "pattern" bargaining of this type is now nearly nonexistent in the private sector. As a result, the union wage premiums for private-sector workers give us a relatively accurate picture of how unions affect wages in the private sector. But pattern bargaining practices may exist in the public sector, where unions have managed to keep approximately a third of the workforce organized for decades now. Especially in those states with exceptionally high public-sector unionization rates—states like New York—union-negotiated wages may be pacesetters for nonunion contracts. Thus in those high union locales a reduced premium in the public sector may indicate union strength, not weakness.

How does one test for these possible union effects on nonunion wages? There is no straightforward path to follow, but one strategy is to focus on a few sets of targeted wage comparisons. The first is a cross-sector comparison between similar workers in the same states. Take New York, for example, where over two-thirds of the public-sector workforce is unionized. If public-sector unions are able to deliver wage benefits to their members *and* to others working for state and local governments, then you might expect the wages of government employees to match or exceed the wages of their private-sector counterparts. For this comparison to be meaningful, one must compare wages of private- and public-sector workers with similar demographic profiles, education levels, and years of experience in the labor force. The second comparison focuses solely on the wages of public-sector workers, and exploits differences among states in public-sector unionization rates. The states used for the comparison must be chosen with caution, given all the ways in which state-level factors influence wage rates. The goal is to compare the wages of public-sector workers—union and nonunion—in a state with a high public-sector unionization rate to the wages of public-sector workers—again, union and nonunion—in a similar state that lacks a large public-sector union presence.

What makes this second comparison especially difficult is that, as Figure 2.1 reveals, public-sector unionization rates tend be strongly patterned by region. The goal here is to compare the wages of workers in the same region, given large regional differences in wage rates. Pennsylvania and Maryland are adjoining states, with their largest cities separated by less than one hundred miles. Yet since the early 1980s, unionization rates among state and local workers in Pennsylvania are nearly 40 percent higher than in Maryland. Given this difference, it may be that public-sector unions are more effective in raising nonunion wages in Pennsylvania compared to its southern neighbor.

These two sets of comparisons round out the investigation of the wage benefits of public-sector unionization. The aim is to determine whether the comparatively low union wage premiums established previously mask the ability of public-sector unions to shape wages among union *and* nonunion workers.[44] Table 2.2 presents the results from this investigation. I examine two types of workers in California and New York, two large states with above-average public-sector unionization rates. The first comparison focuses on the predicted wages for full-time, white female workers in California with a high school diploma and at least ten years of potential labor market experience.[45] The average weekly wage for a unionized private-sector worker fitting this profile is $827. Her nonunion counterparts average $685 a week, nearly equivalent to what similar nonunion workers in the public sector earn. Yet the unionized private-sector worker's weekly wage is over $50 higher than that of the unionized public-sector worker. Thus this particular comparison shows reduced union wage premiums in the public sector, and substantially higher union wages in the private sector.

Let's examine the next wage profile. Here we are focusing on the weekly wages of male workers with a high school diploma and average potential experience levels of at least two decades. These workers live in New York. Similar to the prior comparison, we see larger union-nonunion differentials among private-sector workers, and substantially higher wages for unionized private-sector workers compared to those in the public sector. As for those public-sector workers who do not belong to a union, their wages *lag* those of nonunion private-sector workers.

These comparisons provide indirect evidence that strong public-sector unions in the United States do not appear to raise the wages of nonunion government employees, at least not enough to surpass the

Table 2.2 Wage predictions, full-time white workers with a high school diploma

	Public	Private
California female, 10+ years experience		
Union	$776	$827
Nonunion	$686	$685
New York male, 20+ years experience		
Union	$979	$1,060
Nonunion	$841	$878

Source: Author's compilations. Data come from the CPS-MORG files, 1983–2009.
Note: Sample restricted to employed wage and salary workers, ages 16 to 64.

wages of similar types of nonunion workers in the private sector. I chose the demographic pairings for these comparisons with the twin goals of providing information on a diverse set of workers while maintaining sample sizes sufficiently large for reliable estimates. Examinations of other possible pairings result in a similar pattern: Public-sector unions' ability to raise nonunion wages above and beyond their private-sector counterparts appears quite limited.

The final wage analysis focuses on public-sector workers only, except now I am comparing the wages of workers in Maryland to those in Pennsylvania. The hypothesis here is that if public-sector unions raise the wages of nonunion public-sector workers substantially, then nonunion workers in Pennsylvania—with its higher public-sector unionization rate—will outearn nonunion, public-sector workers in Maryland. Here we again compare wages of male high school graduates with substantial labor market experience who work full time for the state or local government. In Pennsylvania, these nonunion workers average $731 a week. In Maryland, similar nonunion workers average over $100 more. The second comparison is between highly educated African American female workers with at least two decades of potential labor market experience who work for the government but do not belong to a union. Once again, those in Maryland earn more than their northern neighbors.

What are we to make of these results? First, I should emphasize the need to treat them with caution. While I match workers according to demographics, education, and potential experience, a range of other work-related differences could explain some of the wage discrepancies on display. Small sample sizes prevent me from disaggregating further to compare workers with even more similar profiles. That said, I believe they do challenge the notion that the smaller union-nonunion wage differentials we have seen in the public sector stem from government unions' abilities to raise wages for all public-sector employees. The evidence instead suggests that the smaller wage gains public-sector unions deliver for their members are just that—smaller, and not due to substantial spillover to nonunion workers.

Of course, wages are not the only issue that concern labor unions. Unions have long played a leading role in expanding health insurance, pensions, and other benefits to wage earners in the United States and beyond. And much of the controversy surrounding public-sector bargaining in recent years relates to the nonwage benefits unions have secured.

The inability of public-sector unions to deliver wages commensurate with those we see in the private sector needs to be compared to how well they deliver on benefit packages. We will focus on this issue next.

Benefits

In May 2011, a group of labor unions representing public- and private-sector workers in Illinois committed a million dollars to an ad campaign aimed at stopping lawmakers in the state from slashing their benefit packages.[46] Attempts to rein in union contracts are a perennial feature of political disputes in the United States, as the discussions of Wisconsin, Ohio, and other states earlier in the chapter make clear. What made the situation in Illinois unique is that the ad campaign's primary target was not Republican state leaders. In Illinois in 2011, there were no Republican state leaders. Control of the House, Senate, and governor's seat rested with Democrats. The unions' media blitz attacked Democratic officeholders for their attempts to increase employee contributions to health care and pensions among state workers. The battle in Illinois highlights an important development in public-sector bargaining: In recent years, fights over benefit cuts have truly been bipartisan affairs. Unions on the defensive have sued over a dozen states to force them to honor their contractual obligations and pay out promised benefits. These include Republican strongholds as well as traditionally Democratic states like Massachusetts. And the battle in Illinois and elsewhere has illuminated an important success of many public-sector unions. Benefit packages among government employees are often quite substantial, making them an obvious target during economic downturns.

How successful have public-sector unions been in delivering robust benefits to their members compared to organized labor in the private sector? Two major components of fringe benefits—health insurance and pensions—are particularly germane to this discussion. I begin with an investigation into unions and health insurance provision.

Unions in the United States have long fought for an expansion of health insurance to workers. In the post–New Deal years, unions invested heavily in lobbying for national health care coverage for all Americans. The defeat of these efforts focused many unions' attention on securing health insurance coverage for their own members through collective bargaining with employers. During World War II many employers, constrained by wartime wage controls, offered health care coverage as a recruitment tool to lure workers in a tight labor market. Unions eagerly added these plans to contract negotiations, bargaining to extend their reach and to decrease employees' share of total costs. Early investigations of union effects on employer-provided health insurance—research largely focused on the private sector—found that unions had a sizable impact on health insurance coverage.[47] For example, in their classic 1984 work on unions, *What Do Unions Do?,* labor economists Richard Freeman and James Medoff found that unionized employees were more likely to be covered by employer-provided health plans, and that the employers contributed a greater share to health care premium costs in union firms compared to non-union ones.[48] Recent work corroborates this general pattern, whether using surveys of employers or of employees.[49] And this work continues the tradition by decomposing various aspects of employer-provided health care insurance, looking at whether the insurance is offered by the employer, the scope of eligibility, who enrolls, and what the total coverage rate is for employees at establishments where health insurance is provided.

For example, in their investigation of union effects on health insurance provision, the economists Thomas Buchmueller, John DiNardo, and Robert Valletta found that deunionization explained about a third of the decline in employer-provided health insurance coverage in the United States between 1983 and 1997.[50] The coverage rate takes into account whether or not the firm offers health insurance, and if it does, to whom, and whether those workers offered insurance enroll in the employer's plan. The measure then is the product of three rates: the offer rate, the eligibility rate (which measures the percentage of employees offered insurance), and the take-up rate (which measures the rate at which employees who are offered insurance enroll or "take up" the offer). The take-up rate can be seen as a proxy of the insurance plan's quality. A high take-up rate likely indicates a high-quality plan, such as one that covers a wide range of treatments or medical conditions and does so at a low relative cost to the employee.

Decomposing health care coverage in this matter is important for at least two reasons. First, it highlights various dimensions of health insurance provision, and how firms' relative generosity on one dimension may correspond with stinginess on another. A firm may offer health insurance to most of its employees, and therefore have a high offer and eligibility rate. But if few of those eligible for employer-provided insurance actually enroll in the plan, the firm's coverage rate will be low. Conversely, a firm may offer a robust benefit package to just a select few employees, resulting in a high take-up rate, but a low rate of eligibility. The quality of employer-provided health insurance plans varies widely, as does the fraction of costs borne by the employer. For example, the retail giants Costco and Walmart both offer health insurance to some of their employees. Costco covers a much higher percentage of premium costs than Walmart, and does so for a larger fraction of its workforce, since the waiting period for new part-time employees to enroll in Costco's insurance plan is much shorter than at its rival.[51] As a result, Costco's eligibility *and* take-up rate is higher than Walmart's. Just recently, Walmart announced that part-time workers who average less than twenty-four hours a week are ineligible for any of the firm's insurance plans, restricting eligibility even further.[52]

Second, union effects on the various dimensions of employer health insurance may vary between the public and private sectors. The economists Henry Farber and Helen Levy found that employer-provided health care coverage is much more widespread in the public sector than the private sector.[53] Is this due to the greater organization rates among government workers? And along what dimension or dimensions of health insurance provision does the coverage disparity emerge? Private-sector unions may be most influential in getting firms to offer health insurance in the first place. In the public sector, unions may be more successful at expanding eligibility. Past research has found that unionized employees in the private sector are between 3 and 6 percentage points more likely to "take up" their employer-offered plan than nonunion workers, once the employees' firm size is taken into account.[54] How public-sector unions score on this crucial dimension of health insurance provision remains unexamined.

In fact, much of what public-sector unions do to secure quality health care coverage for their members remains unexamined. The research on the topic either focuses exclusively on private-sector workers and firms, or uses data with both sectors combined, obscuring any sectoral differences. What we do know is that politicians are quite eager to rein in spending by cutting union-negotiated health plans among government employees. How extensive are these plans? And how does their rate of take-up and overall coverage compare to what we see in the private sector?

Two main sources of data are available to answer these questions.[55] The first is the CPS's Benefits Supplements surveys conducted in 1988, 1993, 1995, 1997, and 1999.[56] The second source of data is the CPS-March series from 1988 to 2009. I extend past research on the topic by separating out sectoral differences in unionization effects on the various dimensions of employer-provided health insurance, relying on the periodic CPS Benefits Supplements. Figure 2.5 presents the results of this analysis. In the figure I report the rates at which respondents work at firms that offer health insurance, the eligibility rates among those offered insurance, the take-up rates among the eligible, and finally the overall coverage rate. The series averages the results from the five years in which unionization and health care measures are included in the same survey and asked of the same set of respondents.

As shown, offer rates run very high among union members in both sectors, and are nearly universal among public-sector union members. If you are a public-sector worker who belongs to a union, it is almost certain that your employer offers health insurance to at least some of the employees at your work site. In the private sector, differences in offer rates between union and nonunion workers are substantial, averaging 15 percentage points across 1988 to 1999. Differences in offer rates are much smaller among government employees as government-sector employers offer health insurance at high rates for union and nonunion workers.

Thus private-sector unions seem especially effective at getting employers to offer health insurance in the first place. Where public-sector unions seem most effective is in expanding eligibility. The union-nonunion difference in eligibility in the public sector is 11 percentage points, a difference about twice as high as found in the private sector. So whereas nearly all employers in the public sector offer health insurance to at least some of their workers, public-sector unions appear effective at expanding the class of workers eligible for health care. In the private sector, if your employer offers health insurance, you are likely to be eligible for the plan, whether you belong to a union or not.

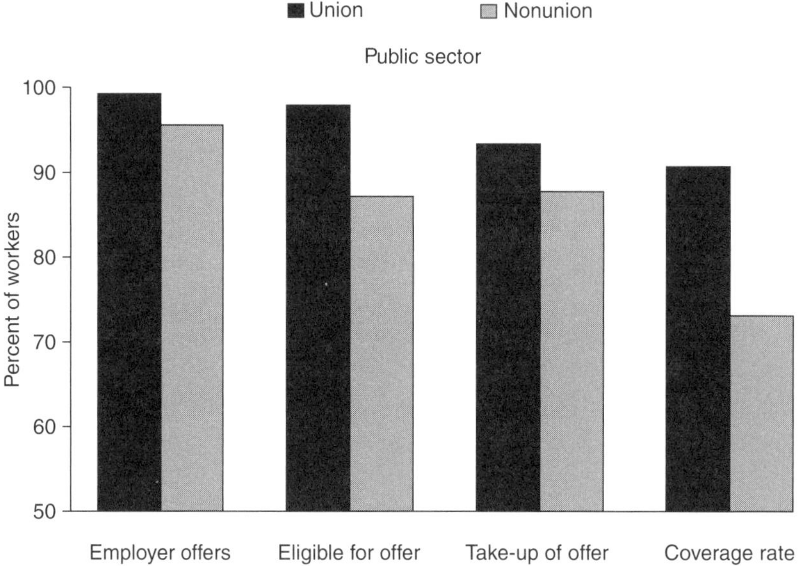

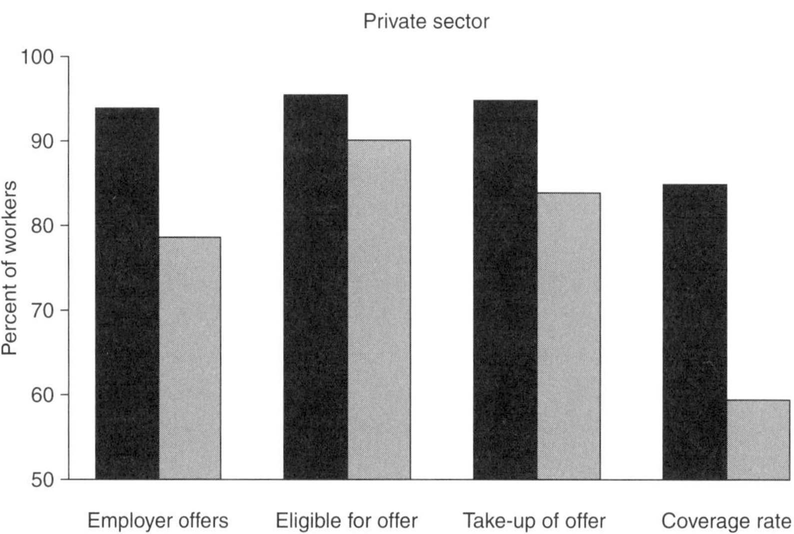

Figure 2.5. Union/nonunion differences in health insurance provision, 1988–1999. *Note:* Sample restricted to employed wage and salary workers, ages sixteen to sixty-four. *Source:* Author's compilations. Data come from CPS Benefit Supplements, various years.

The eligibility rates for nonunion private-sector workers exceed those found among nonunion government workers for every year examined.

What about the proxy for insurance quality and cost—the take-up rate? Here too the union-nonunion difference is much higher in the private sector. What explains this sectoral discrepancy? Take-up rates among public-sector nonunion workers are quite high, nearing 90 percent in most years. Based on these numbers alone, it appears that unions exert a stronger effect on plan quality and cost in the private sector. In the public sector, if you are eligible for a health insurance plan, you are more likely to take it—union or not—suggestive of higher-quality and less expensive plans.

The coverage rate captures the overall union effect on health insurance provision in the workplace. Figure 2.5 indicates that unions may play a large role in expanding employer-provided health insurance to workers, especially in the private sector. Between 1988 and 1999 less than 60 percent of nonunion private-sector workers received health insurance from their employer, compared to 85 percent of unionized workers. Public-sector differentials are not as sizable, but they are still substantial: 73 percent of nonunion government workers received employer-provided health insurance. Among unionized workers, nine in ten did—an exceptionally high rate of health insurance provision.

I emphasize that unions *may* play a large role in health care provision because the results displayed in Figure 2.5 fail to adjust for many of the factors besides union membership found to influence the provision of employer-provided health insurance. Take establishment size: Past research suggests that employer-provided health insurance plans are much more widespread in larger firms.[57] Unionization, too, is concentrated in firms with large workforces. Thus what appears to be a strong role for unions in increasing health insurance coverage rates for their members may simply reflect the fact that large firms are more likely to offer health insurance plans, and large firms are more likely to be unionized. To test whether the raw differentials revealed in the figure hold up to comparisons between similar types of workers in similar occupations, industries, and firms, I estimated a range of adjusted rates for all four dimensions of the health insurance provision process. For brevity's sake I present only two: take-up and overall coverage rates.[58] I restrict the analysis here to the April 1993 supplement, as two key controls—firm size, and tenure at one's firm—overlap only in that year.

Figure 2.6 displays the raw differences in take-up and health insurance coverage between union and nonunion workers, and then displays the differences adjusted for the influence of potentially confounding factors such as firm size. Two findings are especially notable. First, among public-sector workers, the union effect on both insurance take-up and coverage remains relatively similar whether we look at a simple cross-tabulation (the raw difference) or the adjustment that controls for a host of factors found to influence health insurance take-up and coverage. That is, adjusting for firm size, tenure at the firm, and other demographic, economic, and geographical characteristics has no impact

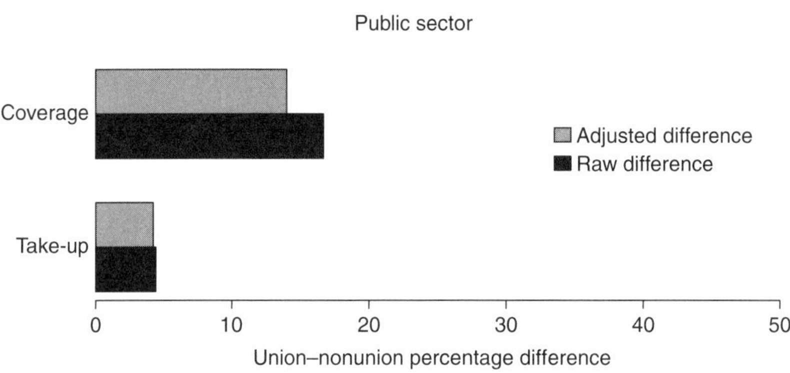

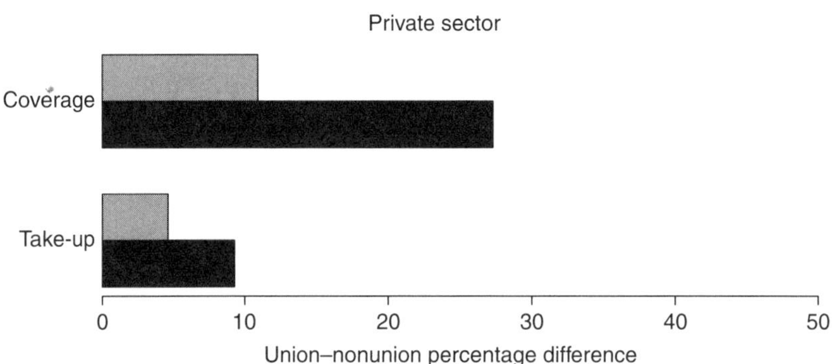

Figure 2.6. Health insurance coverage and take-up, union and nonunion workers, 1993. *Note:* Sample restricted to employed salary and wage earners, ages sixteen to sixty-four. *Source:* Author's compilations. Data come from the CPS Benefit Supplement, 1993.

on the union/nonunion difference in take-up rates. Unionized public-sector workers have a take-up rate nearly 5 percentage points higher than nonunion workers. The adjustment reduces the coverage rate, but only slightly. Even after controlling for all the different factors that affect employer-provided health insurance coverage, union members have a 14-point advantage over nonunion government employees.

What about the private sector? Here we see that the adjustments make a large difference. The union effect on insurance take-up is nearly halved, while the effect on the overall coverage rate is 60 percent less than the raw difference indicates. An examination of the underlying model reveals that firm size and firm tenure are key predictors of health insurance coverage in the private sector, and help to explain why the adjusted differences are so much lower than the cross-tabulations. Once these factors are accounted for, the union effects are marginally larger in the public sector than the private sector.

While the focus on the CPS benefit supplements suggests that—in 1993 anyway—public-sector unions were slightly more effective than private-sector unions at increasing the take-up and overall coverage rates for their members, the CPS-March data sets allow us to see if this advantage holds when examining the premium costs of employer-provided health insurance. And the CPS-March helps expand the investigation beyond 1993. For the final health care analysis, I tease out factors that determine whether an employer pays for all or only some of its employees' health insurance premiums. This examination is limited to those workers enrolled in their employer's health care plan, and limited to the roughly two decades between 1988 and 2009.[59]

Table 2.3 presents the results from this investigation. What I do here is analyze the relative impact of a range of predictors—including union membership—on whether respondents pay nothing or pay a portion of their employer-provided health care premiums. Based on the results, I then predict the percent of respondents who report paying no premium costs.[60] So, for example, as we see in the first row of the public-sector column, the probability that a union member's employer pays for all of the member's health care costs is 2.9 points higher than it is for an otherwise similar nonmember. We can describe the union effect, then, as about 3 percentage points. Keep in mind that these are model *predictions,* not actual distributions of who pays for some versus none of his or her health insurance premiums. The goal here is to isolate the effect of

Table 2.3 Differences in the probability that employer pays for health care, 1988–2009

	Percentage-point difference	
	Public sector	Private sector
1. Union vs. nonunion	2.9	17.1
2. 1988 vs. 2009	19.9	24.6
3. 25th vs. 75th income percentile	0.0	−1.5

Source: Author's compilations. Data come from CPS-March series.
Note: Sample restricted to employed wage and salary workers, ages 16 to 64.

key predictors like unionization while controlling for other influencing factors.

How does the union effect compare to other key determinants of health insurance costs? Table 2.3 also shows the effects of two other factors: year and income. The rising costs of health care—and employers' response to the increases—are evidenced by the temporal effect. Over the decades covered by this analysis, firms became much less likely to cover their workers' entire insurance expenses. For example, in the public sector, firms' likelihood of covering all premium costs was 20 points higher in 1988 than in 2009. We can describe the public-sector temporal effect, then, as roughly seven times as large as the public-sector union effect. Income levels, on the other hand, show no relationship to health care costs, at least among those employees lucky enough to be enrolled in their employer's insurance plan.

Private-sector comparisons are displayed in the right-hand column of the table. We know from the prior analyses that public-sector unions appear slightly more effective at increasing employees' take-up and overall coverage rates. But here we see that for those workers already covered by their employer's plan, private-sector unions have a much larger effect than unions representing government workers at eliminating premium costs for their members. Union members enrolled in employer-provided health insurance have a 17-point advantage over nonmembers when it comes to avoiding health insurance premium costs.[61] Indeed, all the effects presented in the table appear larger for private-sector employees, and none more so than the year under examination. In 2009, the probability that a private-sector firm covered all of the health insurance costs of its workers was a full 25 percentage points lower than in 1988, indicative of recent employer efforts to shift rising health care costs onto their employees.

❁ ❁ ❁

I have bigger issues than who sues me. Get in line.

—New Jersey governor Chris Christie[62]

So proclaimed New Jersey's chief executive in early 2011. Governor Christie was responding to threats from public-sector unions to sue the state over what the unions viewed as his abrogation of pension agreements. If there is any labor-related issue more divisive among state legislators and governors in capitals across the country than state-employee health care costs, it is pension obligations owed to state and local workers. Unions—public and private—have long bargained for employer-provided retirement packages. What remains unclear is whether unions representing private- or public-sector workers are more influential in obtaining these plans. I provide the first investigation into this issue, again relying on the CPS-March series.

The pension-related questions in the CPS are much less detailed than those pertaining to employer-provided health insurance, limiting my focus simply to whether the worker receives a pension from his or her employer. This ignores other critical factors, such as the worker's share of contribution to the pension, and whether the pension is a defined benefit plan or a defined contribution plan. But the analysis does provide a broad understanding of where unions are most influential in negotiating an employer-provided plan in the first place.

I show the results of this investigation in Table 2.4.[63] The results indicate large effects for unions in both sectors—but a much larger one in the private sector. Among private-sector union members, the probability of receiving an employer-provided pension is 21 points higher than it is for nonmembers. In the public sector, the union advantage is roughly half as large. Firm size again has a strong effect on pension provision, as does the respondent's income. Earners in the 75th percentile of the wage distribution are much more likely to receive a pension on their job than those in the bottom quartile.

Table 2.4 Differences in the probability of enrollment in an employer-provided pension plan, 1988–2009

	Percentage-point difference	
	Public sector	Private sector
1. Union vs. nonunion	11.0	20.7
2. Firm size <25 vs. 1,000+	−10.8	−37.0
3. 1988 vs. 2009	5.5	0.9
4. 25th vs. 75th income percentile	−12.0	−22.4

Source: Author's compilations. Data come from CPS-March files.
Note: Sample restricted to employed wage and salary workers, ages 16 to 64.

What those results mask, however, is the overall rates of pension provision among government workers. Part of the smaller union effect in the public sector may be due to the higher general rate of pension provision. And indeed analyses of the underlying data bear this out. In the public sector, 88 percent of workers receive a pension from their workplace, compared to just 63 percent of private-sector workers.

Who Is Represented in the Public Sector?

The wage benefits of union membership and the union influence on health insurance cost-sharing and pension provision are smaller for unionized government workers compared to private-sector union members. On the other hand, unions representing public-sector workers seem to have a larger impact than those representing private-sector workers on health insurance take-up and coverage, after accounting for other key factors influencing those dimensions of health care, such as firm size. What is left to explore is the characteristics of those who actually benefit from these union efforts. That is, what is the composition of union members in the private and public sectors in today's labor force? We know that the labor movement in the United States is now predominantly a public-sector phenomenon. What we need to find out is what this means in terms of who gets represented. We will focus on one year in particular—2009, one of the first in which the total number of public-sector union members outnumbered those in the private sector.

Other research on this topic has revealed some critical sectoral differences in union memberships. For example, Blanchflower's investigation into what predicts whether a worker will belong to a union finds that education has a negative effect on private-sector representation, and a positive effect in the public sector.[64] That is, highly educated workers are less likely to belong to a union in the private sector, and more likely in the public sector, after accounting for other important factors that pattern union memberships in the United States.

Table 2.5 presents public- and private-sector union memberships broken down by key characteristics such as race, gender, education, and income level. The first notable divergence is the stark differences in overall unionization rates. The public-sector rate in 2009 was fully 32 percentage points higher than the private-sector rate.[65] Racial and ethnic differences between union members and nonmembers in either sector are quite small. Not so when it comes to sex: Here we see that two-thirds of private-sector members are male, compared with slightly

Table 2.5 Composition of the union and nonunion workforce by sector, 2009

	Public sector 40% union		*Private sector* 8% union	
	Union	Nonunion	Union	Nonunion
% Full time	91.9	82.5	86.6	79.6
% Male	43.2	41.2	66.3	51.7
% Married	70.0	63.8	63.5	57.0
% White	74.0	71.8	68.4	68.4
% Black	10.6	12.6	10.9	9.1
% Hispanic	10.1	9.8	14.5	16.2
% Other	5.3	5.8	6.3	6.3
% HS dropouts	2.0	4.0	9.1	11.7
% HS grads	17.0	19.7	37.0	28.1
% Some college	26.2	27.7	33.6	30.8
% 4 years or more	55.1	48.8	20.3	29.4
Median weekly earnings	$928	$677	$812	$558
Mean age	44	42	42	38

Source: Author's compilations. Data come from the CPS-MORG files.
Note: Sample restricted to employed wage and salary workers, ages 16 to 64.

over half of private-sector nonmembers and well under half of public-sector workers, union and nonunion. The concentration of organized labor in the public sector means the increasing representation of female workers relative to males.

There are similarly stark inter-sectoral differences by education. Slightly over half of all private-sector union members in 2009 had at least some college experience. But that means that nearly half had only a high school diploma or less. Compare that to union members in the public sector, where over four in five members had some college experience. Replicating Blanchflower's 2006 unionization model with 2009 data finds that private-sector workers with four years or more of college were significantly less likely to belong to a union than workers with just a high school diploma.[66] Among public-sector workers, the opposite was true. Thus the increasing proportion of unionists in the public sector is disequalizing in terms of education. It is disequalizing in terms of income as well: Both union members and nonmembers in the public sector outearn their private-sector counterparts. As unions concentrate in the public sector, their historical role representing those with comparatively low education and income levels is reduced.

Where does this leave our analysis of public-sector unions? We know that public-sector workers, union and nonunion, are more affluent and highly educated than those in the private sector. They are also more likely to be women. We learned earlier that public-sector unions are less effective at delivering wage gains and at negotiating pension coverage for their members. Public-sector unions, on the other hand, are marginally more effective at boosting take-up and overall health insurance coverage rates, although the sector differences here are not dramatic, as evidenced by Figure 2.5. In general, the influence of public-sector unions on the working conditions of their members appears less substantial than in the private sector. And thus what unions do in the public sector differs from their roles in the private sector. Whom they represent differs as well.

We have also learned that the prospect for union growth in the public sector appears limited, both because of huge state-level variation in public-sector bargaining laws, and because of the dramatic stability in the public sector's share of overall employment. More recently we have witnessed a concerted assault on the very ability of public employees to bargain collectively. Thus it is quite unlikely that a rapid expansion in public-sector unionism is around the corner. Much more likely is further contraction. That leaves the private sector, in which over four-fifths of all Americans are employed. We have already learned that private-sector union wage premiums remain substantial, along with unions' abilities to deliver retirement and health packages for their members. In the next chapter, we will continue this focus on the private sector and investigate what the dramatic decline of organized labor in the private sector means for wages and inequality in modern America.

3

Wages and Inequality

Chapter 2 examined the implications of a labor movement increasingly dominated by its public-sector members. But despite dramatic reductions in union rolls, many private-sector American workers remain organized. After all, a 7 percent organization rate in an economy with over one hundred million private-sector workers translates to millions of unionized individuals.[1] Similar to decades past, the remaining pockets of the private sector that are organized tend to be concentrated in particular industries in particular areas. Research has found that nonunion workers in these heavily unionized sectors often benefit from a strong union presence.[2] In this chapter I focus on what private-sector unions continue to do for their remaining members, and for unorganized workers in labor markets where unions retain a presence. I end the chapter by situating union decline and unions' impact on worker pay within broader trends in wages and inequality patterns in the private sector as a whole.

Union Members

In early 2008, the domestic auto industry in the United States almost collapsed. A huge government loan helped salvage Chrysler and General Motors. The conditions attached to federal funds called for a radical restructuring of the companies' labor contracts. Ford managed to stay afloat without a federal bailout, but only after securing steep cuts in wages and benefits from its workforce. The concessions sought by policymakers and employers alike aimed to align the American autoworkers' contracts with those offered by foreign auto companies operating plants in the United States. The United Auto Workers (UAW) fought to delay the most painful changes, but ultimately recognized its terrible bargaining position. For union workers at Chrysler and GM, intransigence would jeopardize the federal bailout, risking the implosion of the companies, and precipitating massive layoffs of thousands of union members. For union workers at Ford, holding fast to the existing contract might necessitate a federal bailout, exactly what the company and union hoped to avoid. Thus, during the height of the negotiations, the UAW issued a statement supporting the need to move its contracts toward those of companies like Toyota and Hyundai, agreeing that "any restructuring plan should ensure that the wages and benefits of the domestic automakers should be competitive with those paid by the foreign transplants."[3]

Yet moving union contracts toward those offered by the foreign transplants risked undermining a key basis for the union itself. The foreign manufacturers operating in the United States are nonunion, and offer lower wages and leaner benefit packages as a result. Not only that: their operations are concentrated in the South, where wage rates—union or not—tend to be low. Nonetheless, the agreements negotiated in 2008 and 2009 included early buyouts of many older autoworkers, the freezing of cost-of-living adjustments (COLAs), and the introduction of a two-tiered wage system in which new hires would be offered as little as $14 an hour, half of what more senior workers earned. These adjustments helped lower the labor cost differentials between the "Big Three" and foreign manufacturers, and helped rescue the domestic auto industry.

Three years later the UAW and the auto companies returned to the bargaining table under much different financial circumstances. The firms were profitable again and rapidly expanding their product lines. And still management wanted cost differentials narrowed between their contracts and those of their nonunion competitors. Spokespersons for Ford argued that "we cannot continue to have a cost gap with the competition."[4] The UAW, on the other hand, wanted to claw back its prior concessions, since, after all, a "cost gap with the competition" is one of the reasons an autoworker may prefer union over nonunion employment.

Today, the nonunion foreign manufacturers set contract standards for the rest of the industry.[5] For example, in recent years Ford has used

Toyota's contract with its factory workers in Georgetown, Kentucky, as a benchmark in negotiations. It used to be the reverse. Walter Reuther, legendary leader of the UAW during the union's heyday in the mid-twentieth century, once remarked that his union was "the vanguard in America," composed of "the architects of the future."[6] He had right to be boastful. The contracts Reuther negotiated with auto manufacturers, including 1950's "Treaty of Detroit," provided automatic annual COLAs alongside bonuses stemming from increases in productivity, as well as generous pension packages. These contracts set the industry standard and served as a broader benchmark for union negotiations in various industries seeking to capitalize on the postwar economic boom. Disruptive strikes by restive autoworkers laid the groundwork for the generous contracts Reuther and others were able to deliver. In contrast, recent contracts with GM and Chrysler included no-strike pledges.

If these developments in auto manufacturing are any indication, union firms increasingly look to their nonunion competitors as the "vanguard" to follow. This reversal raises fundamental questions about unions' ability to raise wages for their members. Raising members' wages is and always has been a core priority for organized labor. Union leaders rarely want wage differentials between union and nonunion establishments to get out of control, as excessive premiums place organized establishments at a competitive disadvantage. Union workers are also unlikely to support outsized wage premiums that could endanger their job security. What unions desire—and often work to implement where and when possible—is to "take wages out of competition." Taking wages out of competition in a particular industry entails establishing a firm wage floor so that rival firms won't compete by undercutting the prevailing wage levels. Instead, competition between firms is based on innovation and other non-wage factors. The unionized firms in the industry may pay higher wages than the floor, but not high enough to affect competitiveness.

While this scenario has proven especially difficult to establish and maintain in the fractured, decentralized collective bargaining environment in the United States, it once prevailed in industries like automotives. In the early 1970s, nearly three-quarters of all nonmanagerial autoworkers were organized.[7] Wage differentials between the unionized workforce and the small fraction of autoworkers that remained nonunion averaged about 13 percent back then—substantial, to be sure, but not nearly as large as the overall union wage premium in the private sector. Unionized establishments in the auto sector remained competitive for at least three reasons: First, the industry was so heavily organized that there simply weren't many nonunion establishments to compete against. Second, the union-nonunion pay differential wasn't so great as to place unionized plants at a competitive disadvantage. While union members outearned nonunion autoworkers, the wage floors established in the industry prevented much undercutting on labor costs. Indeed, the average weekly wage for nonunion autoworkers in the 1970s was about $110 more per week than during the first decade of this century. And finally, import penetration and the related establishment of foreign manufacturers' U.S.-based plants remained small.

These conditions broke down in more recent years, as foreign automakers increased their share of the U.S. market and opened plants across the southern United States that paid drastically lower wages than the Big Three. The union-nonunion wage differentials that prevailed in the industry some thirty years ago widened dramatically. Average wages among organized autoworkers in recent years were roughly $300 a week higher than those of unorganized autoworkers, a difference of over 30 percent. In some cases the cost differentials exceeded 50 percent. For example, in Chattanooga, Tennessee, a Volkswagen plant that opened in 2011 offered its workers a wage and benefit package worth less than half of that of a typical Ford worker.[8]

If unable to establish standardized wage floors, unions are in the business of delivering for their own members. As we learned in Chapter 2, across the past few decades union wage premiums in the private sector remained substantial, averaging about 25 percent over nonunion workers. But as shown in Figure 2.4, the union wage premium in the private sector dipped slightly in recent years. It may be that as union strength waned in the private sector, so too did the labor movement's ability to secure high wages for its members. The new contracts among Detroit automakers certainly suggest that the union wage premium may be in decline. To explore whether unions remain effective at raising wages for their members, I first estimate annual union wage premiums for private-sector workers disaggregated by sex. The analysis largely follows my strategy in Chapter 2 in which I compared union wage premiums in the public and private sectors. The goal again is to isolate, to the extent possible, the independent effect on one's wages of belonging to a union. This involves accounting for many of the other dominant influences on wage rates, including demographic factors like age, education levels, race, and gender. And since union penetration has always been concentrated both geographically and by industry and occupation, the statistical analyses include numerous controls for industry, occupation, and where one lives.[9]

Figure 3.1 presents union wage premiums by sex over time. The wage premium series represent the percent higher wages a union member

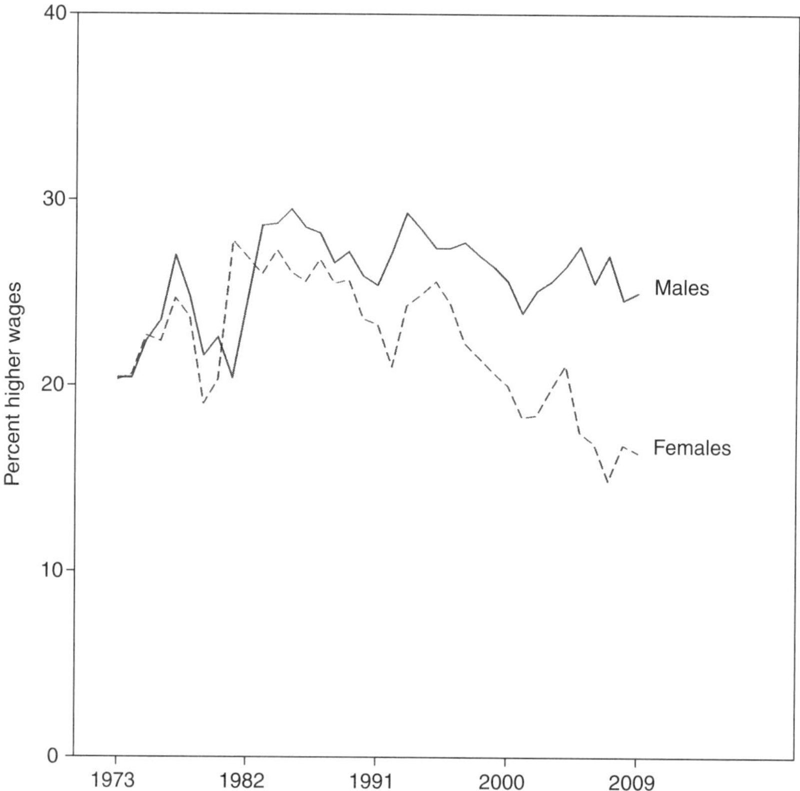

Figure 3.1. Union wage premiums in the private sector, 1973–2009. *Note:* Sample restricted to employed workers, ages sixteen to sixty-four, with positive wages. *Source:* Author's compilations. Data for 1973–1981 come from the CPS-May files; data for 1983–2009 come from the CPS-MORG files.

receives over an otherwise similar nonmember, derived from analyses of annual Current Population Survey (CPS)-May and CPS-MORG files.[10] Both the men's and women's trend lines were roughly equivalent at the beginning of the series. In 1974, for example, unionized men and women in the private sector enjoyed wages 21 percent higher than their nonunion counterparts. By the mid-1980s, men's union wage premiums exceeded women's, and the gap continued to grow through the early years of the twenty-first century.

The female series reveals a union wage advantage that drifted downward over time. After peaking in 1981, women's union wage premiums bottomed out at 15 percent in 2007. What explains this drop? A few developments seem particularly noteworthy. In the early 1970s, roughly half of the female unionized workforce in the private sector was employed in manufacturing, the traditional redoubt of organized labor. By 2009, that fraction had fallen to approximately 13 percent. In more recent years unionized women were disproportionately employed in the professional service industries working jobs such as health care aides, orderlies, or educators in private schools. Many of these occupations require a college education—the fraction of female unionists with at least a college degree more than doubled over the past quarter century—and the union-nonunion pay differential is smallest among the highest educated.

Men's union wage premiums never fell as low as women's, and the dominant trend in the men's series is stability. Despite drastic declines in unionization rates over the period covered by this analysis, the wage advantage among unionized men remained remarkably stable, averaging 26 percent between 1973 and 2009.[11] These results are surprising given recent decades of membership losses and concession bargaining. They point to unions' continuing ability to maintain pay differentials with unorganized workers, at least up through 2009.[12]

What explains the durability of the male private-sector union wage premium? First, unlike the composition of female union members, most private-sector male unionists remain employed in traditional blue-collar occupations like manufacturing, construction, and transportation. In construction and transportation, in particular, union members outearned nonunion workers by a wide margin. Second, movements, or the lack thereof, in the union wage premium depend on a number of factors. One of them is organized labor's impact on nonunion wage rates, a topic to which we now turn.

Nonmembers

> It would be acceptable to say that the activities of many unions in the United States are benefiting many nonmembers; in other words, unions are doing much good for people who do not pay them any dues.
>
> —Fred K. Foulkes, 1980[13]

Management professor Fred K. Foulkes's survey of large nonunion firms from over three decades ago found strong evidence that nonunion firms at that time often looked to their organized counterparts for guidance in setting wage and benefit rates. The spread of these union-established scales helped raise wages for nonunion workers. It also helped compress the overall distribution of wages at workplaces union and nonunion alike. And it likely helped keep the union wage premium in check, as many nonunion firms sought to approximate the wage rates set by unionized establishments.

Unions' influence on pay generally has two effects. First, organized labor helps raise wages among less-educated and blue-collar workers, thereby narrowing the pay distance *between* these workers and others. Second, the standardized wage schedules negotiated by unions reduce the spread of wages among similar groups of workers, narrowing inequality *within* those similar groups. Thus we can speak of unions' between-group and within-group effects on inequality. And past work has shown that these effects on wages and inequality extend well beyond the ranks of the unionized.

For example, in earlier research I examined how union density influenced wage inequality between workers and their managers. I measured the pay distance between nonprofessional, nonmanagerial workers and their managers in particular industries and regions. What I found was that pay discrepancies between workers and their managers were lower in those industries and regions that had higher unionization rates. What drove this dynamic was unions' ability to raise wages among average workers—I found no evidence that unions reduced managerial pay. In fact, in those industries and regions that were highly unionized, lower-level managers tended to have comparatively *higher* wages. I argued that union-negotiated wage standards reverberated up the pay scale. The pay boost that average workers received often precipitated upward wage adjustments for those occupations directly above nonsupervisory workers. However, the wage gains for average workers dwarfed the positive effect of unionization on managerial compensation, reducing inequality between workers and their supervisors in those industries and regions where unions remained strong.[14]

Managers are nonunion by definition, so my finding revealed one pathway through which unions affected nonunion wages. In that particular case, unions narrowed between-group inequality, with the groups defined as workers and their managers. Other research has focused on union threat effects that occur when nonunion employers match union pay scales to forestall an incipient organizing drive.[15] Management professor Mathew Bidwell described how in prior decades "companies were very worried about unions and the possibility of strikes. They treated their employees well so they wouldn't join a union."[16] This treatment helped lower within-group inequality since it resulted in higher wages for workers who might otherwise be tempted to unionize.

On the other hand, standard economic theory suggests unions may *increase* between-group inequality through the disemployment effects of the union wage premium. In this account, high union wages force employers to lay off existing workers or reduce new hiring, increasing the labor supply in nonunion sectors. This increased supply exerts a downward pressure on wages in unorganized sectors, widening between-group inequality. Empirical evidence for this dynamic is quite thin, however. One study of union effects on wages in the 1970s and 1980s did find some evidence for negative spillover (or "crowding" effects) at the industry level, but also found that at the city level unions operate to raise the wages of nonunion workers.[17] In a more recent study of the hospitality industry in Nevada, economist C. Jeffrey Waddoups found that the highly unionized sectors in Las Vegas did not affect wage levels in the trade sectors, where unionization rates are comparatively low.[18] Finally, sociologist Peter Catron's analysis of what caused unemployment during the recent recession revealed that belonging to a labor union *lowered* one's probability of being laid off.[19] Negative effects of unions on nonunion wages through disemployment appear to be minimal.

In a recent investigation Bruce Western and I pointed to yet another way in which nonunion workers benefited historically from a strong labor movement. We argued that organized labor in the United States often supported standards of "fair pay" that extended beyond its own membership. These efforts took various forms—ranging from union leaders' public speeches in support of greater equality, to their lobbying of elected officials for policies that would narrow wage dispersion, to union participation in formal institutions such as wartime pay boards that developed wage and price guidelines. Depending on their particular manifestation, we suggested that these efforts lowered between- and within-group inequality. And our analyses indicated they did, especially within-group inequality. In industries and regions where unions were strong, nonunion wages were generally higher, and inequality among nonunion workers generally lower compared to areas where organized labor had failed to establish a presence.[20]

But our analyses suggested that this effect on nonunion wages and wage dispersion had declined over time; unions' influence on broader pay standards appears to be waning. We have learned that unionized workers continue to outearn nonunion employees. And we have learned that the size of the union wage premium has held remarkably steady among private-sector men. But the population of unionists has shrunk considerably—unions are delivering for a smaller and smaller slice of the working population. Thus organized labor's overall influence on labor markets increasingly depends on whether and how it affects nonunion workers' wages. After all, a large union wage premium means little if only a tiny fraction of the population receives it.

And unions' impact on nonunion workers' wages has implications for the union wage premium. A stable union wage premium can result from either unchanging average wages among union and nonunion workers or from both groups experiencing relatively comparable wage increases or decreases over time. During the immediate post–World War II decades, the dominant trend was steadily rising wages for union members and nonmembers in those labor markets where unions had established a sizable presence. Organized labor negotiated generous pay packages for its members, which many nonunion firms used as benchmarks, leading to rising wages for the majority of nonprofessional, nonmanagerial workers. What has been happening recently?

To answer this question I first extend my prior research and analyze what influence unions have had on nonunion wages in recent years. To accomplish this I examine how the unionization rate in a nonunion employee's industry and region affects his or her wages.[21] To the extent that unions continue to raise wages for those not in unions, nonunion workers in heavily organized industries and regions should have higher wages than similar workers in unorganized labor markets. Why the focus on industry-region unionization rates? Employers often look within regions and industries for guidance in setting wages. And unionization rates along with pay scales vary significantly across industries and regions. While looking within states might better capture local labor markets, in larger industries, especially capital-intensive industries where unions once concentrated, pay standards stretch across state lines.[22]

Figure 3.2 presents the results of an analysis investigating how industry-region unionization affects the wages of private-sector workers who do not belong to a union. The outcome variable, weekly wages, is in log form, and thus we can interpret a point estimate of, say, 0.44, as indicating that a nonunion worker in an industry-region with a 100 percent unionization rate has, on average, a weekly wage 55 percent higher than a nonunion worker in an industry-region with a 0 percent unionization rate (since $e^{.44} = 1.55$). That stylized example is, of course, logically impossible, since the respondent is not in a union, so no industry region is composed of all union members. But what about an industry region with a 20 percent organization rate compared to one where just one in ten workers is organized? Here an estimate of 0.44 suggests that the nonunion worker in the more heavily unionized industry region has 5.5 percent higher wages than the one who works in an industry region with a 10 percent organization rate, given the 10-point unionization differential.[23]

For our purposes, the static point estimates are not as important as the trend lines.[24] The trends indicate that among both men and women, unions' ability to raise wages among nonmembers declined dramatically. Among men, the union influence on log weekly wages for nonmembers fell by over 40 percent between 1973 and 2009. Among women, the drop-off was just as substantial, and the magnitudes of the unionization effects on nonmembers were much smaller.

Thus while unions in the private sector continue to raise wages for their own members, their ability to shape pay standards among nonunion workers has diminished. Given decades of membership declines,

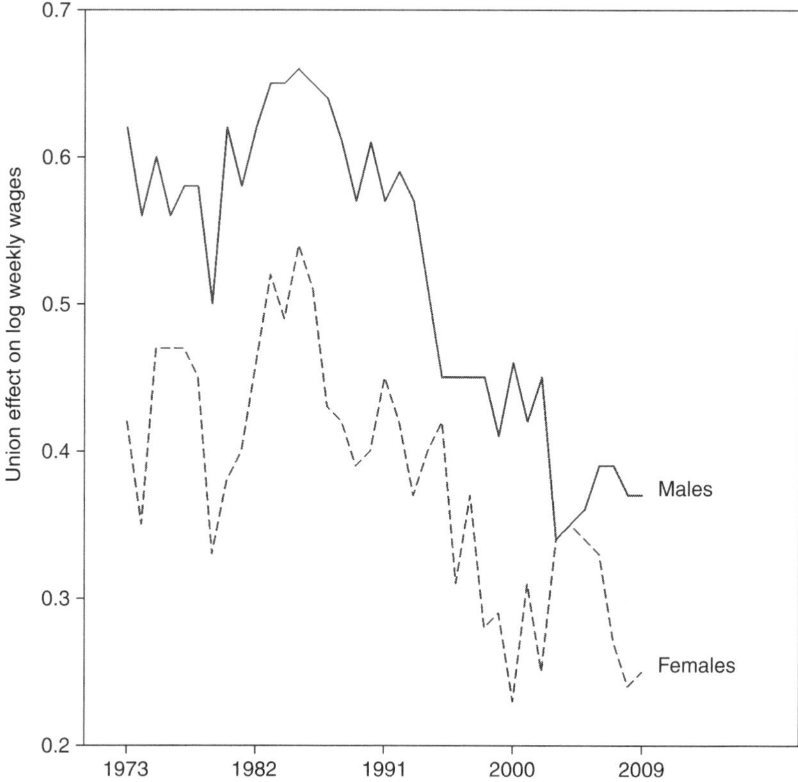

Figure 3.2. Union wage effects on nonunion workers in the private sector, 1973–2009. *Note:* Sample restricted to employed nonunion workers, ages sixteen to sixty-four, with positive wages. Point estimates represent the industry-region unionization coefficient from regressions estimating log weekly wages. See the text and Data and Methods Appendix for further details. *Source:* Author's compilations. Data for 1973–1981 come from the CPS-May files; data for 1983–2009 come from the CPS-MORG files.

this diminishment likely reflects in part the declining threat unions pose to nonunion employers. With little organizing to speak of, the typical nonunion employer today has little incentive to match union wage standards. As Bidwell summarized: "Unions are on the decline. It's easy to quash them if they try to organize."[25]

It is also likely that declining union rolls eroded the impact of the labor movement as a voice for wage equity in the labor market. In the past, according to labor activist Richard Yeselson, unions could claim "a broad institutional legitimacy grounded in their ubiquitous presence within economics, politics, and even culture."[26] Today, acting as just another interest group in the political sphere, as a cultural actor whose voice has been muffled by decades of decline, and as an institution without the power to establish and maintain wage-setting rules, unions increasingly fight a rearguard battle on behalf of their own members only. And, as the recent turmoil in the auto industry indicates, the wage and benefit standards of nonunion companies increasingly set the contours of this battle.

The Big Picture

The focus of the chapter so far has been on union effects on members and nonmembers' wages. What such a focus obscures, however, are broader wage and inequality trends in the private sector. Widening the frame helps us contextualize the union findings. We know that the male union wage premium has held steady for decades. But this information indicates nothing about broader developments in male wage levels over the period. A sizable union effect means something different if everyone's wages are dropping than if all workers are enjoying rapid wage growth. We also know that the equalizing effect of unions on nonunion wages has fallen considerably. What does that mean for developments in private-sector inequality? Where do unions fit into the bigger picture of wage and inequality trends?

Figure 3.3 plots median weekly wages in constant 2007 dollars by sex and union membership for full-time workers. The goal here is simply to capture what has been happening in private-sector pay as union influence has receded. Unsurprisingly, unionized men had the highest median wages over the three and a half decades covered by the data. Yet the wage trajectory for unionized males in the private sector was remarkably flat. In 2009, median wages stood less than a percentage point higher than where they were in the mid-1980s. Among nonunion men, wage levels actually decreased relative to levels in the early 1970s. This pattern helps us understand the union wage premium trends we saw earlier. For men, unions have simply managed to forestall the wage erosion experienced by unorganized workers. Wage growth among women has been steady, increasing by over a third for both union and nonunion workers, as rising female

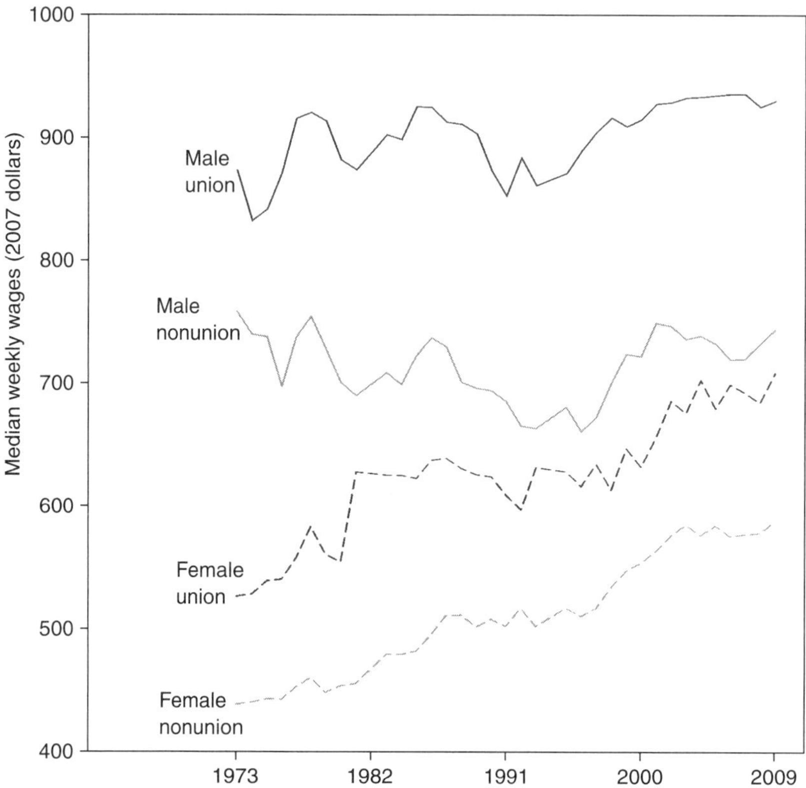

Figure 3.3. Median weekly wages for full-time private-sector workers, 1973–2009. *Note:* Sample restricted to employed workers, ages sixteen to sixty-four, with positive wages. *Source:* Author's compilations. Data for 1973–1981 come from the CPS-May files; data for 1983–2009 come from the CPS-MORG files.

labor force participation and the successes of the women's movement helped pry open occupations that had been previously limited to men.

What about wider trends in inequality? Figure 3.4 presents 90/10 weekly wage ratios for men and women, again disaggregated by union membership. The 90/10 ratio is a commonly used measure of inequality, and represents the ratio of 90th-percentile wage earners to those in the 10th percentile—the higher the ratio, the greater the inequality.[27] Similar to the median wage picture, the sample I use is restricted to full-time workers in the private sector.

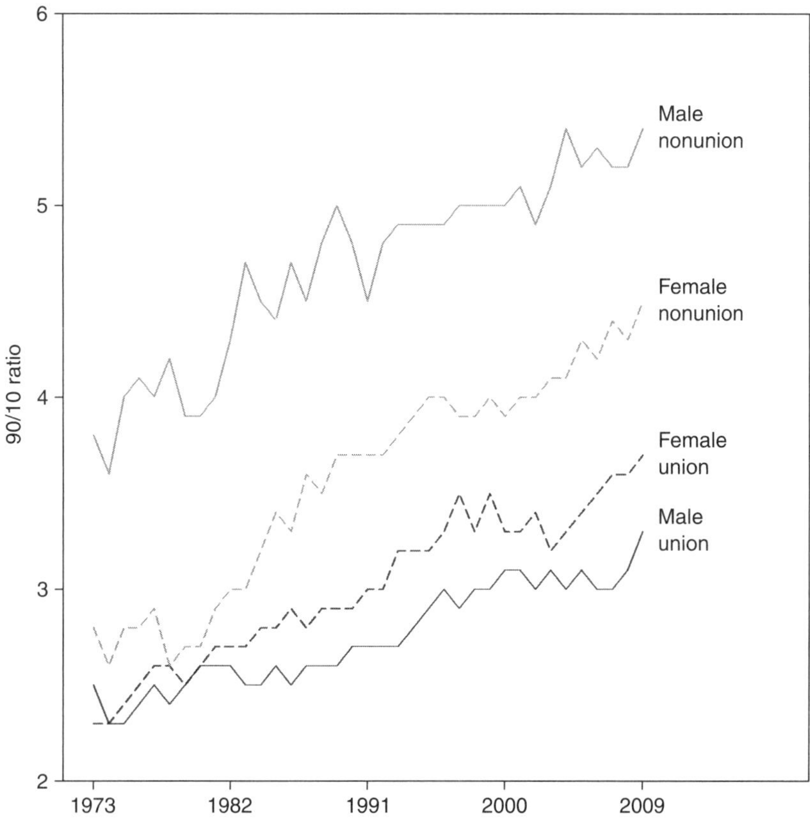

Figure 3.4. Wage inequality among full-time private-sector workers, 1973–2009. *Note:* Sample restricted to employed workers, ages sixteen to sixty-four, with positive wages. Point estimates represent 90/10 weekly wage ratios. *Source:* Author's compilations. Data for 1973–1981 come from the CPS-May files; data for 1983–2009 come from the CPS-MORG files.

Unlike the median wage trajectories, inequality trend lines do not show much of a gender discrepancy. Inequality has increased for both men and women, unionized or not. Among nonunion men, 90/10 ratios have grown by over 40 percent between the early 1970s and 2009. Yet the rise in inequality among unionized male workers was also substantial, growing by nearly a third over the same period. Female wage inequality increased even more, rising over 60 percent across the series. The rise was nearly equivalent for unionized and nonunion women.

Many factors have contributed to wage stagnation among private-sector men and steady wage growth among private-sector women. Technological advances alongside rising competitive pressures resulting from globalization have de-skilled certain jobs, while the steady integration of high-paying occupations like law and medicine have boosted female pay in the private sector. Likewise, the rise in pay inequality among men and women has plenty of antecedents. Researchers have identified increasing demand for skilled labor resulting from the introduction of new technologies, and changes in pay-setting practices as likely sources of contemporary inequality trends—to name just a few. The decrease in unionization is surely not the only story here. But there is no doubt that the collapse of the labor movement is implicated in the wage and inequality trends shown above. When the labor movement had organized over a third of the private-sector workforce, it stood as a cultural voice for pay equality and a political actor with influence unsurpassed among other interest groups. This influence often materialized in pay-setting institutions that raised the wages of average workers—union and nonunion—while holding inequality in check. The removal of the key countervailing power in the economy and polity had a direct impact on private-sector wage and inequality levels.

Moreover, evidence points to important *indirect* impacts of unions on wage trends. Take technological changes at the workplace—a common explanation for widening wage gaps and stagnant wages for low-skill workers. In his in-depth investigation of a plant restructuring, the sociologist Roberto Fernandez found that unions operated to temper and direct technological change in ways that moderated pay inequality and limited layoffs.[28] Other research found that merit-based pay was less common in unionized firms, and merit-based pay is associated with higher levels of wage dispersion.[29] With unions in retreat, organized labor's mediating impact on major workplace transformations such as technological upgrades has waned, as evidenced by the growth in inequality among union members.

Today, unions continue to raise wages for their own members. While the private-sector union wage premium for women has fallen, it remains substantial. For men, the wage advantage attributable to union membership has held relatively constant for a quarter century. And the evidence I present in Figure 3.2 suggests that unions continue to boost wages for nonunion workers in heavily organized industries and regions, although unions' influence has fallen considerably over time. In the backdrop of these trends are shrinking memberships. As Figures 3.3 and 3.4 make clear, these increasingly constricted union effects occur in a broader context of wage stagnation for private-sector men, and rising wage inequality for private-sector men and women.

The long-term effects of the new contracts hammered out between the domestic auto manufacturers and the UAW will not be known for years, given how recently the restructuring occurred. In all likelihood, they will significantly reduce the union wage premium in the auto industry, but not by propping nonunion wages up, as occurred in the past, but by forcing union wages down. During organized labor's heyday, the auto industry served as a forerunner of wider trends in the nation's economy. If that remains true, then the overall union wage premium should decline as defensive unions agree to peg labor contracts to their increasingly dominant nonunion competitors.

The recent rounds of labor negotiations in the domestic auto industry were notable not only by their emphasis on concession bargaining, but also by what was missing. In the past, gigantic strikes paralyzed huge swaths of the economy, including in the auto industry, as unions sought to increase their leverage at the bargaining table. In the fall of 1958, for example, Walter Reuther's UAW called Ford workers off their assembly lines to pressure management into accepting the union's demands for increased pay, severance packages for idled workers, and increased unemployment insurance. On the morning of September 17, nearly one hundred thousand Ford employees stretching across twenty-four states walked off their jobs. Management settled within six hours.[30]

Ford's nonmanagerial workforce today is less than half as large as it was back in 1958. Unlike GM and Chrysler, Ford did not enter its 2011 round of negotiations hamstrung by a no-strike pledge. But nobody at Ford struck. As the next chapter makes clear, strikes rarely happen anymore.

4

Strikes

Let me make one thing plain: I respect the right of workers in the private sector to strike. Indeed as president of my own union I led the first strike ever called by that union.

—President Ronald Reagan, 1981[1]

In the fall of 1980, leaders of the Professional Air Traffic Controllers Organization (PATCO) drew up a list of contract demands to present to the Federal Aviation Administration (FAA). Membership was restive. During the prior decade, even as compensation for other federal employees outpaced inflation, the purchasing power for the average air traffic controller fell. According to labor historian Joseph A. McCartin, President Jimmy Carter's administration "had been disastrous for air traffic controllers," allowing real wages to decline and simultaneously stripping the workers of early retirement and a popular program that granted immunity to controllers who reported violations to the FAA.[2] After Senator Ted Kennedy's failed effort to oust Carter from the top of the ticket in the Democratic primary battle, PATCO faced a political dilemma. Endorsing Carter "was impossible when his FAA was doing everything it could to weaken PATCO's negotiating position" in advance of upcoming contract talks.[3] That left two options: not endorsing anyone in the presidential contest, or throwing PATCO's support behind the former governor of California, Ronald Reagan. The union went with Reagan.

After all, prior to entering politics, Reagan served as president of the Screen Actors Guild (SAG). And during his tenure he led his fellow actors into their first strike against the Hollywood studios. Terms of the eventual settlement included minimum wage boosts for actors and stuntmen, a retirement plan, and a health fund that Hollywood producers initiated with a $375,000 contribution.[4] During his Hollywood years, Reagan's support of organized labor was not all-encompassing—like many union leaders of his day, he regularly denounced Communist influence in the labor movement. Nonetheless, he was twice elected president of SAG, and resigned only when he began producing motion pictures. His support of unions did not end with his entry into politics. Early in his first term as governor of California, he signed an act allowing for collective bargaining between local governments and their employees. During his tenure as governor, public-sector workers initiated over one hundred illegal strikes, and both the outcomes and tone taken by the governor suggested a politician willing to work with public employee unions. As McCartin summarized: "Nearly all strike settlements included amnesty clauses, and in only sixteen cases were any punitive actions taken against strikers. Reagan never campaigned against public sector unions or specifically encouraged tougher sanctions against their strikes."[5]

And thus after Reagan's landslide in the 1980 election, PATCO leaders approached contract talks with cautious optimism. When negotiations dragged on into the spring of 1981, the union decided that the only way to get the government's undivided attention was through an explicit strike threat. The union set a walkout date for later in the summer, and hoped that the threat of a shutdown would prod the government to meet its demands. Weighing the decision, PATCO's leaders looked at Reagan's own history as a union president, his experience negotiating with unions during his governorship, and how the federal government had responded to public-sector strikes in the past. Prior administrations dealt with dozens of illegal work stoppages in the years before the PATCO dispute, and in just 20 percent of them had any strikers been fired.[6] The air traffic controllers' union also looked to its own recent experience engaging in sick-outs for clues about what action the federal government might take if they struck. The union had always been successful in winning back all the jobs for workers temporarily sanctioned for their participation in illegal job actions.[7] The union then had little reason to believe that the president would "break dramatically with precedent" by firing all striking workers permanently and dismantling their union.[8] At the time, this was a nearly unthinkable outcome. Members overwhelmingly rejected the last in a series of government contract offers in late July, and on August 3, 1981, organized air traffic controllers walked off their jobs across the country.

The decision proved an immediate disaster. The president first issued a forty-eight-hour ultimatum for the striking workers to return to their jobs. In his announcement Reagan stressed his support of private-sector work stoppages, citing his own experience as a union leader, but rejected the right of government employees to strike. When the deadline passed, and PATCO members failed to report to work, Reagan summarily fired over eleven thousand strikers, slowly replacing them with supervisors, nonstriking employees, and members of the military. The president's actions did not stop there. He barred the striking PATCO workers from ever returning to federal employment, and his Federal Labor Relations Authority decertified the union later in the fall.[9]

* * *

> Since the eighties, it has been insane to go on strike. Every strike ends in disaster.
>
> —Thomas Geoghegan, 1991[10]

Nervous private-sector union leaders watching the PATCO walkout and its aftermath might have taken solace in a few distinctive characteristics of the strike. One, it occurred in the public sector. Back in the early 1980s, government workers made up only a small portion of the total unionized workforce. And government unions operated according to regulations different from those governing their private-sector peers, including a ban on strikes by federal workers. The PATCO strike was expressly illegal, and thus Reagan could (and would) claim that his government was simply upholding the law. Two, private-sector union leaders could point to Reagan's vocal support for private-sector strikes, reiterated during his forty-eight-hour ultimatum to the PATCO workers. Because of the legal prohibitions against walkouts among many types of government employees, and the small fraction of the workforce employed by the government, public-sector strikes were comparatively rare. Thus private-sector union heads might have hoped that the lessons of PATCO did not apply to them.

They were wrong. Less than two years after the PATCO dispute, unionized copper miners in Arizona legally walked off their jobs to protest drastic wage and benefit cuts. Unbeknownst to the workers, their employer—the giant Phelps Dodge Corporation—anticipated the walkout, and had been preparing a contingency plan behind the scenes for some time. The company would use the strike as a pretext to replace permanently thousands of union workers and to dismantle the patterned bargaining that had governed the copper industry during the preceding decades. According to labor lawyer Jonathan D. Rosenblum, the lesson of the Phelps Dodge strike to private employers was clear: "If you can't live with a union, then kill it, legally, with permanent replacements."[11]

Since the 1938 Supreme Court decision *NLRB v. Mackay Radio & Telegraph Co.*, the hiring of permanent replacement workers has been legal. But for decades private-sector employers avoided the tactic—it simply fell outside the normative practices of collective bargaining. During the 1980s, it became widespread.[12] Once the practice was established in high-profile disputes such as the air traffic controllers' walkout and copper miners' strike, the mere threat of hiring permanent replacements would often suffice to bring a union to its knees. In late 1991 the once-mighty United Auto Workers (UAW) authorized a strike against Caterpillar, a major producer of construction equipment. The union was attempting to maintain pattern bargaining in the construction manufacturing industry by pegging compensation increases at Caterpillar to what workers at John Deere received. Caterpillar was committed to breaking the pattern, and after months of a bitter standoff, the company began taking applications for replacement hires. Thousands poured in, the union quickly called off the strike, and workers returned to their jobs under a temporary contract that the UAW had previously rejected.[13]

You don't have to reach as far back as PATCO, Phelps Dodge, or even Caterpillar for examples of strikes ending in disaster for the workers involved. In the fall of 2003, tens of thousands of grocery workers walked off the job following a prolonged contract dispute with their Southern California employers. Soon nearly fifty thousand additional area grocery employees joined them—against their will—when rival grocery chains locked them out in a telling display of capital solidarity. Five long months later, management approached the union with a contract proposal that would freeze wages at previous levels, ratchet up employee contributions to health coverage, and institute a two-tier compensation and benefit package in which new hires would receive much lower wages and leaner benefits than existing employees. Union strike funds had run dry, whereas management, with a combined net revenue topping $100 billion, showed no signs of capitulating, and workers were eager to return to their jobs. The union accepted management's offer, and nearly 90 percent of the eligible rank and file voted to ratify the deal. The long-idled grocery workers returned under the new contract in early March 2004.[14]

What began as an attempt by California grocery workers to reverse recent increases in their out-of-pocket health care costs and to secure wage gains ended with a wage freeze, no end to rising medical costs, and the introduction of differential pay structures at the workplace. Added to that were the millions of dollars in lost wages and benefits. From the workers' perspective, the Southern Californian work stoppage was a disaster. And according to the labor lawyer Thomas Geoghegan, it was a disaster experienced by other workers whose unions were "insane" enough to call them off their jobs in the aftermath of PATCO, Phelps Dodge, and many others.

These preceding examples point to a fundamental shift in the relationship between unions, employers, and the use of the strike. The strike has always been a gamble, but if these examples are at all representative, during the 1980s the odds of success became much steeper. Figure 4.1 presents evidence that private-sector unions heeded the lessons of Phelps Dodge and other work stoppages gone wrong by dramatically scaling back on striking. The solid-line series represents the annual number of strikes involving one thousand or more workers between 1947 and 2009. Why only large strikes? The Reagan administration's hostile policies toward organized labor extended all the way down to government spending on labor research. Early in the president's first term, Bureau of Labor Statistics (BLS) budget cuts prevented the agency from keeping track of strikes involving fewer than a thousand workers. I obtained some of the missing information after filing a Freedom of Information Act request with the Federal Mediation and Conciliation Service (FMCS). With the exception of the airline industry, parties unable to resolve contractual disputes must file with the FMCS prior to any work stoppage, as specified in section 8d of the National Labor Relations Act (NLRA). The FMCS provided data on private-

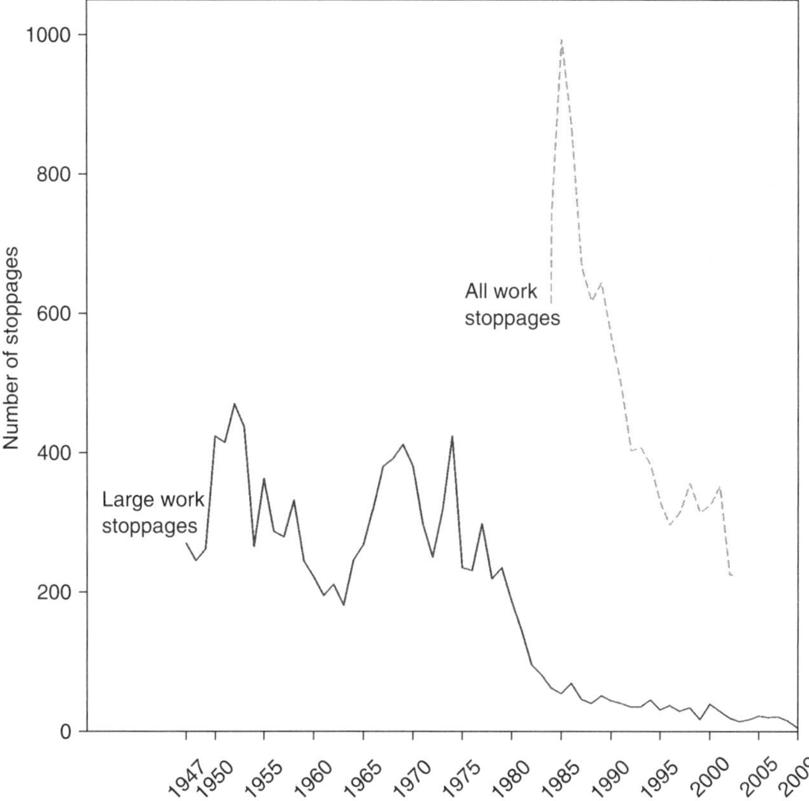

Figure 4.1. Work stoppages in the United States, 1947–2009. *Note:* Series do not distinguish between strikes and lockouts. The BLS series includes public-sector stoppages; the FMCS series is restricted to private-sector stoppages. *Source:* For large strikes, data provided by Bureau of Labor Statistics historical Work Stoppages file. For all strikes, data provided by the Federal Mediation and Conciliation Service.

sector strikes of all sizes occurring between 1984 and 2002. This truncated series is represented by the dotted line in the figure.[15]

Despite a labor force that has grown dramatically over the past half century, the number of work stoppages involving a thousand or more workers has plummeted. The series peaks in the early 1950s, when between four hundred and five hundred large strikes occurred annually. It plunges throughout the 1980s and 1990s, and bottoms out in 2009. That year, only five strikes involving one thousand or more workers occurred in the country.

Strikes of such size have always constituted a small fraction of the total number of work stoppages in the United States.[16] Thus the large-strike series may be unrepresentative for any number of reasons. For example, the demise of smokestack industries throughout the Midwest and Northeast meant a reduced number of organized factories employing thousands upon thousands of workers. It could be that the decline we see in the large-strike series may be capturing the fracturing of union members into smaller establishments throughout the country. The FMCS series suggests otherwise. The dramatic declines in work stoppages are not due to the particularities of large strikes. Despite an uptick in the mid-1980s, during the last decades of the twentieth century, strike activity in the private sector fell by well over two-thirds. The FMCS data also included information on the number of workers involved in each stoppage. In 2002, for example, around eighty-seven thousand private-sector workers, representing about a tenth of a percent of the private-sector workforce, participated in a work stoppage.

Why Have Strikes Declined? And Why Does It Matter?

Whether one focuses on the BLS or FMCS series, strike declines have spanned periods of tight labor markets and periods of steep recessions. This apparent decoupling of strike activity from the business cycle, like the dramatic decline of the strike itself, is novel. Past research emphasized the importance of economic conditions in accounting for trends in industrial disputes. Union fortunes, and with them the deployment of the strike, often depended on boom times when labor leaders could bargain with management from a position of relative strength. This linkage of strike rates with broader economic conditions has been borne out in certain historical periods, especially during the middle decades of the last century. For example, the incredibly high strike activity of the late 1940s and early 1950s corresponded with a full-employment economy (along with employer efforts to reduce wages back to prewar levels). Work stoppages in the closing years of the 1960s followed a similar pattern. Low unemployment triggered a massive increase in walkouts, falling during the second half of the 1970s with the declining fortune of the U.S. economy.[17]

That pattern no longer holds. Take the last period of full employment in the United States, the late 1990s. The tech-fueled economic boom provided unions with a fertile bargaining ground from which to strike against management for higher wages. While inflation remained low, a low jobless rate combined with tepid wage growth in core union industries should have prodded union leaders into assuming a proactive stance at the bargaining table. As Figure 4.1 makes clear, it did not. The recent decline in work stoppages no longer seems tied to short-term fluctuations in the business cycle. Unions rarely struck in the full-employment economy of the late 1990s, and they rarely struck when tougher economic times hit, such as during the steep recession that began in 2007.

Could strike decline actually indicate a growth in union power? Research on European labor movements has suggested that strike rates have historically followed an inverted U-shaped curve, where stoppages increased during the early stages of working-class organization, leveled off as labor became firmly institutionalized within the polity, and then declined as the working class shifted its focus to the political arena. In these nations, decreasing strike activity accompanied an expansion of the welfare state, as powerful labor movements succeeded in delivering for their members politically without enduring the hardships that striking entails.[18] Strike declines, then, may herald an increase in union power. Is this what has happened in the United States? Did strike declines correspond with an expansion of the welfare state and the growing political clout of the labor movement? Hardly. If anything, welfare entitlements were scaled back in the 1980s and 1990s, yet strikes continued to decline. And as we will learn more about in Chapter 7, the political clout of labor unions has fallen along with membership rolls.

Another possible explanation for the drop-off in strike activity is greater labor-management harmony at the bargaining table. Yet as strike activity plunged, unions filed unfair labor practice (ULP) charges at record rates. Indirect evidence suggests that many of these charges were responses to employer illegalities. And contrary to recent patterns in strike activity, employers' testing of existing labor law *does* seem related to economic conditions. The filing of ULPs increased during periods of high unemployment. The sociologist Holly McCammon suggests that employers used periods of slack labor demand to their advantage when confronting unions, and that often these tactics violated the law, triggering the counteraction of ULP charges by unions.[19] Yet we should not view unions' increasing use of ULPs as a substitute for the strike.

Whereas in periods when organized labor was strong the strike represented an offensive tactic, the filing of ULPs in more recent years is in many cases a defensive response to employer aggressions against existing unions.

Perhaps bargaining remains contentious, but the various parties have just gotten better at it. That is, maybe the steep drop-off is due to more-effective bargaining strategies from unions and management—perhaps a growth in transparency forestalling the need to strike? Past work in labor economics characterized strikes as bargaining mistakes due to either asymmetric information, imperfect information, or information uncertainty between the competing sides.[20] If all parties have perfect knowledge of their bargaining partners' negotiating schedules, strikes should not occur. In this framework, strikes are avoidable, and represent a misreading of an employer's or union's contract stipulations. Strikes distort the eventual settlement and cause substantial losses to all parties involved in the interim period.

In certain cases that may well have happened. The various negotiating parties may simply have grown better at reading one another over time. But here it is important to qualify the strain of labor economics that characterizes stoppages simply as mistakes. First, much of this work discounts research in political science and sociology demonstrating the political and cultural components of striking. Walkouts help generate solidarity, which is necessary to maintain unity against management offensives, and solidarity often translates to power—a vital good in confrontations with employers.[21]

Strikes may generate power in another way as well. The threat of a walkout has the potential to increase worker power at the bargaining table. After all, the threatened withdrawal of labor represents one of labor's most important points of leverage in negotiations. But the threat must appear credible. An employer unworried about a strike will simply discount the possible costs of a walkout. And during contract negotiations the surest way that a strike threat gains credibility is if the union has struck before, especially in the recent past, where the costs remain fresh in the memories of all parties involved. Thus the dramatic decline in strikes in the United States likely signals more than increasing efficiency in bargaining. It likely signals a decisive loss of leverage for organized labor.

Historians often divide strike activity over the twentieth century into three distinct periods coinciding with the rise and fall of the labor movement. Prior to passage of the NLRA, strikes were often unruly and violent, pitting workers against employers and state agents. Indeed, according to historian Jeremy Brecher, before the 1930s "the government frequently acted systematically as a strikebreaker."[22] Many of these strikes spiraled out of control into full-blown racial and ethnic riots. In the spring of 1907, for example, a longshoremen strike settlement precipitated a major riot in lower Manhattan. Following an agreement with their employers, striking dockworkers returned to their jobs to find their replacements heading the other way. As reported by the *New York Times*, they attacked the hundreds of strikebreakers—mostly Italian immigrants and African Americans—with "cotton hooks, clubs . . . and paving stones."[23] Those strikebreakers who managed to avoid the longshoremen still faced the wrath of union sympathizers in the neighborhood. Strikers' wives proved especially formidable foes, simultaneously assaulting the fleeing replacement workers and the police who had been called in to quell the uprising. The *New York Times* recounted that one woman, armed with an iron poker, "had knocked down three Italians, and was pounding them on the head with the poker when the police rescued the men." Another woman was found "seated upon an Italian and was pounding him with a baseball bat."[24]

These chaotic, often violent labor disputes of the turn of the century soon gave way to mass organizing strikes by the nation's fast-growing industrial unions. Unlike in the early decades of the twentieth century, support by the state in the form of the Roosevelt administration's pro-union policies during the New Deal era propelled the labor movement and convinced many employers to accept unions at their firms. By the close of World War II, the legitimation of organized labor in the law, alongside steady union growth, helped regularize bargaining relations between unions and management. This growth provided labor with the organizational base from which workers could successfully strike against their employers. And strike they did. At the height of the post–World War II strike wave, for example, nearly five million American workers walked the picket line annually.[25] Even by the mid-1970s, when union representation rates had begun to decline, over five thousand strikes shook the American economy each year.[26]

Because of the peculiarities of U.S. labor law, by the mid-twentieth century, trade unions no longer initiated work stoppages for organizing purposes on a large scale, as they had in decades past. In particular, following passage of the NLRA, courts interpreted the law to protect the right of *unions* to strike, not workers. As a result, according to Brecher, "only an extremely narrow range of strikes were legally protected. Generally, they had to be called by a union . . . and they could only be about wages, hours, and working conditions."[27]As a result, strikes largely occurred over compensation, and were primarily confined to periods of contract renegotiation.

Research has found that during this period strikes and the threat of strikes in certain sectors raised the wages of workers relative to their nonstriking, unionized peers. Substantial strike funds coupled with the damage that prolonged work stoppages caused employers, especially in capital-intensive industries, enabled a well-established labor movement to deploy the strike to achieve wage and benefit gains for its members. For example, using a 1979 employee survey, sociologist Michael Wallace and his colleagues found evidence that workers who had directly participated in a strike in their past had higher wages than otherwise comparable nonstrikers.[28] In a study focusing on the printing and publishing industry, sociologist Arne Kalleberg and his colleagues argued that during particular periods strike frequency increased labor's share of total income, especially during the first few decades following World War II—a finding echoed in the work of fellow sociologist Beth Rubin.[29] An active union with a history of striking simply had more leverage in negotiations with its employer than a relatively dormant one. For the entire labor movement then, falling strike activity may actually represent a real financial loss, and a clear sign of declining power.

What did a successful strike look like? Take the rubber industry strike of 1967. In the postwar decades, a handful of firms dominated rubber production and processing in the United States. All were organized by the United Rubber Workers. In the spring, contracts expired at the five major rubber firms: Goodyear, Firestone, General Tire, Uniroyal, and B. F. Goodrich. Coordinating contract expirations was a common union practice during this period of pattern bargaining, where settlements with one firm often served as the basis for agreements with others in the industry. In late April, workers at three of the five companies struck, demanding increased wages, pensions, vacation time, and unemployment benefits. Workers at the other two firms followed suit later that spring. In return, the employers banded together and developed a generous three-year pay and benefit package that they unveiled to the union in early June. The package's broad outlines would apply to all production workers at the striking firms. One by one, the union settled with the rubber companies, and the rank and file ratified a resulting contract that in broad form duplicated the employers' coordinated package. The firms would raise workers' total compensation by over 5 percent, and increase employer contributions to supplemental unemployment insurance while adding paid vacation days based on seniority. Workers at Uniroyal held out the longest, agreeing to return to their jobs in late July after ratifying a contract that "largely duplicated" the agreements made at their rival firms, as reported by the *Wall Street Journal*.[30]

Or take the 1933 strike at the Hormel meatpacking plant in Austin, Minnesota. The timing and economic setting of the Hormel conflict differed from the major walkouts that were to come in important ways. For instance, unlike the industry-wide walkout that shook the rubber industry three decades later, the Hormel strike largely predated pattern bargaining whereby a contract agreement between a leading firm and major union provided the outline for industry-wide wage and benefit standards. And rather than benefiting from a fast-growing economy like that of the late 1960s, Hormel workers struck during disastrous economic conditions that rendered organized labor relatively quiescent. But the stoppage would prove a harbinger of strikes to come in two key ways.[31] First, its target: After escorting (and none too gently) the company's CEO, Jay Hormel, and other top managers from their offices, the strikers zeroed in on the company's product by leaving twenty million pounds of meat on racks, threatening to spoil if the impasse did not end soon. Second, the result: While the union did not achieve all its demands, it secured substantial wage gains for various classes of employees following arbitration.[32] For decades, the Hormel meatpackers of Austin enjoyed generous contracts, with regular wage increases, profit-sharing agreements, and a provision to allocate certain jobs to disabled war veterans.

Today the slaughterhouse remains, but under new management. Over the years, Hormel has "outsourced" much of the butcher work to in-house companies, who then deliver their product to the Hormel packaging plant next door. The practice has allowed Hormel to steadily whittle away at its once-generous labor contracts. A brutal strike in the mid-1980s, precipitated by management's unilateral demand of a 23 percent wage cut, further reduced employees' living standards. That strike pitted union members against union members, as the national United Food and Commercial Workers union begged the local to back away from its bargaining position. While the national union urged the local to call off the walkout, the governor of the state called in hundreds of National Guardsmen. Troops clad in riot gear cleared a pathway for replacement workers to maintain production.[33] Despite this state involvement, the strike dragged on for over a year, and ended when the national union put the local into receivership and agreed to wage rates a penny over the company's last offer.[34]

This most recent Hormel strike is typical of stoppages during the third and most recent era. So what changed? Why today does the typical strike "end in disaster" for the workers involved? As noted, the decline doesn't seem driven by the business cycle, by more harmonious or transparent bargaining practices, or by the increasing power of the labor movement. It does seem clear that the broader employer assault on labor unions that began in the 1970s helped stymie strike activity. The hiring of permanent replacements, moving operations to nonunion facilities in the aftermath of a strike—these tactics would make any rational union leader think twice about calling members off the job. And declining membership rates shrank the pool of potential strikers, although strike declines outpaced membership losses.

It also may be that part of the decline in strike activity reflected organized labor's realization that strikes rarely accomplished what they had in the past. For example, strike activity may no longer lift workers' wages. In prior research I investigated this issue by linking the detailed FMCS strike information to Current Population Survey (CPS) data.[35] The strike data provided by the FMCS contained measures on the number of workers involved in a dispute, the strike's duration, location, date, employer name, union name, and company product. Ideally, to test the hypothesis that strikes led to wage increases for the participating workers, we would match these firm-level strike data to firm-level data on pay rates and unionization levels. Unfortunately, no such comprehensive data set exists. Instead, I used the employer name and product information provided in the FMCS data to link each strike to a three-digit Standard Industrial Classification code. I categorized over ten thousand strikes by the industry and locality in which they took place. This served as the necessary bridge to link the FMCS data to data from the CPS. I used these industry codes, along with the region in which the strike occurred, to create a data set composed of strike rates, wage rates, and assorted other workforce characteristics at the detailed industry-region level. While data limitations prevented measuring the direct impact on one's wages of participating in a strike, the data analyses did indicate whether those union members in industries and regions with comparatively high strike rates had higher wages than members in industries and regions where strikes were rare.[36]

The results showed that the positive influence of strike activity on wages—whether restricted to the entire workforce, to the highly unionized sector, or to those industries within the highly unionized sector that have maintained the strongest union presence—has disappeared. In contrast with earlier eras, strikes no longer affected workers' wages. Strike activity also failed to narrow worker pay dispersion. I examined whether a high strike rate correlated with lower levels of wage inequality at the industry-region level. It did not.[37]

A few caveats about this research are in order. Given the level of data aggregation, my analysis could not detect the typical outcome of an individual strike. It may be that in the contemporary era unions call for strikes only when faced with the most desperate situations, such as a plant closing, rapid downsizing, or severe pay cuts. Even a "successful" strike under such adverse circumstances is only likely to restore the status quo, and is unlikely to translate into real wage growth for the workers involved. Or, strikes may now be a sufficiently rare event that even a strike settlement that does lead to wage increases for the workers involved fails to reverberate across similar firms, leading to a minimal overall effect on wages. That is, given the relative infrequency of strikes, employers may no longer feel threatened by them. Finally, the results may indicate an increased use of lockouts by employers. As I mentioned earlier, no work-stoppage data distinguishes between strikes and lockouts, so the lack of a positive strike effect may reflect the increased willingness of employers to lock out their workers in order to secure wage cuts and other concessions.

It could also be that the dominant type of strikes in the immediate post–World War II period—namely, strikes over economic issues—has fallen in frequency compared with other types of walkouts. Making use of earlier BLS strike data, Wallace calculated that for the entire post–World War II period, strikes over wages rarely fell below half of all work stoppages, rising to over two-thirds by the early 1980s.[38] Strikes over job security issues (layoffs, tenure arrangements, and the like) remained relatively infrequent from the 1950s onward. However, it may be that strikes over job security issues now loom larger as workers scramble to retain their positions or seniority arrangements in the workplace. No data on strikes during the last few decades distinguishes between types of work stoppages, and a lack of a wage effect may be partly driven by a growth in disputes over job security or other contentious issues in the workplace.

We also learned in Chapter 3 that despite the severed connection between strikes and wages, the union wage premium remains sizable. It is clear then that the near disappearance of strike activity—a prominent example of what unions no longer do—has not eliminated unions' abilities to secure wage gains for their members. But the broader context is important to keep in mind. From the 1980s onward, as strike activity plummeted and unionization fell to its lowest rate since the 1920s, average wage levels remained stagnant. The unions that survived were able to maintain sizable premiums during a period of growing inequality and flat wage levels for the broad middle of the distribution. By contrast, when unions were strong, large and active memberships generated premiums in a context of rapidly rising wages for most nonprofessional, nonmanagerial workers. Union wages were higher than nonunion wages, but wages were growing for nearly everyone. Strikes likely helped union members maintain this pay differential despite robust wage growth for the entire working class. Also, the union wage premium describes union members' wages relative to nonmembers. It does not tell us whether members in particularly active unions earn more than their peers in unions that do not strike. Especially in an era where belonging to a union and striking are both low-frequency occurrences, the overall union wage premium is a particularly coarse indicator of the effectiveness—or lack thereof—of work stoppages.

The decoupling of strikes and wages suggest one explanation for why unions are so reluctant to strike these days—strikes simply don't work to increase labor's share of available income. For those few strikes that did occur in recent years, they tended to be "nasty, brutish, and long," according to Brecher, with many employers digging in to shed existing contracts and sometimes the unions that negotiated them.[39] As a result, what was once labor's most powerful and prominent weapon in wage and benefit negotiations has nearly vanished from the American economic landscape.

5

The Timing Was Terrible

Deunionization and Racial Inequality

The decades surrounding the turn of the twentieth century proved inauspicious for the emergence of a strong African American presence in the labor movement. Early growth in U.S. unions coincided with often violent attacks on African American nonunion workers.[1] Increases in low-skill immigration from Europe resulted in intense competition for jobs among immigrants and U.S.-born whites, leading many native workers to organize in unions to protect their privileged economic position. This growing competition between European immigrants and native whites would lead to violence against African Americans, given black workers' subordinate position in the economy and their nearly universal exclusion from protective institutions like labor unions.[2]

While strikes were not a necessary condition for white unionists to attack nonunion blacks, they often proved a sufficient one. Employers' recruitment of African Americans as replacement workers frequently spurred antiblack violence.[3] During a Chicago meatpackers' strike in the summer of 1904, for example, picketers attacked an African American worker along with his ten-year-old son, gouged the eyes of another black strikebreaker, and fatally stabbed a black worker suspected of strikebreaking.[4] A strike in the same city just eight months later proved even more incendiary. According to the historian William M. Tuttle, Jr., "the hostility of striking whites toward strikebreaking Negroes had been generalized into hatred for the black race as a whole."[5] Full-scale rioting ensued, with fatalities on both sides. Unionists often threatened nonunion African Americans with lynching. And, on occasion, they followed through. During a meatpacking strike in Oklahoma City in 1922, enraged picketers kidnapped a black strikebreaker named Jake Brooks from his home, drove him six miles into the woods, and hanged him from a tree.[6]

Many white unionists and union sympathizers associated all African Americans with "scabbing." Subsequent work by historians has concluded that blacks made up a minority of strikebreakers during this bloody period in America's labor history, yet the image of blacks crossing picket lines remained etched in the popular imagination.[7] For those blacks who did cross lines, strikebreaking presented a rare opportunity for them to earn relatively decent wages, albeit for short durations and often under the constant threat of violence. Unless faced with labor strife, most industrial employers turned to African Americans only if the pool of native whites and immigrant workers had run dry, and the dominant craft unions simply kept blacks out. White workers, immigrants and natives, would make up the vast majority of union members for generations, and many union leaders fought hard to keep it that way.

As the nation's trade unions policed their racial boundaries, they pressed the state for official recognition and protection as organizations granted the legal right to bargain with employers. These political efforts culminated in congressional passage of the National Labor Relations Act (NLRA), commonly referred to by the name of its chief sponsor, Senator Robert Wagner of New York. Shepherding the bill through Congress required gaining the votes of powerful southern Democrats, who insisted on a provision excluding agricultural and domestic workers from the law's purview.[8] These exemptions had the intended effect of keeping the majority of the African American workforce unorganized and exploited. In 1935, the historic year in which President Roosevelt signed the Wagner Act into law, less than 1 percent of all union members were black.[9]

This would change remarkably quickly. In recent years no population has been more overrepresented in labor unions than African Americans, at least in the private sector. But African American unionization rates would peak just as private-sector union rolls began to plummet, suggesting that deunionization has contributed to racial wage inequality in recent decades. In this chapter, I address two primary questions: Given the contentious history between blacks and organized labor, why have African American unionization rates surpassed those of white workers for decades, and how has union decline exacerbated black-white wage inequality?

Organized Labor and African Americans

Figure 5.1 displays unionization ratios for black and white women and men between 1973 and 2009. Each series represents the African Amer-

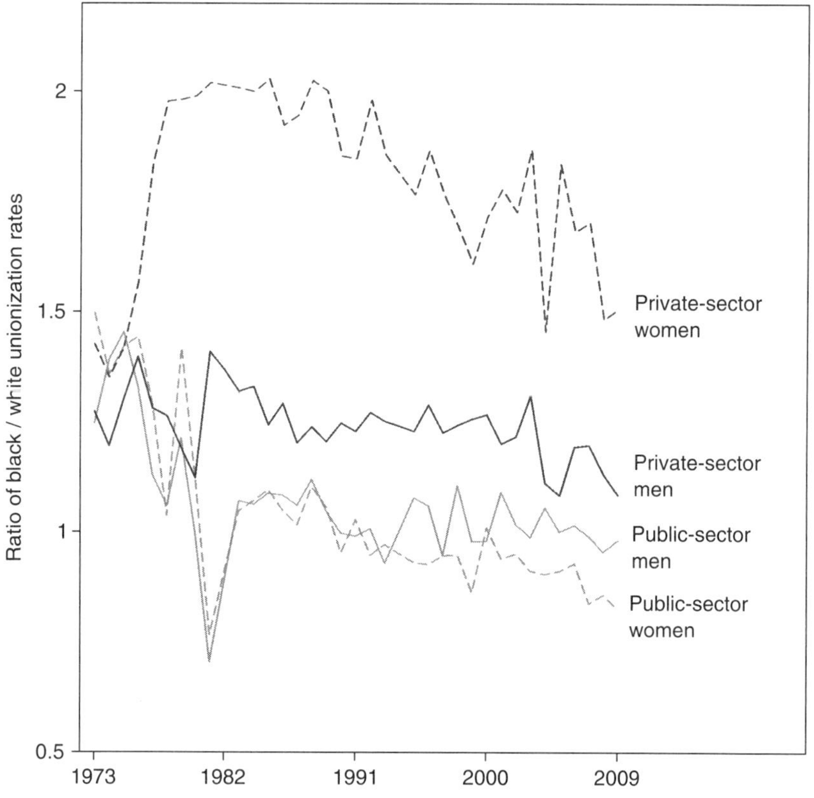

Figure 5.1. Ratio of black/white unionization rates, 1973–2009. *Note:* Sample restricted to employed workers, ages sixteen to sixty-four, with positive wages. *Source:* Author's compilations. Data for 1973–1981 come from the CPS-May files; data for 1983–2009 come from the CPS-MORG files.

ican unionization rate divided by the white unionization rate by sex and sector. As shown, private-sector unionization rates for African Americans have exceeded those of whites for decades now, especially for female workers. Despite the stereotypical image of the blue-collar male union member, unionization rates for African American females rose dramatically during the 1960s and 1970s, with nearly one in four black women in the private sector belonging to a union by the end of the 1970s. Their organized presence was not limited to traditionally female-dominated industries, either. During the end of the 1970s, half of all black female union members in the private sector worked in manufacturing, and another 10 percent worked in communications. In the heavily industrialized Midwest, the historical anchor of America's manufacturing base, rates of unionization for African American females working in the private sector peaked at 40 percent.

These high rates for black, private-sector females translated into large black-white female differentials in unionization. For decades the black female unionization rate was twice as high as the rate of white females. Corresponding race differentials among males never reached such magnitudes. In 1979, a year in which female organization rates peaked, the private-sector black-white unionization ratio for females stood at 2 to 1. Among males, the ratio stood at 1.2 to 1. Yet the organizing advantage among black males was still substantial for most of the years covered here. Even as late as 2000, the unionization rate for white males in the private sector was nearly 25 percent less than the corresponding rate for black males.

By contrast, public-sector unionization gaps largely disappeared by the early 1980s. This was true for both sexes. While black males and females were more organized than whites in the public sector during the early-to-mid 1970s, these advantages diminished quickly.[10]

What the ratios on display in Figure 5.1 obscure is the scale of private-sector organization among black and white workers throughout the past decades. As shown in Figure 5.2, this scale was tremendous, especially among black men. By the early 1970s, nearly 40 percent of black men in the private sector belonged to a union. These men were concentrated in the production and transportation industries. Indeed, over 60 percent of black male union members worked in manufacturing, and another 10 percent worked in transportation. Common occupations included machine operatives, assembly-line workers, and forklift and truck drivers.

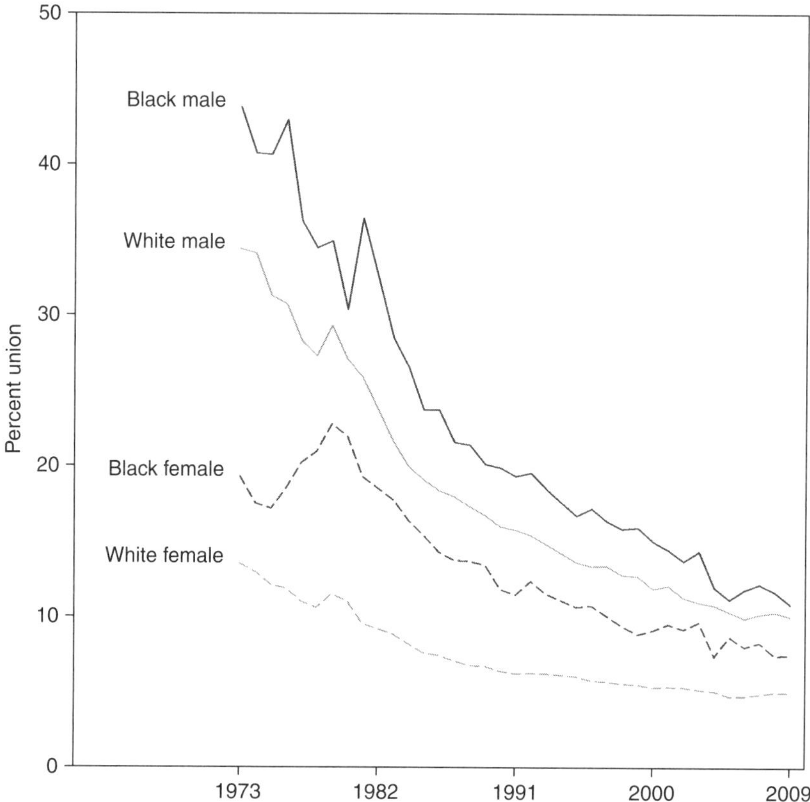

Figure 5.2. Private-sector unionization rates, 1973–2009. *Note:* Sample restricted to employed workers, ages sixteen to sixty-four, with positive wages. *Source:* Author's compilations. Data for 1973–1981 come from the CPS-May files; data for 1983–2009 come from the CPS-MORG files.

Both sets of industries experienced severe deunionization from the early 1970s onward, and the fraction of the workforce employed in manufacturing plummeted during the last decades of the twentieth century.[11] These trends are reflected in the steep declines in organization rates for African American men. Yet still over a third of the African American male private-sector workforce belonged to a labor union until the early 1980s, and over a fourth did until the mid-1980s.

Rates among African American females never approached these levels, but as noted, they were once substantial. A fifth of the black female workforce was unionized until the early 1980s, and fully one in seven black private-sector female workers belonged to a union throughout the mid-1980s. These unionized women were spread across the occupational spectrum, although like their male counterparts they concentrated in a few highly organized industries. Among production workers, many unionized black women worked as assemblers, sewers and stitchers, and packers and wrappers. Among nonproduction workers, many unionized black females worked as telephone operators, nurses' aides, and janitors. Given negligible organization rates just decades before, this turnaround for black workers—male *and* female—represents a dramatic historical reversal. The entrance of nearly a quarter of the private-sector African American female workforce into labor unions by the 1970s is especially impressive, given the double disadvantage African American females faced just decades earlier. Not only did many private-sector unions exclude blacks from their ranks, but gendered occupational hierarchies largely consigned black women to a few exclusively nonunion occupations that paid little and offered even less opportunity for advancement.[12]

What caused this reversal? Existing research on the topic points toward two related explanations. The first is the labor-market-position theory of unionization. A "positional" theory of union organizing focuses on the ways in which relatively stable industrial, occupational, and geographical factors affect unionization. According to this theory, a particular group's unionization rate will vary according to how its employment patterns map onto those labor-market positions within the economy where it is relatively easier or difficult to organize. To the extent that the population is employed in particular occupations and industries that organizers have had little luck penetrating, its unionization rates will run low, regardless of the group's desire for or past experience with unions. Conversely, to the extent that the group is in the economic locations that have proven most amenable to union efforts, its rates should run comparatively high.

Which positional factors are most important? One factor operating against organization is high labor costs relative to other factors in production.[13] And in industries with high wage bills combined with largely unskilled employment, the barriers to unionization are especially substantial. Not only do employers' incentives against unionization rise with relative wage costs, but the substitutability of labor lowers workers' bargaining leverage. Smaller firms have proven harder to organize as well, as monitoring costs are low, thereby negating a potential benefit of union presence, and the productivity gains spurred by union grievance procedures are likely lower in establishments with few employees.[14] In modern capitalist economies such as that of the United States, these characteristics—high wage bills, unskilled employment, and smaller firms—are found in many service industries, and contribute to the comparatively low unionization rates found in that sector.

Industry *location* affects unionization costs independent of characteristics specific to the industry itself. For example, state-level differences in labor laws and the (related) less union-friendly political environment of the South may depress unionization rates, other factors held constant. Occupation factors into unionization patterns as well. It has proven to be more difficult to organize white-collar workers—with their well-defined career ladders, higher levels of workplace autonomy, and greater pay—than their blue-collar counterparts, who are less likely to identify with management in battles over representation.[15]

In the specific case of African Americans, a positional theory suggests that blacks happened to be in those labor-market positions most amenable to organizing at the time when mass unionization accelerated in the United States. The capital-intensive manufacturing sector, with large, hierarchically arranged firms, constituted the unionized core of the economy in mid-twentieth-century America. The great migration northward during the early and middle decades of the twentieth century brought millions of African Americans into the expanding industrial centers of the Midwest and Northeast, areas dominated by these large, capital-intensive factories. Another million southern blacks who remained in the region left their farms for the factories of Memphis, Atlanta, and other southern cities. While unionization rates in the South never approached the levels in other regions, during the middle decades of the twentieth century unions found success in factories all over the United States, including in pockets of the traditionally antiunion South.

What accounted for the success of unions in factories? Because of relatively low wage bills and strict divisions between managers and floor workers, manufacturing plants proved easier to organize than other sectors of the economy, and provided the growing labor movement with millions of potential members. Low wage bills relative to the other costs of production lessened employer opposition to unionization drives, while strict divisions between workers and their managers lessened employee opposition to unionization, since the average worker saw little possibility of moving up into the managerial ranks.[16]

These structural factors made production work particularly susceptible to organizing efforts. At the same time many manufacturing employers were desperate for employees, shifting bargaining leverage toward workers—and toward their union representatives. The mass migration of African Americans to cities all across the country was spurred in part by the labor demands generated by a nation gearing up for war. According to the historian Karen Anderson, labor shortages in the World War II era "posed the most serious challenge in American history to the traditional management preference for white male labor in primary-sector jobs."[17] Women constituted over half of those African Americans entering the paid labor force during the war years. Among employed black women, the percentage working as domestic servants fell by 25 percent during the early 1940s as the fraction working in production occupations nearly tripled.[18] And while core production industries like auto remained predominantly male, their racial demographics changed dramatically in the mid-twentieth century. The proportion of black autoworkers, for example, more than doubled during World War II, and then doubled again in the immediate postwar decades.[19]

Overt discrimination by unions against African American workers would continue for years, especially in the craft unions affiliated with the American Federation of Labor (AFL). And the labor movement had to overcome the wariness many blacks felt toward unions as a result of the often-brutal treatment white unionists and union sympathizers meted out to blacks in prior generations. However, as fast-growing industrial unions found success organizing large manufacturing firms, "unions had little choice but to try to diversify," according to political scientist Paul Frymer, given African Americans' growing concentration in the industrial cores of many cities.[20] Historian Eric Arnesen has suggested that the "historic breakthrough" in the relationship between African Americans and organized labor came with the rise of the Congress of Industrial Organizations (CIO), a confederation of unions intent on organizing the mass-production facilities that employed so many African Americans.[21]

The United Auto Workers (UAW) was one of the fastest-growing CIO affiliates and quickly established itself as one of the most racially progressive unions in the United States. A 1941 UAW strike against Ford sought full union recognition for workers, including dues-checkoff and closed-shop provisions. Hundreds of black employees stayed on as strikebreakers, spurring the UAW to seek out local black leaders to gain their support. Before long, "black workers, whose participation in union activities had lagged well behind those of most whites, became among the most steadfast UAW members."[22] This type of outreach to African Americans helped overcome the labor movement's historic legacy as exclusionary organizations, and allowed CIO affiliates to sign up blacks in factories all across the country. At the onset of World War II, African American participation rates in the CIO unions were double their rates in the AFL-affiliated unions.[23]

The changing demographics of the labor movement redounded to organized labor's governing hierarchy, so much so that by mid-century "no labor leader could appear as anything but a racial liberal if he or she aspired to national influence," according to labor historian Nelson Lichtenstein.[24] Take Walter Reuther: Reuther assumed the helm of the UAW in 1946, a position he retained until his death in an airplane crash in 1970. Reuther's UAW provided key financial support for the 1963 civil rights march on Washington, and Reuther spoke at the gathering. Partly because of these efforts, Reuther's union had gained the loyalty of the thousands of African Americans working the production lines in auto and other factories—those locations in the economy where industrial unions found great success organizing.

By the 1970s African Americans had the highest unionization rates of any racial or ethnic group. These rapidly rising organization rates stemmed from more than blacks' overrepresentation in those industries where unions had found great success. The legacy of discrimination and continuing impediments to upward mobility concentrated blacks in nonsupervisory, nonmanagerial *occupations* eligible for union organizing.[25] African Americans, especially females, remained blocked from most of the high-skill, high-paying occupations that either were ineligible for union organizing, or featured low demand for unionization. Thus high unionization rates for blacks may have resulted from their location in both the industries and occupations where unions have been successful. If these high rates of organization stem largely from blacks' labor-market location, then analyses that account for workers' industry, occupation, and other relevant positional factors should find rates of unionization among blacks similar to those of whites. Such a finding would buttress the positional theory of unionization.

❁ ❁ ❁

> The blacks just weren't treated right, until they got that union. We didn't see freedom until we got that union in!
>
> —Irene Branch, employee of Memphis Firestone[26]

On the other hand, African Americans' high rates of unionization may result from more than where they are situated in the labor market. Unions, on average, offer higher pay and better benefits than do otherwise similar nonunion jobs. Unions may also protect against inequitable treatment by bargaining for and often delivering more standardized and transparent pay and promotion policies, as well as clearly delineated procedures to handle shop floor grievances.

For much of the twentieth century, organized labor hardly provided African Americans a refuge from racism. Discriminatory practices among unions ranged across locals and over time. As political scientist Michael Goldfield maintained, in the earlier decades of the century, with few exceptions, AFL affiliates varied only "in the degree and forms of implementation of extreme racist practices."[27] Increasing competition from CIO unions at mid-century would temper these practices in some locals, but the integration of many craft industries remained a quarter of a century away. The CIO's record was less overtly racist, especially among locals with leftist leadership.[28] Successful organizing drives in mining, steel, and, as we have seen, auto were notable for the unions' deliberately inclusive strategies.[29] But, according to industrial relations professor and civil rights leader Herbert Hill, even the most progressive unions "engaged in a variety of discriminatory practices."[30]

And even the most progressive unions had to deal with a rank and file often vehemently opposed to integration. So-called "hate strikes" erupted in plants all across the country as blacks sought entry into positions and organizations they had long been denied. In 1943, for example, after the introduction of black women into a rubber plant because of wartime labor shortages, thousands of white women walked off the job, demanding separate bathroom facilities. As Anderson maintained, many of these stoppages emerged because whites "feared that blacks were dirty or diseased."[31] Union leaders watching such events worried about the risk that integration could pose to the morale and dedication of their existing members, or to those potential members still adamantly opposed to integration.

Moreover, when it came to race, numerous unions were not progressive at all. Holdouts included railway unions and many of the elite craft organizations. It was only in the late 1960s and early 1970s that these unions began to integrate their ranks and end discriminatory practices, owing in part to legal coercion and the mounting financial strain of lawsuits.[32]

Still, the "variety of discriminatory practices" a unionized African American worker could expect in her local was often preferable to what she would experience in an unorganized job. Missing from many accounts of unions' racist practices is the fact that it was often worse for blacks in unorganized workplaces. Irene Branch's story suggests that the union provided her and her fellow black rubber workers some semblance of freedom in the workplace. While racist treatment would continue, the union served as an important mechanism for redress that was simply absent in unorganized workplaces.[33] Or take construction unions, often identified as among the most stubborn and recalcitrant when it came to matters of race. During the late 1960s and 1970s, the Richard Nixon administration took various steps to force construction unions to integrate and provide African Americans access to highly desired apprenticeships. It was certainly the case that many construction unions had systematically excluded blacks from the most privileged positions for generations. Yet as historian Judith Stein has recounted, "The nonunion labor pool was hardly buoyant water for blacks. Actually, unionized contractors had better racial records than the nonunion ones."[34] During the mid-1970s, the fraction of minority apprentices in union programs was twice as high as the fraction in nonunion ones.[35]

As a result, when unions began to diversify, many African American workers looked to them as potential protection against economic and racial inequity.[36] As Lichtenstein explained, "To African-Americans . . . long subject to the capricious exercise of an ethnically coded set of discriminations, the very bureaucratization of labor relations inherent in mass unionization had an impact that was liberating in the world of daily work life."[37]

The "liberating" impact of unionized work speaks more to what African Americans confronted in nonunion settings than to the racially progressive policies of many unions. Nevertheless, this historical evidence suggests that African American overrepresentation in organized labor may not simply be due to their concentration in labor-market sectors easy to organize. The second dominant explanation for African Americans' concentration in labor unions is what I term the "protectionist" theory of unionization. It refers to the protection against discriminatory treatment that organized labor may provide black workers.

How would one differentiate between positional and protectionist explanations? If African American workers seek union jobs to escape discriminatory employers in the nonunion sector, then accounting for their labor-market location should still result in higher rates of organization than whites. That is, an African American working in the same industry, occupation, and area as a comparable white worker should have a higher probability of being in a union. Now, "protection" here is not directly observed. The Current Population Survey (CPS) lacks information about why individuals enter particular jobs, or how they feel about unions. This lack of information precludes a purely causal interpretation of the findings. Yet there is substantial historical and public opinion research to buttress the protectionist argument. As indicated by Branch's quote above, historical research reveals a strong desire among many African Americans for the bureaucratized, standardized routines of union employment—a desire reflected in the accounts of scholars Nelson Lichtenstein and Robert Korstad, as well as in Michael Honey's oral histories of African American workers.[38]

Regarding public attitudes toward organized labor, the economist Richard Freeman and politics and law professor Joel Rogers found that African Americans' support of unions was higher than other groups'.[39] In fact, in their models of union support, the most powerful predictor of pro-union attitudes among nonunion workers was race. In recent years, nonunion black workers were nearly 30 percent more likely to support a unionization drive than otherwise similar nonunion white workers. Among other factors, the authors attributed this finding to "the exceptional vulnerability of blacks in the job market" and their "need for protection against discrimination."[40] As I explained in Chapter

1, I do not feel that the relative popularity of organized labor tells us much about union decline. Not only has overall demand for unions remained high in the United States, but no amount of pro-union sentiment can overcome a disadvantageous economic position and employers steadfast in their opposition to unionization. But the comparatively high demand for union protection among blacks may tell us something about their higher unionization rates relative to whites occupying similar economic positions and working for employers with similar stances toward unions. This is especially true during earlier years when unionization rates remained substantial. Thus in concert with the historical research, this prior work on union attitudes helps contextualize any findings of elevated unionization rates for African Americans—and helps point these potential findings toward a protectionist interpretation.

To test positional and protectionist explanations of African American unionization rates, I again utilize the CPS-May and CPS-MORG files from 1973 to 2009. The data provide information on a range of factors found to influence one's likelihood of belonging to a union, including demographic information like age, race/ethnicity, and sex, positional characteristics like industry, occupation, and sector, and geographical characteristics such as the state in which the respondent resides. The empirical task here is to assess how well these variables explain differences in unionization rates between black and white workers. If these core positional variables account for all the variation in black and white unionization probabilities, then there is little room for racial differences in the desire for union protection to account for blacks' higher organization rates. On the other hand, if the statistical analyses that include key positional variables still reveal large group disparities in unionization, then I interpret the difference as consistent with a protectionist theory of unionization. But we have to be cautious with our interpretations, given that the associations we draw are indirect—"protection" in this analysis is inferred, not directly observed.

Despite this drawback, the analysis I present below represents one of the most comprehensive investigations into African Americans' engagement with the labor movement in modern America. The goal is to compare workers in similar economic positions, in similar locations, and with similar demographic characteristics, save for their race. These tests treat whether or not the respondent belongs to a labor union as the dependent variable. And what we are most interested in assessing is whether one's union membership "depends on," in the statistical sense, the respondent's race—namely whether or not he or she is African American. To accomplish this, the statistical tests measure whether or not blacks have elevated or depressed unionization rates once we account for all the previously discussed factors that affect unionization. The total number of these factors exceeds fifty in the annual models I present in Figure 5.3.[41] Given the small differences in unionization rates between blacks and whites in the public sector, I limit these analyses to private-sector workers.

In Figure 5.3 I present the results from the unionization analyses. The point estimates in the figure represent the odds of unionization for blacks relative to white workers. In any given year, an odds ratio above one indicates a higher probability of unionization for blacks than whites. I break the results out by sex, given the larger racial disparities in unionization among females than males evident in Figure 5.1. I include a "race/ethnicity model" series as a baseline comparison for the positional series. Aside from the respondent's race/ethnicity, the baseline series does not account for any other factors influencing union membership. Among private-sector men, this baseline adjustment averages 1.3 over the years covered here, indicating that black men have, on average, roughly a third higher odds of unionization compared to whites. Among private-sector women, the equivalent series averages a much higher 1.9, revealing that black women average nearly twice the odds of white women of belonging to a union. The baseline estimates for men and women trend slightly downward over time, following the general pattern of declining unionization rates for all groups.

The "positional" series adjusts for the respondents' labor-market position, along with a host of other factors that pattern unionization. This adjustment actually *increases* African American odds of belonging to a union relative to whites. Once you compare black workers and white workers who live in similar areas, who do similar types of work, and who have similar education and age levels (among many other characteristics), blacks' likelihood of being in a union is higher than when comparing blacks and whites in general. This is especially true among women. African American odds ratios peak in the 1980s at just under 2.5 to 1. Even by the end of the series, when unionization rates among all groups have declined precipitously, African American females have

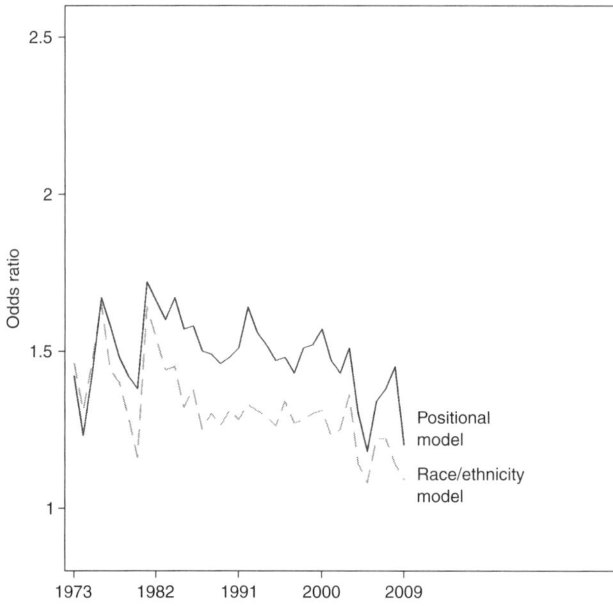

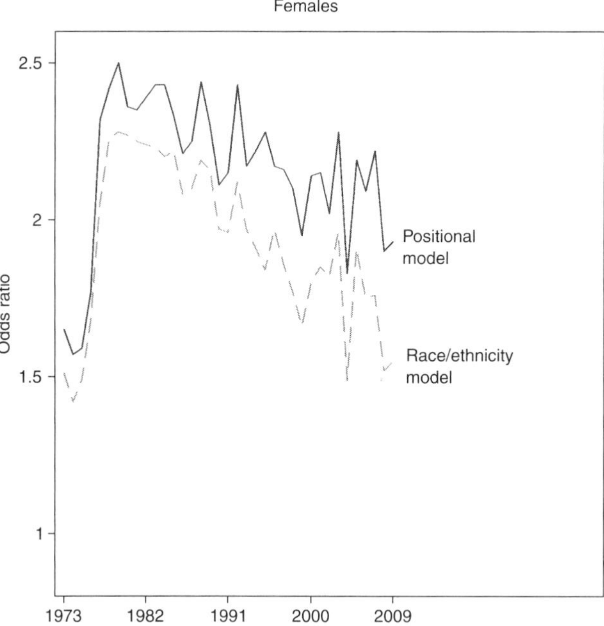

Figure 5.3. Blacks' odds of unionization, 1973–2009. *Note:* Sample restricted to employed workers, ages sixteen to sixty-four. *Source:* Author's compilations. Data for 1973–1981 come from the CPS-May files; data for 1983–2009 come from the CPS-MORG files.

nearly twice the odds of being in a union compared to otherwise similar white females. While the African American effect is not as large among men, they still have roughly 1.5 times the odds of belonging to a union compared to white men across the series.[42]

These results provide strong evidence that blacks' overrepresentation in private-sector unions is not solely reducible to their concentration in highly unionized labor-market positions. Indeed, accounting for labor-market position results in higher African American unionization odds. The results, then, are consistent with the protectionist hypothesis. African American overrepresentation in unionized jobs stems in part from the protections unions may provide against employer discrimination. It is not that labor-market position does not matter. In these analyses your industry, occupation, and where in the country you work are powerful predictors of whether or not you will be unionized. It is just that once you compare blacks and whites in similar positions, blacks are much more likely to belong to a labor union.

In past work I have explored alternative ways of measuring union participation among blacks and whites. In one investigation, my colleague Meredith Kleykamp and I used the National Longitudinal Study of Youth (NLSY), a panel data set of nearly thirteen thousand individuals ages fourteen to twenty-two when first surveyed in 1979. Unlike the CPS, the NLSY measures respondents' Armed Forces Qualifying Test (AFQT) scores, a test of verbal and math ability. These scores provide a proxy for unmeasured skills often used in econometric analyses. After adjusting for respondents' AFQT scores, we found that African Americans were more likely to belong to a union than whites, similar to the results shown here, although the gender differences were more muted.[43] In another analysis we used the CPS to construct one-year panels and tested whether blacks were more likely to join a union than whites.[44] They were, providing further evidence that the results on display in Figure 5.3 are not due to the particularities of the data set I use or to my estimation strategy.

The preceding findings help answer *why* African Americans are overrepresented in private-sector unions. The next step is to answer *how* this overrepresentation affects economic inequality between black and white workers. African Americans' disproportionate concentration in unions means that deunionization has likely hit their economic fortunes especially hard. And deunionization has likely contributed to contemporary patterns of racial wage inequality, given blacks' overrepresentation in a labor-market institution suffering from decades of decline. In what follows I assess how deunionization has shaped racial wage inequality in recent decades. Since black-white differences in unionization rates are negligible in the public sector, and have been for some time, my primary focus is on private-sector workers. Given that racial differences in unionization rates are more pronounced among females, it is likely that deunionization's role in exacerbating black-white inequality is larger among females than males. But before we get to that, we first need to understand what has been happening to racial wage inequality in the United States.

Black-White Wage Inequality in the Modern United States

In Figure 5.4 I plot whites' wage advantages over their African American counterparts for men and women in the private and public sector.[45] Let's begin with men. As shown, racial wage gaps among men are large, persistent, and exceed those of females throughout the years covered here. Among male public-sector employees, white wage advantages have declined a bit in recent years. In the private sector, the trend line is quite flat, at least since 1990.[46] The level of inequality among private-sector males surpasses that of private-sector females for every year covered by this analysis. And male racial wage inequality is not due to differences in hours worked. Pay disparities between black and white males are comparable to the ones shown here if I limit the sample to full-time workers only. A portion of these persistent gaps is due to whites' overrepresentation among top-end earners. Yet limiting the sample to the bottom 95 percent of wage earners only reduces racial wage disparities by 7–8 percentage points in recent years.

Explanations for this stubborn racial wage inequality tend to focus on African American males' overrepresentation in the highly industrialized, core manufacturing cities of the Midwest and Northeast. Deindustrialization would hit these urban areas especially hard, with the transformation to a postindustrial economy creating new jobs that former factory workers often lacked the skills to perform. Take Detroit: In 1947, city leaders could boast of over 338,000 jobs in manufacturing. Three decades later, the number had fallen to 153,000.[47] Postwar automation in the auto factories rendered many positions obsolete—positions

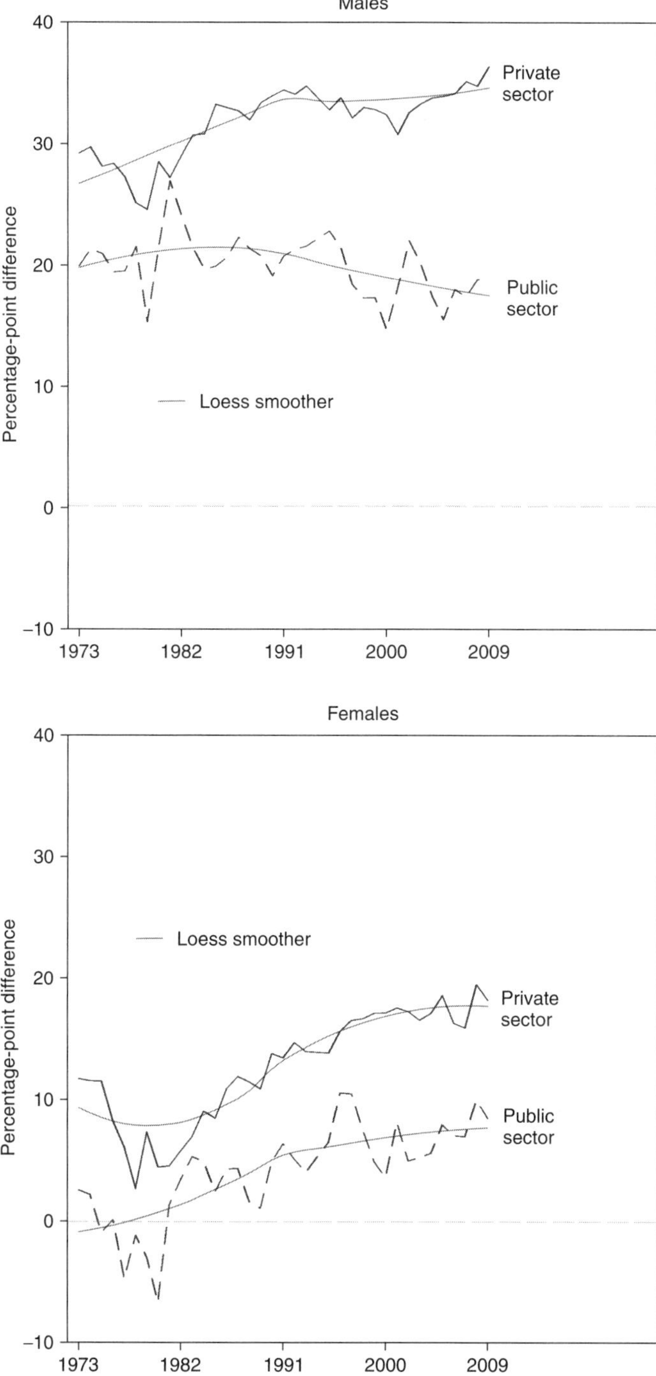

Figure 5.4. Racial wage inequality, 1973–2009. *Note:* Y axis represents the percentage-point difference in mean wages between whites and African Americans. Sample restricted to employed workers, ages sixteen to sixty-four, with positive wages. *Source:* Author's compilations. Data for 1973–1981 come from the CPS-May files; data for 1983–2009 come from the CPS-MORG files.

disproportionately held by black men. Ford's sprawling River Rouge complex, for example, employed nearly ten thousand black workers. Technological upgrading and other managerial changes sliced the River Rouge workforce in half during the 1950s.[48] Even those new jobs that former factory workers could perform were often located well beyond city limits now dominated by shuttered plant gates and growing deterioration.[49]

Analyses of racial wage gaps in the public sector are much less extensive, but existing work points to individual-level factors like skill differences between black and white workers, and to differences in occupational placement. Black males in the public sector, on average, seem to have lower levels of "human capital" or job-relevant skills, and are concentrated in public-sector occupations that pay less than others.[50]

On the bottom of the figure I plot the corresponding racial wage gaps series for private- and public-sector women. The trend lines here tell a different story from what we see for men. After almost reaching parity by 1980, wage inequality between black and white women nearly tripled during the 1980s and 1990s.[51] Explanations for the earlier narrowing focused, among other possibilities, on occupational shifts among African Americans during the period, including the entrance of large numbers of black women into relatively well-paying government jobs.[52] Among government workers, African American females had reached parity with their white counterparts by the late 1970s. Over the subsequent decades, relative wage gains for public-sector whites would steadily grow, settling at a 5 percentage-point wage advantage over African Americans. But as shown, the initial decline and subsequent increase in female wage differences are not confined to the public sector. Indeed the *private-sector* differentials are more pronounced, and the increases in inequality over time more stark. By 1980, mean wages for white females in the private sector were only 4 percentage points higher than African American women's wages, down from 12 points in the early 1970s. During the 1980s white women's wage advantage doubled, and then nearly doubled again between 1989 and 2009. As the economists John Bound and Laura Dresser concluded: "The news for African American women, once heralded as an equal opportunity success story for their near wage parity with white women, is not good."[53]

What does the preceding picture tell us about deunionization's possible role in affecting black-white wage inequality? Among male private-sector workers, recent years of union decline occurred alongside relative stability in black-white wage gaps, at least for the last two decades covered by the data. These large and relatively stable pay disparities combined with the comparatively small differences in union membership rates between black and white males in the private sector suggest a minor role for deunionization in explaining contemporary patterns of economic inequality. That is not to say that union decline has not affected the wage *levels* of black men. In her exhaustive analysis of race and ethnic wage inequality in metropolitan labor markets, the sociologist Leslie McCall concluded that for African American males, "unionization is the strongest source of high relative wages, even after considering a wide range of other labor market characteristics."[54] But given their organization rates, unionization was a strong source of high relative wages for white men as well, likely attenuating the effect of union decline on male racial wage gaps. The economists John Bound and Richard Freeman have argued that deunionization played only a small role in explaining racial wage gaps (as opposed to levels) among young males in the workforce. They found that union decline explains only about 5 percent of the overall trend, although deunionization's contributions were greater among young men with low education levels, and among young men in the Midwest.[55]

Among female private-sector workers, on the other hand, declining union memberships in recent decades corresponded with a steep increase in female wage inequality. And earlier we learned about the large racial gaps in organization among female private-sector employees, providing further evidence that union decline exacerbated racial wage inequality among private-sector females. What little work that has been done on women's racial pay inequality and organized labor tends to emphasize the importance of *public-sector* unions for blacks' economic advancement during the 1960s and 1970s.[56] As we have seen, racial gaps in public-sector unionization rates are essentially nonexistent for most of the years covered in this book, and public-sector unionization rates have held quite steady for some time, leaving little room for government unions to account for recent developments in public-sector wage inequality. This is true for public-sector men as well.

Thus, whatever role deunionization has played in exacerbating racial wage inequality between black and white workers, it is clear that the impact is largely limited to the private sector. Given white men's high organization rates, combined with the consistently large racial wage gaps among private-sector men, there is little room for union decline to account for a large portion of male racial wage inequality. Among women, the story is different. Black females' organization rates were twice as high as whites for decades, and black-white wage disparities were not nearly as stark. The consequences of black female overrepresentation in unions and subsequent union decline have been largely overlooked.

Measuring Deunionization's Impact on Black-White Wage Gaps

The quantitative analyses at the beginning of the chapter assess various groups' unionization probabilities. In statistical terms, they treat union membership as the dependent variable, and test whether and to what extent different independent variables affect respondents' probabilities of belonging to a union. The task now is a bit different. Instead of trying to predict union membership, the goal is to isolate how union membership affects wages among workers, similar to the tests I describe in Chapter 3. That is to say, I now treat union membership as an independent variable, along with numerous other factors that influence how much money an individual makes at his or her job.

Isolating the causal effect of union membership on wages turns out to be a complicated dilemma with ultimately imperfect solutions, an issue I explore in great detail in the Data and Methods Appendix. The CPS data sets do contain a rich battery of relevant variables, and have been used by labor economists and other researchers interested in measuring union wage premiums across time and place.[57] I follow the lead of this past work on the topic and utilize various series of the CPS to capture how unions influence wages, and to reveal how deunionization has contributed to racial wage gaps between 1973 and 2009.

Many of the factors that help predict whether a worker belongs to a labor union also help structure wage returns for workers. Take the industry one works in: Unionization is heavily patterned by industry. Historically, union presence in certain industries such as auto manufacturing was substantial, while organized labor had—and continues to have—extraordinary difficulty gaining traction in service-sector industries such as retail. Inter-industry wage rates vary as well. Even after all the recent turmoil in the U.S. auto industry, the typical auto plant worker's hourly wage is much higher than that of an individual staffing the checkout counter at a local KFC, even if these two workers have the same amount of work experience and levels of education. Any analysis of wages then must include adjustments for industry. Similar to the statistical analyses I presented in Chapter 3, my estimates of the union wage premium contain controls for broad industry categories.

Occupation is also an important economic variable that influences both unionization probabilities and wage rates. Members of certain occupations, such as managers, are prohibited by law from joining a union, while pay rates for top-tier occupations and bottom-rung ones vary widely. Comparisons between nonunion and union workers, then, should be made between individuals in the same industry and occupation. The final economic factor relevant to my analyses of union wage effects is hours worked per week. Since the outcome variable of interest is inflation-adjusted weekly wages, lacking a control for time spent at work could result in misleading comparisons. Take two observationally similar individuals, paid the same hourly rate, except that one works full time and the other part time, and the full-time worker belongs to a labor union while the part-time worker does not. Someone who works only part time will report a weekly wage well below that of a full-time worker, leading the analyst to conclude that the unionization of the full-time worker accounts for the wage difference, when it is actually due to a difference in hours worked.[58] Hence the need to control for hours worked.

Aside from those economic factors, investigations into the union wage premium control for a range of demographic and human capital characteristics long found to affect wages. These include potential workforce experience, race, education, and marital status.[59] Like in the prior analyses of unionization, I also add year and a set of detailed state-grouping "fixed effects," as well as controls for urban/rural locale. All told, my analyses of the union wage premium include nearly ninety relevant control variables, lending confidence that the union wage premiums revealed are due to union membership and not other confounding factors.[60]

Unions and Black-White Wage Inequality in the Private Sector

The results from the quantitative analyses indicate that deunionization has substantially lowered wage levels among both black and white men and exacerbated racial wage inequality among women. I begin by estimating race-specific union wage premiums and wage inequality in recent decades. Table 5.1 shows the results of this investigation. Specifically, it displays the remaining racial wage gaps among nonunion workers, and the union wage premiums for both black and white private-sector workers after adjusting for all of the correlates of wages included in the analyses. Since many of the dynamics generating pay differentials differ by sex, I generate the premiums from two different analyses: one for private-sector women, the other for private-sector men. The table presents estimates of black-white weekly wage inequality and union wage premiums averaged across the entire time period under analysis.

Table 5.1 Black/white wage inequality and union wage premiums

	Percent higher weekly wages
Private-sector women	
White wage advantage (nonunion)	8
White union wage premium	24
Black union wage premium	22
Private-sector men	
White wage advantage (nonunion)	17
White union wage premium	28
Black union wage premium	30

Source: Author's compilations. Data for 1973 to 1981 come from the CPS-May files; data for 1983 to 2009 come from the CPS-MORG files.

Note: Sample restricted to private-sector workers ages 16 to 64 with positive wages. The weekly wage advantage and union premiums generated from wage models that control for a range of demographic, economic, and geographic factors found to influence wages, adjusted with the appropriate CPS weights.

The results reveal that the African American wage deficits displayed in Figures 5.4 and 5.5 are not entirely due to racial differences in the economic, demographic, and geographic characteristics included in the analyses. Among nonunion private-sector men, whites maintain 17 percent higher wages than similar African American males. This disparity is much lower than the observed differences presented in Figure 5.4, but still quite substantial. Disparities are similar among unionized men, as indicated by the comparable union wage premiums among black and white men. It is unlikely that deunionization can account for much of this residual inequality, since African American unionization rates among private-sector men were never much greater than the rates for white men. Nonunion white women's weekly wages remain 8 percent higher than black women's. As with their male counterparts, this level of inequality is roughly similar among female union members, since the union wage premium does not differ much between white and black women. Unlike the case with men, however, the black female union wage premium is slightly lower than the premium for white women. These female racial wage gaps are smaller than the raw differences in black and white female wages presented in Figure 5.4, indicating that some of the observed differences in female inequality result from racial variation in the control variables included in my analyses.

The union wage premiums displayed here reveal little differences by race, an issue I explore further in the Data and Methods Appendix and in prior work with Meredith Kleykamp.[61] Regardless of why unionization does not increase the pay of blacks substantially more than whites, it still raises pay above the level of those who do not belong to a union. The union wage premiums displayed here average about 26 percent. That is, an average worker in the United States who belongs to a union earns an estimated 26 percent higher weekly wage than an otherwise similar nonunion worker. These large union wage premiums imply that declining union presence in the private sector has contributed to stagnant wage levels for both black and white men, given high organization rates among both sets of workers back in the early 1970s through the early 1980s. They also suggest a substantial role for deunionization in exacerbating black-white wage disparities among women, given the racial discrepancies in unionization.[62]

To what extent did union decline exacerbate racial wage inequality and reduce wage levels over the preceding four decades? To answer this question, I use the estimates generated from the cross-sectional premium models (displayed in Table 5.1) to predict black-white wage disparities under two scenarios, displayed in Figures 5.5 and 5.6. First, I generate annual wage estimates for blacks and whites, allowing unionization to decline as it does in the data, and estimate the African American wage penalty over time. We can interpret this scenario as the white wage advantage over black workers after adjusting for all the factors found to influence wages that I include in the analyses. Second, I generate annual estimates of black and white wages after fixing unionization at its

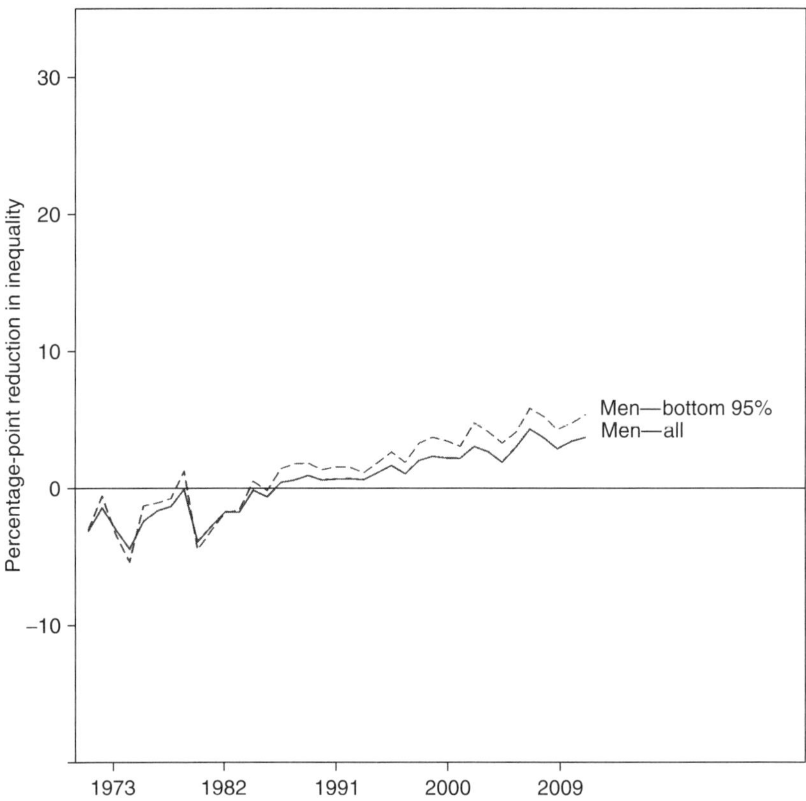

Figure 5.5. Male counterfactual inequality estimates, 1973–2009. *Note:* Y axis represents the percentage-point reduction in inequality had no deunionization occurred. See the text for further details. Sample restricted to employed workers, ages sixteen to sixty-four, with positive wages. *Source:* Author's compilations. Data for 1973–1981 come from the CPS-May files; data for 1983–2009 come from the CPS-MORG files.

1973 race-specific levels for males, and at its 1979 race-specific levels for females. I then estimate the black wage penalty under this alternative scenario—the "counterfactual-predicted" inequality series. The counterfactual asks what inequality would look like had unionization levels not declined from their peak in 1973 for men, and their peak in 1979 for women.

In the figures I present the overall percentage reduction in black-white wage inequality had unionization in the private sector remained at its highest levels, calculated by subtracting the two series and dividing by the counterfactual-predicted series. Inequality estimates are

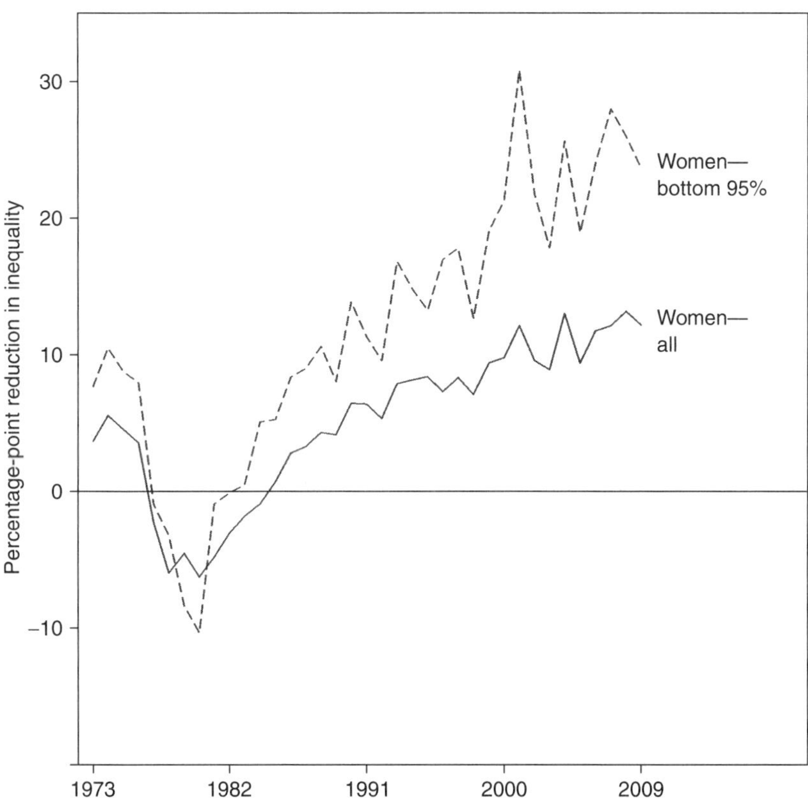

Figure 5.6. Female counterfactual inequality estimates, 1973–2009. *Note:* Y axis represents the percentage-point reduction in inequality had no deunionization occurred. See the text for further details. Sample restricted to employed workers, ages sixteen to sixty-four, with positive wages. *Source:* Author's compilations. Data for 1973–1981 come from the CPS-May files; data for 1983–2009 come from the CPS-MORG files.

sensitive to the inclusion of top earners in the sample, and with the exception of a few occupations, such as airline pilots, unionization rates among top earners are comparatively low, especially among men. So I supplement the counterfactual exercise with a similar analysis limited to the bottom 95 percent of wage earners, and present the corresponding reduction in inequality for these truncated samples.

Let's begin with men. In Figure 5.5 the counterfactual series fixes male unionization rates at their 1973 levels, since that is the year private-sector union levels peaked for black and white men between 1973 and 2009. It is important to emphasize here that male private-sector unionization rates actually peaked much earlier—back in the 1940s and 1950s. The CPS did not begin asking respondents about membership until 1973, preventing a full accounting of deunionization's influence on private-sector male wages. The results from my analysis, then, should be seen as a conservative estimate of the impact of union decline on wage levels among men.

The figure reveals what I hypothesized previously. Since unionization rates do not differ dramatically between white and black men for most of the period covered here, deunionization does not reduce black-white wage inequality all that appreciably. The counterfactual line for all male workers indicates that by the end of the series union decline has exacerbated black-white inequality by about 3–4 percent. Estimates using the truncated sample reveal an effect roughly a third larger. What these male inequality trend lines obscure, however, is deunionization's impact on male wage *levels*. For black men in 2009, average weekly wages in the truncated sample would be over $50 higher had no union decline occurred. For full-time workers, that translates to an annual loss of income of $2,600. White male workers also experience a similar weekly wage loss as a result of union decline, blunting deunionization's impact on black-white wage inequality.

What about private-sector women? In Figure 5.6 I conduct the same set of analyses on women, with one minor change. Instead of fixing unionization at its 1973 race-specific levels, the counterfactual series here fixes female unionization rates at their 1979 levels, since that was the year private-sector union levels peaked for women between 1973 and 2009. As shown, deunionization has contributed greatly to growing racial wage disparities among women. By 2009, compared to the model-predicted series, black-white weekly wage gaps would be 12 percent lower, barring private-sector union declines from 1979 onward. Within the truncated sample of female earners, the corresponding reduction reaches 30 percent in recent years. For example, in 2001, white workers' wage advantage in the sample restricted to the bottom 95 percent of female earners was 6.3 percentage points; absent union decline in the private sector, the difference would have been 4.8 points. Thus had 1979 unionization rates prevailed in 2001, overall inequality between black and white females would be approximately 31 percent lower than the model-predicted series.[63] These inequality effects stem from the absolute gains unions provide African American females. In 2007, without any private-sector deunionization, weekly wages for blacks would be nearly $14 higher. For whites, wage levels would increase by less than $6 a week.

As we will learn more about in the next chapter, past upsurges in U.S. unionization have propelled many disadvantaged populations' economic ascent into the middle class. This was not true for African American men—for a while. Most unions either explicitly or through more indirect routes barred black males during the first upsurge of organized labor in the United States. Indeed, according to the historian Robert Korstad, even during the 1930s and into the 1940s, "to have any chance of bringing white workers into the CIO, many unions had to publicly disavow any intention of promoting social equality."[64] And the CIO unions were, in general, far more progressive on racial matters than their peers in the AFL. But by mid-century African American men flooded into the rapidly expanding labor movement, spurred on by the production demands and labor shortages of the wartime economy. There they would enjoy a few decades of steady membership gains prior to organized labor's decline. By the early 1970s, over 40 percent of private-sector black men belonged to a labor union, a striking turnaround from just decades before. They joined private-sector unions that had previously organized a large fraction of the white male labor force. Organized labor's fortunes would soon turn, and with them, the economic progress of working-class men of all racial and ethnic backgrounds. In recent decades, both black and white male unionization rates in the private sector declined precipitously, and the drop-off among black men was steeper. By the early years of the twenty-first century, private-sector unionization rates between black and white males had largely converged. This decline in private-sector organization rates played little role in exacerbating the substantial and persistent racial wage inequality among males. Weekly wages for both black and white men would be around $50 higher today had private-sector unions remained strong.

Even when African American men were effectively banned from the majority of unions, they were at least eligible for employment in certain occupations sought after by immigrant and low-skill native white laborers. Not so for African American women. Whites effectively blocked African American females from these positions, consigning them largely to farming and domestic service.[65] Passage of the NLRA rested on the exclusion of these two occupations from the law's reach, guaranteeing the continual subjugation of the female African American workforce. Racial and gender oppression thus doubly segregated black women, both from the employment niches offering any opportunity for economic advancement and from the key labor-market institution situated between the employer and the employee.

In 1940, 60 percent of employed black women worked as domestic servants. Opportunities for black women did open up during the armament phase and the war itself. The fraction employed in domestic service fell by a quarter in the run-up to the war, and the portion employed on farms fell by half. The fraction of employed African Americans in production nearly tripled during the war.[66] Yet as the conflict ended, many of these women were unable to retain their positions. As Anderson has argued, "their concentration in contracting industries, their low seniority, and their sex contributed to employment difficulties in the post-war period."[67] For example, under pressure from the Fair Employment Practices Commission, St. Louis's General Cable Corporation hired black women in its production divisions during the war. After the war, "the cord assembly department, where the company had assigned most of its women production workers, was closed. . . . No black women survived the cutbacks."[68] Black men, on the other hand, remained a large presence in the company despite the postwar retrenchment.

Rapid occupational ascent for African American women followed in the 1960s and 1970s, stemming from the civil rights and women's movements, and the resulting legal pressure on employers. Lawsuits and the growing threat thereof also helped open up labor unions to black women. By the end of the 1970s, two in five black female private-sector workers in the Midwest and nearly one in four nationwide belonged to a labor union. Corresponding rates for white females never approached these levels. After decades of struggle, African American females joined African American men in private-sector unions in unprecedented numbers.

But the timing was terrible. Black females' membership rates peaked just as private-sector unionization began its dramatic descent. Take AT&T, the largest private-sector employer in the country in the early 1970s, and one with over half a million union workers. During the 1970s AT&T entered into a five-year consent decree with the federal government, agreeing to diversify positions held traditionally by white males. The results were impressive, with women joining the managerial ranks in significant numbers, and increasing their share of largely unionized, blue-collar positions by a third. During the decree years, the percentage of black women in outside craft positions doubled, and their share of the inside craft positions increased by roughly a quarter.[69]

Yet AT&T's overall employment levels barely budged during the decade, and this stability was driven by a large increase in the number of officers and managers—nonunion occupations that remained disproportionately white. Among the core blue-collar occupations, overall employment levels dropped because of increasing automation and other technological improvements.[70] Here we see black women making significant gains in declining industries organized by declining labor unions.

Or take the case of the Memphis Furniture Company in the late 1970s. By that time, Memphis Furniture employed a predominantly black, female production workforce. It remained nonunion. An organizing campaign began in earnest in 1977, with Coretta Scott King arriving to speak to the workers, and neighborhood churches and civil rights organizations lending financial and organizational support.[71] In 1980, Local 282 of the Furniture Workers of America successfully organized the plant after a bitter, protracted strike. But within a few years, the company shut its doors. According to Ida Leachman, one of the union's organizers—and herself an African American woman—the plant closing "brought down the local."[72]

Thus African American women were unable to consolidate the economic advantages gained through a durable presence in a strong labor movement, further disadvantaging a population long accustomed to economic marginality. And the collapse of the labor movement helped set African American females back in terms of racial wage parity. After nearly matching white females' wage levels during the late 1970s, black women would see interracial wage gaps rise throughout the final decades of the twentieth century. Deunionization helps explain a good part of the contemporary disparity. Had unionization rates remained at their peak levels, black-white wage differences among private-sector females would be between 10 percent and 30 percent lower than today.

What the preceding analyses and discussion largely ignore is the role unions once played in supporting the livelihoods of other minority populations. Early successes of organized labor in this country stemmed in part from the energies and commitment of millions of immigrants and their offspring, who in turn benefited from a fast-growing labor movement. In the next chapter we will explore whether a similar dynamic is now occurring between labor unions and the nation's largest ethnic group, Hispanics.

6

Justice for Janitors?

Deunionization and Hispanic Economic Assimilation

Eliseo Medina was born in 1946 in Central Mexico, the son of migrant farmworkers. His family made the journey north in the mid-1950s to pick fruit in the fields of Delano, California. After finishing eighth grade, Medina quit school to join his siblings and parents in the grape, orange, and tomato farms that dominated the California countryside, farms that relied heavily on foreign workers. There he toiled away his adolescence, until a strike led by the legendary leader of the United Farm Workers (UFW) Cesar Chavez galvanized Medina. He quickly joined the union, launching a career in organized labor that would take him from California to Texas, Florida, and beyond—including the floor of the Senate Judiciary Committee, where Medina would testify in favor of an overhaul of the nation's immigration policies.[1]

According to the author and activist Randy Shaw, over the past thirty years Medina was probably responsible for organizing more workers into unions than anyone else in the United States.[2] Medina's successes spanned industries and unions. After leaving the UFW in the late 1970s, Medina helped lead organizing drives for the American Federation of State, County, and Municipal Employees and the Communications Workers of America before joining the Service Employees International Union (SEIU) in 1986. The SEIU dispatched the itinerant organizer to revitalize its flagging local in San Diego. In just a couple of years, Medina helped orchestrate a remarkable turnaround, more than quintupling the union's membership.[3] Thereafter Medina rose rapidly up the SEIU's leadership ranks, winning a seat on the international's executive board in 1996 and assuming the position of secretary treasurer in 2010. Medina served as a key strategist for a series of high-profile victories during his ascent, including the unionization of seventy-four thousand Californian home health care aides in 1999—the largest organizing victory in generations.[4]

Medina's remarkable rise in the labor movement is all the more impressive given his heritage. It was only in 2000 that the American Federation of Labor and Congress of Industrial Organizations (AFL-CIO) abandoned its restrictionist stance toward immigration. Prior to that reversal, the major union federations had looked warily upon foreigners, concerned about employers' use of them as strikebreakers, and as general sources of cheap labor that would help depress wages. There also existed a long-standing belief on the part of many unionists that new arrivals brought with them un-American norms and values—cultural predispositions that rendered them "unorganizable." This was felt to be especially true for transient groups looking only for short-term economic opportunities (and thus unlikely to settle in the United States), and for imported laborers such as Chinese workers in the nineteenth and early twentieth centuries.[5]

Yet Medina's case was not without precedent. Despite the often contentious relationship between organized labor and immigrants, many American union leaders came from abroad. Take Sidney Hillman. Hillman was born in the village of Zagare, Lithuania, in March 1887. Hillman descended from a long line of merchants and rabbis, and relatives impressed with the young boy's obvious perspicacity hoped that he too would follow tradition and practice his faith for a living. They were soon disappointed, as Hillman's teenage rebellion took the form of active participation in radical groups. Hillman distributed pamphlets, raised funds, and delivered speeches during the failed Russian Revolution of 1905. When the tsarist crackdown came, Hillman worried he would be targeted. First fleeing under an assumed name to England, Hillman eventually made his way to the garment factories of Chicago. There he put his past activist skills to work and helped organize the Amalgamated Clothing Workers Union. The effort would prove a challenge for a number of reasons, including mutual antagonisms and language impediments dividing the disproportionately foreign-born workforce.

Hillman's solution was to create numerous locals based on nationality, including separate ones for Lithuanians, Italians, and Poles.[6]

The Lithuanian immigrant from the village of Zagare would go on to become one of the most influential union leaders of his day, a close adviser to President Roosevelt, and, as we will see in the next chapter, a powerful political figure who helped reshape electoral politics in the United States. Twice appearing on the cover of *Time* magazine, Hillman had a tremendous impact on the shape and structure of the U.S. labor movement. And Hillman was not the only early American labor leader born outside the United States: Samuel Gompers, founder of the AFL, was from London; Harry Bridges, founder and longtime leader of the International Longshore and Warehouse Union, hailed from Australia; and many other leaders were the sons and daughters of immigrants. Indeed, the labor movement's great upsurge between the Great Depression and World War II relied heavily on European immigrants and their children, with many arrivals assuming top leadership posts in the nation's fast-growing unions. In the early decades of the twentieth century, nearly a third of the union leaders in the United States were born outside the nation's borders.[7]

The relationship between unions and immigrants was mutually beneficial, as rapidly growing labor unions helped facilitate the economic incorporation of European immigrants in the early and mid-twentieth century.[8] During the labor movement's peak, unions helped provide a firm economic foundation for these otherwise disadvantaged populations, propelling millions up the class ladder and out of ethnic ghettos. In immigrant communities throughout the Midwest and in northeastern cities, a union card was often the family's ticket to the middle class. In the process, the labor movement transformed America, helping to assimilate the famous Ellis Island arrivals of our textbooks into the nation's economy and polity. Many of these arrivals, buoyed by the economic benefits of union membership, would go on to shape the distinctive economic and political character of mid-twentieth-century America. Sidney Hillman, for one, would emerge as a key policy architect of the New Deal's economic programs.

What about today? Since the 1965 Immigration and Nationality Act abolished preexisting country quotas, the immigrant and second-generation populations in the United States have expanded dramatically. Over the past forty years, the fraction of the active workforce that is foreign born has more than tripled.[9] This growth is especially pronounced for arrivals from Spanish-speaking countries, especially Mexico. However, unlike many of the earlier waves of migrants, arrivals in recent decades encounter an increasingly union-free economy. Past research on organized labor in America points to immigrants as a necessary ingredient to unions' initial rise and subsequent success.[10] Can recent newcomers repeat this pattern and help inject organized labor with energy and vitality seemingly sapped from American-born workers? And what does our nearly union-free economy portend for recent immigrants and their offspring struggling to gain an economic foothold in their new country? This chapter addresses these two questions, focusing on the nation's largest minority population, Hispanics.

The Historical Context

The history of the American labor movement is at once a story of inclusion and upward assimilation of previously marginalized groups, and of virulent racist and xenophobic tendencies. This is a story we saw play out for African Americans in the prior chapter, and it is a similar story for immigrant populations of generations past. Asians, particularly Chinese and Japanese, faced extreme hostility from the early craft unions, exemplified by organized labor's successful lobbying for the Chinese Exclusion Act during the late nineteenth century.[11] The expression of anti-Chinese sentiment extended beyond mere lobbying. In the fall of 1885, white miners of the Knights of Labor slaughtered dozens of Chinese workers in Rock Springs, Wyoming. Yet just over two decades later in the very same location as the massacre, Chinese miners could be found attending United Mine Workers of America meetings alongside other workers eager for the benefits and protection promised by the union.[12] And in more recent years, Asians in the United States (immigrants and U.S. natives) held more pro-union attitudes than whites.[13]

For many decades, organized labor's anti-immigrant policies and practices extended to European arrivals. The fact that the leadership of many early unions came from overseas did not prevent these very same unions from actively lobbying against further immigration during the late nineteenth and early twentieth century. In 1897, for example, the national board of the AFL endorsed a resolution calling for a means test and an educational requirement for all potential newcomers to the United States. Other unions advocated more stringent policies. The New York branch of the AFL, for example, called for a temporary halt to *all* immigration.[14]

Aside from the endemic racism of the time, there was practical economic logic behind labor's stance. A restricted labor supply might bolster labor's position, while a glut of arrivals searching for work might undermine it. Added to this was the aforementioned suspicion that foreigners were somehow less "organizable" than workers born in America, despite the growing body of counterevidence exhibited by the conspicuous overrepresentation of immigrants at the top of labor's hierarchy. The counterevidence extended down to the rank and file, where many immigrant laborers proved the most tenacious supporters of strikes and other industrial actions. In the fall of 1912, for example, restive copper miners in Utah considered a walkout as long hours and rising copper prices failed to produce higher wages. Union leadership urged caution, but were soon overwhelmed by the "foreign element" in the miner's camp. Austrian, Italian, Japanese, and Bulgarian immigrant workers were "insistent upon a walkout," and their sentiment prevailed, as reported by the *New York Times*.[15] Seven years later another mining dispute in Wyoming dragged on longer than the company and many U.S.-born workers desired. Why the lengthy conflict? Striking immigrant workers promised to "shoot anyone" who returned to work.[16] Across the country in New Jersey the mayor of the town of Perth Amboy learned of immigrant laborers' tenaciousness when striking brick makers—largely Bulgarians—stoned the official after mistaking him for a strikebreaker.[17] Fog, apparently, was quite thick at the time.

Why, despite all the counterexamples cited above, did anti-immigrant sentiment prevail among many unionists and their leaders? For many immigrants and their children, the very act of joining a union became part of the process of economic incorporation. In labor historian David Montgomery's words, they saw their membership "as a badge of assimilation."[18] And for many immigrant workers, this badge entitled them to react harshly toward what they saw as the threat posed by even more recent arrivals. Thus, workers who had made the journey from Ireland, England, and Germany decades earlier viewed the latest arrivals from Italy and the European periphery as unorganizable, and thus "unassimilable." This sentiment was echoed among U.S.-born workers, many of whom had fought unsuccessfully to keep the first wave of migrants out of their country, and out of their unions. And it was a sentiment that would be echoed generations later by unionized Italian Americans and others as they themselves viewed the next waves of arrivals with suspicion.

The perennial problem for anti-immigrant unionists is that new arrivals tend to concentrate in those positions of the economy that unions target. The millions of immigrants from Europe who arrived in the United States during the decades surrounding the turn of the twentieth century flooded into the factories, mills, and mines where unions found greatest success. In turn-of-the-century Detroit, for example, over half of all manual workers were foreign born. During the early decades of the twentieth century, Henry Ford's employees were largely immigrants, with the greatest share coming from Russia, Romania, Italy, and Austria-Hungary.[19] As Montgomery recounted, so prevalent were immigrants among manual laborers, "that they produced nothing less than an ethnic recomposition of the American working class."[20] The result was that "even those American trade unionists who were most contemptuous of the newcomers found no alternative to organizing them into their own ranks."[21]

This pattern of simultaneously incorporating newcomers while fighting to restrict any further immigration extended across the twentieth century. It is a pattern evident in the contemporary relationship between the country's Hispanics and organized labor. The onset of severe deunionization in the 1970s, coupled with a dramatic increase in the Hispanic population, rekindled long-standing tensions between organized labor and the nation's Hispanics. In Los Angeles, unionists were "openly hostile" to Hispanic workers pouring into the local labor market during the 1970s and 1980s, according to sociologist Ruth Milkman.[22] Worries about the destabilizing impact of ethnic divisions, especially between Mexicans and native-born whites, motivated some of the hostility. This was a long-standing fear in the labor movement. Throughout the 1920s the AFL pushed to have immigration from Mexico "severely restricted," recounted the historian Harvey Levenstein.[23] Samuel Gompers, an immigrant himself, lobbied unsuccessfully to add Mexico to the list of countries covered by the National Origins Act of 1924. His successor at the AFL persuaded the major Mexican labor federation to lobby its government to restrict emigration to the United States. Even the more radical union leader John Lewis, son of two immigrants from Wales, proposed that the AFL officially oppose immigration from Mexico. His proposal passed at the 1919 AFL convention.[24]

Under the leadership of President John Sweeney and Executive Vice-President Linda Chavez-Thompson, the AFL-CIO finally abandoned its restrictionist stance toward immigration in 2000. Spurred on by fast-growing unions such as the SEIU and leaders such as Eliseo Medina, the AFL-CIO's executive committee issued a statement calling for general amnesty for illegal immigrants in the United States and ending the practice of sanctioning employers for hiring undocumented workers. Announcing that it "proudly stands on the side of immigrant workers," the AFL-CIO reversed over a century's worth of lobbying to curtail migration to the United States.[25] It did so in part because of the rapidly expanding role of Hispanics in American workplaces, and in unions across the country.

The New Arrivals

Today Hispanics are the single largest minority group in the country, accounting for nearly 17 percent of the nation's total population. And today over half of all immigrants in the United States are of Hispanic origin. Despite the post-1965 growth of the immigrant population, the foreign-born in the United States today make up a smaller share of all workers than they did in the early twentieth century. The fraction of the workforce born outside the United States peaked in 1910, when immigrants constituted over a fifth of all workers. Estimates from 2007 indicated that approximately one in six workers in the United States was an immigrant.[26] That 2007 figure represents a post–World War II high—during the 1950s through the 1970s, the proportion of foreign-born in the labor force hovered below 10 percent.

Through the 1960s, a large portion of migrants to the United States came from Europe and Canada. That has changed dramatically, with recent arrivals increasingly coming from Latin America and Asia. Since the early 1990s, Hispanic migrants have made up the single largest category of legal immigrants, and millions more have entered the country illegally.[27] Nearly a third of the current immigrant population is from

Mexico; no other country comes close to matching Mexico's contribution to the U.S. immigrant population.[28] Accompanying the increasing numbers of Hispanic migrants are high birth rates among many Hispanic subpopulations in the United States, further contributing to the growth of America's largest minority group.

The Hispanic category includes a huge and heterogeneous population, ranging from the young Mexican migrant worker who just crossed the southern border illegally to notable public figures such as Marco Rubio, a sitting U.S. senator from Florida born in the United States whose parents migrated from Cuba. What do all these people have in common? Social scientists define Hispanics as those who classify themselves according to one of the Hispanic-origin categories provided on standard surveys. Common Hispanic-origin categories include Mexican, Cuban, or Honduran, as well as broader groupings such as Central and South Americans.

As the proportion of Hispanics in the general population increased dramatically in recent decades, so too has the proportion of Hispanics in the active workforce. In Figure 6.1 I present trend lines of the fraction of employed workers in the United States who self-identify as Hispanic, as well as the fraction of employed workers who are immigrants and Hispanic immigrants for those years in which the data are available. In official government questionnaires such as the census, the ethnic-origin questions are asked separately from those asking about one's race. Thus, a Hispanic can be of any race. However, for the calculations I present in Figure 6.1 and throughout the rest of the chapter, I combine race and ethnic categories and define four mutually exclusive racial/ethnic groups: white, African American, Hispanic, and other. Anyone who defines him or herself as Hispanic, regardless of race, is included in the Hispanic category.

Since the early 1970s, the portion of the employed population that self-identifies as Hispanic has more than tripled. By 2009, nearly one in every seven active workers was Hispanic, up from less than one in twenty thirty-five years earlier. Data on the immigrant workforce are limited to 1994 forward, as that was the first year in which the Current Population Survey (CPS) included questions on country of birth. Even though the truncated series covers just a decade and a half of data, we still see a substantial increase in the percentage of immigrants working in the United States. This rise is due primarily to the growth of the His-

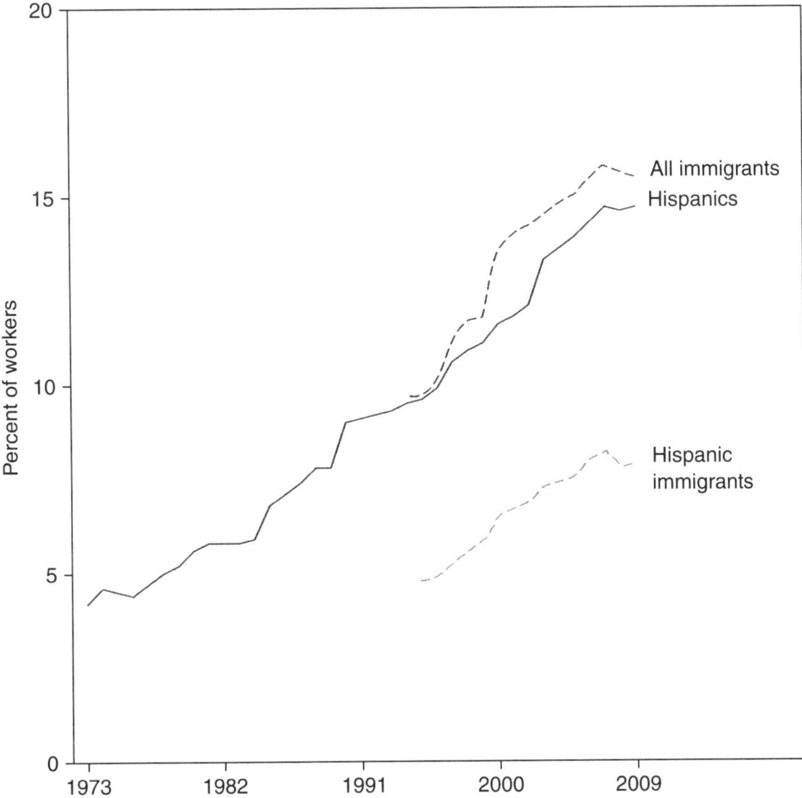

Figure 6.1. Hispanic and immigrant workforce in the United States, 1973–2009. *Note:* Sample restricted to employed workers, ages sixteen to sixty-four. *Source:* Author's compilations. Data for 1973–1981 come from the CPS-May files; data for 1983–2009 come from the CPS-MORG files.

panic immigrant population. The size of and trends in the Hispanic and Hispanic immigrant workforce reveal populations increasingly important to the nation's economy. Academics have wrestled for years over the question of how successfully Hispanics are incorporating economically.[29] Some researchers have identified the beleaguered labor movement as a possible source of upward mobility for Hispanic immigrants and their offspring, and as a site where certain Hispanic subpopulations may utilize their own past experiences with collective mobilization to strengthen unions.[30] It is to these issues that we now turn.

Hispanics and Organized Labor in Modern America

During the 1980s, owners of downtown office buildings in Los Angeles began subcontracting cleaning services. The move relieved them of dealing with janitorial contracts, and ushered in a wave of deunionization among the city's cleaning staff. As the total janitorial workforce in L.A. doubled during the office building boom of that period, the cleaning subcontractors pushed aggressively against union agreements. Their effort coincided with dramatic demographic changes among the city's tens of thousands of janitors. What once was a disproportionately male, disproportionately African American occupation quickly came to be dominated by Mexican and Central American immigrants, many of them female. By 1990, Hispanic immigrants composed over 60 percent of the janitorial workforce in Los Angeles.[31] And unlike earlier decades, when SEIU Local 399 had organized a large fraction of building cleaners, most of these recent arrivals were nonunion.

In 1988, SEIU sent organizers and resources to Local 399 in an attempt to resuscitate unionization efforts among the now-unorganized cleaning service workers. Union losses in prior years stemmed in part from the building owners' switch to subcontractors. These outfits were plentiful, and if one of them happened to organize, building owners could easily replace it with a nonunion alternative. Recognizing the futility of going after individual subcontractors, the innovative campaign that would materialize, commonly known as Justice for Janitors, targeted the building owners themselves. Instead of organizing work-site by work-site, the union identified a specific geographic locale—downtown Los Angeles—and aimed to score large master contracts that established wage and benefit standards for a sizable fraction of cleaning staff in the area. The campaign also focused on generating substantial community involvement in the effort, and often used high-profile protests to raise visibility. These efforts mirrored the community-based strike mobilizations of past immigrant struggles, in which "the network of family savings, ethnic fraternal organizations, grocers, and churches sustained the strikers," as recounted by Montgomery.[32] The SEIU's organizers also sought the help of community leaders. A successful organizing strike in the spring of 1990 that capitalized on support from leading Los Angeles politicians and church officials, including the archbishop of the city, led to substantial wage increases for a segment of the city's janitorial workforce.

Over the coming years, the union would score a string of victories for the largely immigrant, heavily female workforce. In 2000, for example, Eliseo Medina led a successful effort that helped to deliver to Los Angeles janitors wage gains that surpassed those achieved in prior Justice for Janitors campaigns.[33] These victories provided a template for other successful campaigns elsewhere in California, in Houston, and in other locations throughout the United States.[34] The broader Justice for Janitors movement also provided beleaguered unions with a rare source of hope after decades of steady membership losses.[35] And the continuing influx of Hispanics, both immigrant and native-born, into high-growth industries and locales suggested to many union leaders that labor's exclusionary stance of the past must be abandoned should it hope to achieve a firm standing in the future. As Linda Chavez-Thomson, then secretary treasurer of the AFL-CIO, stated in 2000, "Immigrants are not only the history of the union movement, they are its future, its soul, its spirit."[36] Many organizers and academics began to identify the tactics and—crucially—the constituency involved in the Southern California janitors' campaign as key elements of a revitalized labor movement in the twenty-first century.

Over two decades have passed since Justice for Janitors began, enough time to evaluate whether organized labor has gained a foothold in Hispanic communities since the high-profile shift in organizing strategies beginning with the Justice for Janitors campaign. Evaluating the relationships between unions and Hispanics allows us to test theories about the "organizability" of Hispanics in recent decades, and provides insights into the contemporary context of reception for the millions of immigrant and second-generation Hispanic workers. Are they following the lead of earlier immigrant populations and using the labor movement as a springboard to the middle class?

Figure 6.2 provides a picture that highlights some of these issues. It plots the percentage of Hispanics in unions from 1973 to 2009, along with the percentage of Hispanic immigrants in unions over the last decade and a half. For comparison, it includes the overall unionization rate, represented by the dashed line. As with all the analyses in this chapter, I restrict the data to employed workers ages sixteen to sixty-four.

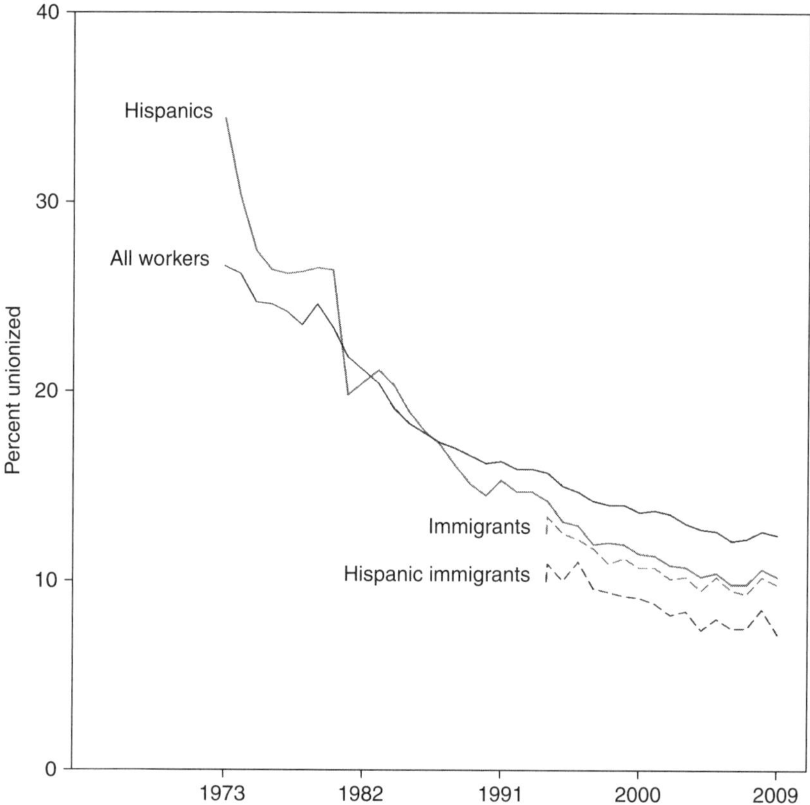

Figure 6.2. Hispanic and immigrant unionization rates, 1973–2009. *Note:* Sample restricted to employed workers, ages sixteen to sixty-four. *Source:* Author's compilations. Data for 1973–1981 come from the CPS-May files; data for 1983–2009 come from the CPS-MORG files.

Hispanic unionization rates peaked in the early 1970s, when over a third belonged to a union. Through the early 1980s, unions organized one in five Hispanic workers. And until that period, the Hispanic rate of organization was actually higher than the overall rate—substantially so in the early 1970s. But over the subsequent two decades, as the Hispanic fraction of the workforce tripled, unionization rates among Hispanics halved. And while the basic unionization *trend* among Hispanics mirrored the broader pattern of deunionization, in recent decades Hispanics' *levels* of organization averaged a few percentage points lower than the overall rate. Organization rates among Hispanic immigrants were a few points lower still. In 2009, the last year of the series, the overall unionization rate was 12.5 percent. Among Hispanics, the rate was 10 percent. And among Hispanic immigrants, it was just 7 percent.

What accounts for these disparities? On the one hand, the low unionization rates among Hispanics in recent years might reflect the changing composition of the Hispanic workforce. If, for example, immigrants make up a larger share of the Hispanic population than in the 1970s and 1980s, this compositional change may explain Hispanics' recent underrepresentation in unions. Research on the timing of union decline and Hispanic growth in certain industries dispels the notion that the growth of the Hispanic population played a large role in deunionization—Hispanics often arrived once union decline was well under way.[37] But an influx of new arrivals—many of them undocumented, and many of them facing language barriers—could raise labor organizers' concern about the "organizability" of these workers, leading unions to focus efforts elsewhere. On the other hand, some scholars argue that many immigrants bring to this country strong union experience and labor solidarism crucial to counteracting aggressive antiunion campaigns by employers, suggesting that the relative decline in Hispanic representation rates is not due to the rise of Hispanic immigration.[38] Instead, relative to decades past, today's Hispanic workforce may simply concentrate in those industries and occupations where the barriers to unionization are exceptionally high. Below I expand on these competing theories, providing a framework for understanding the empirical results.

Solidaristic Theories

In the prior chapter we learned of "positional" and "protectionist" theories of unionization. Here we need to add one more. "Solidaristic" theories of unionization emphasize the ways in which group solidarity, ethnic- or class-based, on the part of Hispanics and Hispanic subpopulations may lower or increase their organization rates. Solidaristic theories suggesting that Hispanics, and especially Hispanic immigrants, will have lower unionization rates tend to take one of two forms. The first emphasizes the destabilizing impact outsiders may have on workplace solidarity. For example, an influx of immigrants into a particular locale may raise the costs of unionization by ratcheting up competition between workers and undermining local solidarity among the working class. Evidence for this version remains quite mixed, however. Whereas one recent study found that increases in immigration are associated with lower unionization rates, another found the opposite.[39] And as noted, the historical record is filled with examples of immigrants demonstrating strong class-based solidarity.

The second variant of solidarity theory suggests that part of the process of economic assimilation for immigrant populations and their offspring involves developing the capacity for class-based collective action in the United States.[40] Such a development is unlikely to occur among the most recent arrivals, who must overcome cultural and legal hurdles to convince themselves and labor organizers that they are prime candidates for unionization. Instead, the class-based solidarity necessary for unionization is likely to develop over time and across generational divides. The historical record offers numerous examples of this pattern. In the mills that dotted the mid-Atlantic states during the early twentieth century, many immigrants from Central and Eastern Europe largely accepted their working conditions and did not agitate for much more than their employers offered. As the sociologist Ewa Morawska recounts, "Their life in Europe as well as in this country had taught peasant-immigrants to keep away from public affairs." Their children, however, "saw things differently, at least regarding their lives as industrial workers," and would go on to be active strike participants and union members.[41] If this version of solidarity theory holds true for Hispanics, we would expect to see higher rates of unionization the longer a Hispanic immigrant has been in the United States, and higher rates of unionization for Hispanics born in the United States, after accounting for other factors that affect union membership.

Likewise, the potential for class-based collective action in the United States should be lower for arrivals who maintain strong ties across borders. Immigrants with a history of cycling between the United States and their home nation are more likely to compare their work conditions in the United States to those experienced in their homeland.[42] This cross-national frame of reference may inhibit any mobilization over unfair pay and work conditions in the United States. Among Hispanic subpopulations, Mexicans move back and forth across the two nations' borders at relatively high rates. If such mobility inhibits the generation of labor solidarity in the United States, we would expect to see lower likelihoods of unionization for Mexican immigrants.

On the other hand, solidarity on the part of new arrivals could work to organized labor's advantage. Many unions now recognize that non-immigrant American workers often lack any experience with unionism or other forms of group solidarity that unions try to capitalize on during organizing drives. Certain immigrants bring to America strong union experience and worker solidarity that could help offset employers' anti-union pressure. [43] And the successes of the Justice for Janitors campaign in Southern California and elsewhere serve as examples in which organizers were able to capitalize on the class-based solidarity exhibited by many Hispanic immigrants. Past research suggests that this solidarity should be most pronounced among non-Mexican Hispanic migrants, because of the significant presence of political refugees and labor activists among that population.[44]

Positional Theory

Solidarity means little if Hispanics concentrate in unorganizable sectors of the economy. As we have learned, a "positional" theory of union organizing focuses on the ways in which relatively stable industrial, occupational, and geographical factors affect unionization. According to this theory, Hispanic unionization rates will vary according to where Hispanics find jobs. To the extent that Hispanics work in particular occupations and industries that organizers have had little luck penetrating, their unionization rates will run low, regardless of their desire for or past experience with unions.

To recount, the most important positional factors include industry, occupation, geographical location, and economic sector. Positional theory would predict that those Hispanics who are disproportionately employed in low-skill service industries—industries with comparatively high labor costs relative to other costs of production—should have lower organization rates relative to others. Those Hispanics employed in the capital-intensive manufacturing sector, on the other hand, should have higher organization rates.

The critical question for our purposes is whether Hispanics and Hispanic subpopulations are more or less likely than nonimmigrant whites to work in labor-market locations where the costs of organization are quite high. And here we have two competing narratives about Hispanic employment patterns. On the one hand is the commonplace belief that Hispanics are concentrated in low-wage, low-skill service and agricultural occupations—occupations like fruit picker, the trade of Eliseo Medina's family. Notwithstanding the scattered successes of the UFW, unions have always found organizing agricultural workers difficult. On the other hand are the less widely known findings from academic studies suggesting that Hispanics as a group have been "more dependent on manufacturing than blacks or whites" throughout much of the twentieth century, as the scholars William Sites and Virginia Parks have argued.[45] Manufacturing served as the anchor of the American labor movement.

Measuring Hispanics' Organization Probabilities

So what explanation best accounts for Hispanics' unionization rates? To test solidarity and positional theories of unionization, I again utilize various series of the CPS from 1973 to 2009. Just as there are no questions directly measuring "protection" in large-scale data sets of the type I analyze, so too are there no questions tapping one's group solidarity. What we have instead is information on a range of factors found to influence one's likelihood of belonging to a union: demographic information like age, race/ethnicity, and sex, positional characteristics like industry, occupation, and sector, and geographical characteristics such as the state in which the respondent resides. The empirical task is to assess how well these variables explain differences in unionization rates among certain Hispanic subpopulations and other groups. If core positional variables account for all the differences between, say, Hispanic immigrants' unionization rates and those of U.S.-born whites, then there is little room for differences in group solidarity to account for variation in organization rates. If the statistical analyses that factor in key positional variables still reveal large group disparities in unionization, then I interpret the difference as consistent with one or another version of solidarity theory. We should be cautious with our interpretations, however, given that similar to the investigation of "protectionist theory" in the prior chapter, "solidarity" in this analyses is inferred, not directly observed.

These analyses treat whether or not the respondent belongs to a labor union as the dependent variable.[46] And what we are most interested in assessing is whether membership in a union "depends on," in the statistical sense, the respondent's race/ethnicity—namely whether or not he or she is Hispanic or a member of a particular Hispanic subpopulation. To accomplish this, the analyses measure whether or not Hispanics have elevated or depressed unionization rates once we account for many of the other factors that influence unionization.[47]

I begin the analyses with annual predictions of Hispanic unionization probabilities from 1973 to 2009 using CPS-May and CPS-MORG data (Figure 6.3). The point estimates indicate Hispanics' odds of unionization compared to white workers. An odds ratio above 1 suggests that Hispanics are more likely to belong to a union, while an odds ratio below 1 suggests the opposite. An odds ratio of 1 (or close to it) indicates no differences in unionization probabilities between Hispanics and the reference group, non-Hispanic white workers. I present two series. The "race/ethnicity model" series only includes race/ethnicity identifiers. That is, it does not take into account the positional and geographical factors that pattern unionization in the United States. This series provides a baseline comparison for the full model series.[48] As shown, the race/ethnicity series trends sharply downward over the nearly forty years covered by the data. Whereas in the mid-1970s Hispanics had one and a half times the odds of unionization of whites, by the late 1990s Hispanics' odds of unionization stabilized at about 20 percent *lower* than those of whites.

What could account for this shift? The "positional" series shows the results of models that attempt to rule out various explanations for the downward trend by comparing statistically similar types of workers. The models account for standard correlates of unionization such as a worker's industry, occupation, sector, potential experience, and where the employee works.[49] Two results from the picture stand out. One, for the majority of the series the point estimates hover close to 1, indicating little variation in union membership probabilities between Hispanics and whites after adjusting for differences in labor-market position and other factors. Up until the 2000s, the unionization probabilities between whites and Hispanics are not much different at all, and they are not statistically significant for most years. For those few years, such as the early 1990s, in which differences remain, they are substantively

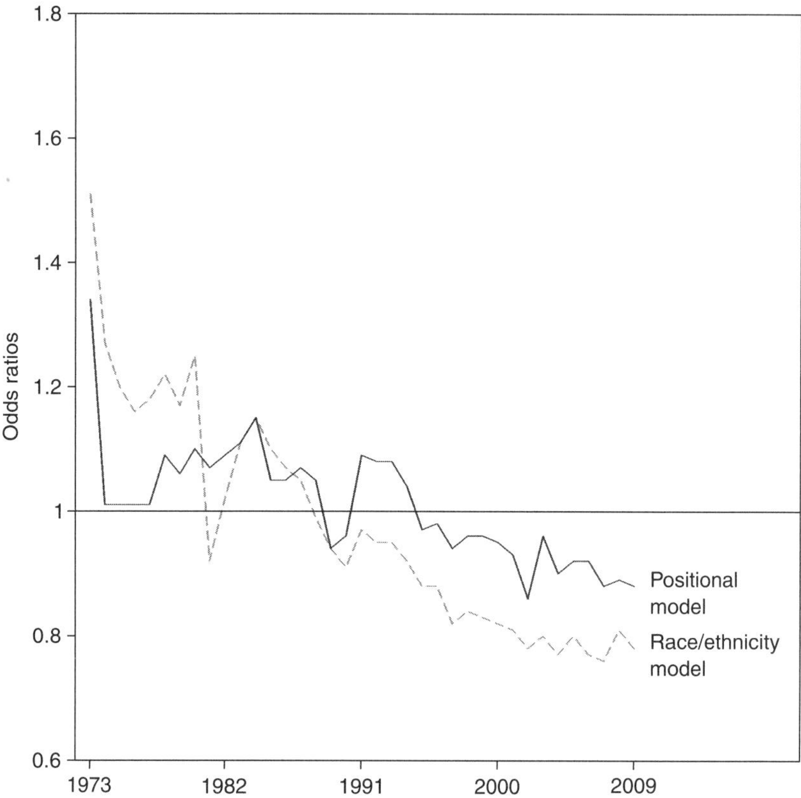

Figure 6.3. Hispanics' odds of unionization, 1973–2009. *Note:* Sample restricted to employed workers, ages sixteen to sixty-four. *Source:* Author's compilations. Data for 1973–1981 come from the CPS-May files; data for 1983–2009 come from the CPS-MORG files.

small. Two, the trend line shows a slightly downward slope. Beginning in the mid-1990s, Hispanics' odds of unionization fall below 1, and between 2004 and 2009, the difference in odds ratios between whites and Hispanics is statistically significant, indicating reduced probabilities of union membership for Hispanics compared to whites in recent years.

This comparison reveals that Hispanics and whites have similar probabilities of belonging to a union for most of the prior decades, after factoring in differences in where the two populations live and work. On the whole, then, solidarity or the lack thereof on the part of Hispanics does not seem to be driving their propensity to join or avoid unions. Nor do union organizers seem reluctant to disrupt existing solidaristic ties by bringing newcomers into the labor movement.

But in recent years we do see a slight change: Hispanics' probabilities of unionization have dropped relative to whites. What could account for this development? We know that the Hispanic population is a huge and heterogeneous lot, and it may be that compositional changes are driving the shifting relationship between organized labor and Hispanics during the early years of the twenty-first century. Solidaristic explanations of unionization focus on discrete subpopulations, such as recent Hispanic immigrants, immigrants lacking U.S. citizenship, or those that cycle back and forth between the United States and their country of origin. I now focus on these groups.

In Table 6.1 I present results from a series of analyses that divides the Hispanic population by citizenship status, national origin, time since immigration, and generation. Each block of results attempts to target specific subpopulations theorized to have high or low probabilities of unionization. For example, past research has found that Mexican immigrants return to their land of origin more often than other migrant groups. This cycling may retard the development of class-based solidarity in the United States.[50] The nationality analyses, then, test whether Mexican immigrants have lower odds of unionization after accounting for key positional characteristics as well as the state in which the respondent lives, and other vital information like potential labor-force experience, gender, and educational attainment. The comparison categories for all the analyses in the table are nonimmigrant, non-Hispanic white workers. I pool across the period to ensure sufficient sample sizes.[51]

I utilize the CPS-March series from 1994 to 2009 for these subpopulation investigations because, unlike the larger CPS-MORG files, the March series includes a measure of firm size. Research has shown that recent arrivals frequently rely on entrenched immigrant networks to find employment.[52] These networks frequently steer migrants to ethnic workplaces, often of small size.[53] By including a firm size measure, I can pinpoint whether unionization differences between Hispanic subpopulations and whites remain after controlling for this important intervening variable. The CPS-March series also includes an indicator of whether the respondent changed addresses in the past survey year. Residential instability may lower one's unionization probability, as

Table 6.1 Odds ratios from regressions predicting unionization, 1994–2009

	All workers	Private-sector workers
1. Citizenship models		
Hisp. nonimmigrant	1.13**	1.23***
Hisp. immigrant citizen	1.16*	1.27**
Hisp. immigrant noncitizen	0.66***	0.69***
2. Nationality models		
Non-Mexican nonimmigrant	1.24***	1.35***
Non-Mexican immigrant	0.86*	0.92
Mexican nonimmigrant	1.07	1.17*
Mexican immigrants	0.77***	0.77***
3. Time-since-immigration models		
Hisp. nonimmigrant	1.14**	1.24***
Hisp. immigrant <5 years	0.54***	0.51***
Hisp. immigrant 5–9 years	0.52***	0.56***
Hisp. immigrant 10–19 years	0.81**	0.88
Hisp. immigrant >20 years	1.05	1.10
4. Generation models		
Non-Mexican 3rd+	1.33***	1.51***
Non-Mexican 2nd	0.98	0.91
Non-Mexican immigrant	0.86*	0.92
Mexican 3rd+	1.03	1.17
Mexican 2nd	1.12	1.16
Mexican immigrant	0.77***	0.77***

Source: Author's compilations. Data come from the CPS-March files, 1994–2009.
Note: Sample restricted to employed workers, ages 16 to 64.
*$p<0.05$; **$p<0.01$; ***$p<0.001$

union job queues are often long. And recent arrivals may also be more likely to move around in search of employment in their new country.

Let's begin with the "Citizenship" block of results. Here we see unionization odds ratios for three different Hispanic subpopulations, first from data that include public- and private-sector workers, and then from data restricted to private-sector workers. Relative to nonimmigrant white workers, Hispanics born in the United States and Hispanic immigrants who are citizens have higher probabilities of being in a union over the 1994–2009 period. This is especially true for private-sector workers, where Hispanic nonimmigrants have 23 percent higher odds of being unionized, and Hispanic immigrant citizens have 27 percent higher odds of belonging to a union than comparable nonimmigrant white workers. Thus there is nothing about being a Hispanic immigrant that impedes one's probability of unionization—so long as you are a citizen. Citizenship status represents a significant divide. Regardless of whether public-sector workers are included in the analyses, Hispanic noncitizens' odds of unionization are roughly two-thirds as high as whites'.

Those immigrants lacking citizenship may differ from citizens in ways that go beyond citizenship status. It may be that noncitizens are more recent arrivals or tend to be from one particular country versus others. The next block of results focuses on national origin, and particularly on whether or not there is something distinctive about Mexican immigrants compared to non-Mexican Hispanics that impedes or increases their likelihood of unionization. As shown, non-Mexican Hispanic nonimmigrants have significantly higher odds of unionization compared to nonimmigrant whites, especially in the private sector. And non-Mexican immigrants in the private sector have similar unionization odds as whites. American-born workers of Mexican heritage have either similar unionization odds as whites, or—when restricting the analysis to the private sector—slightly *higher* odds of belonging to a union compared to otherwise similar nonimmigrant white workers. Here the real dividing line seems to be between Mexican immigrants and others. The odds of unionization for Mexican immigrants are just three-quarters as large as those of nonimmigrant whites.

One version of solidarity theory posits that it takes time, and perhaps even generations, for newcomers to develop the capacity for class-based collective action in the United States. Whether because of their precarious legal statuses, language barriers, or a mind-set accustomed to comparing working conditions in the United States to those of their country of origin, recent arrivals may prove poor candidates for unionization efforts. The Time-since-immigration and Generation sets of analyses buttress this hypothesis. Hispanic immigrants who have been in the United States for less than a decade have approximately half the odds of unionization compared to nonimmigrant whites. Those who have resided in the United States for at least two decades, by contrast, have similar odds of unionization as nonimmigrant whites. Breaking down the

Hispanic population by generation reveals a similar pattern. Third generation or above Hispanics are significantly more likely to belong to a union than similar nonimmigrant white workers. Nonimmigrant Hispanics with at least one parent born abroad have odds of union membership comparable to U.S.-born whites—whether they are Mexican or not. And just as with the nationality models, again we find that Mexican immigrants have the lowest unionization probabilities.

Disaggregating the data into even more finely graded groups of interest, groups like noncitizen Mexican immigrants who arrived in the United States very recently, results in categories with very few respondents, which generates extremely shaky estimates from the statistical models. In supplementary analyses, I investigated whether Mexican immigrants may be overrepresented among those who have not been in the United States for very long. Since we know duration in the United States plays a large role in patterning unionization among immigrants, an overconcentration of Mexicans among the most recent arrivals may explain the Mexican immigrant finding from the nationality models. It turns out that the fraction of Hispanic immigrants from Mexico remains pretty steady along the time-since-arrival continuum. In the CPS-March data sets, roughly 60–65 percent of all Hispanic immigrants are from Mexico, regardless of whether you focus on those who have been in the United States for decades, or on those who arrived within the last five years.[54]

The four blocks of results point to a few conclusions. First, citizenship exerts a strong, positive effect on unionization, perhaps suggesting that citizenship signals incorporation and serves as protection for immigrant workers against employers eager to exploit precarious legal statuses. Similar to other minority populations (most notably, African Americans), once assimilated into the open labor market and protected against threats of deportation, Hispanic immigrants organize at higher rates than U.S.-born whites. Second, all the analyses reveal higher odds of union membership for U.S.-born Hispanics than Hispanic immigrants, and among Hispanic immigrants the results indicate increasing odds of membership with time spent in the United States. This pattern supports the version of solidarity theory arguing that the development of class-based solidarity in the United States takes time, as recent arrivals must navigate language barriers, or shift their frame of reference away from their home country. Third, the analyses suggest that non-Mexican

Hispanic immigrants have higher probabilities of unionization than Mexican immigrants, perhaps indicative of past experiences with collective action and labor organization among these (largely Central American) migrants. The results are also consistent with the argument that higher rates of cycling between the United States and Mexico impede the unionization rates of Mexicans.[55] However, supplemental analyses limited to private-sector workers in firms with one thousand or more workers revealed no significant differences in unionization odds between Mexicans immigrants and non-Mexican immigrants. Thus nationality does not seem to matter all that much among those Hispanic immigrants who find work at very large firms.

What the results obscure, however, is just how strongly key positional characteristics pattern union memberships. Also, while the odds ratios indicate whether the relative probabilities of unionization for Hispanic subpopulations are different from those of U.S.-born whites, their magnitudes are not immediately intuitive. After all, 35 percent higher odds of unionization for non-Mexican, U.S.-born Hispanics may mean very little if the base rate of unionization is extremely low. And we are well aware that the base rates of unionization—in the private sector, at least—have fallen precipitously in recent years. It is worth asking then what best explains unionization among the small fraction of the population that remains organized. Is it one's ethnicity and immigration status? Or where one happens to be situated in the labor market?

In Table 6.2 I answer this question through a series of predicted probabilities based on analyses that include public- and private-sector workers and controls for the respondent's firm size and whether he or she moved in the prior survey year, along with the standard set of positional, geographic, and demographic adjustments. The probabilities reveal the magnitude of the effects of various key predictors of unionization.[56] That is, they help answer the "so what?" question sometimes obscured by researchers' focus on statistical significance. As shown at the top of the table, nonimmigrant white workers have a probability of unionization 2.4 percentage points higher than Hispanic immigrant noncitizens. This difference is much smaller than the effects of key positional characteristics like firm size, sector, and occupation. Workers in firms with one thousand or more employees have a predicted probability of belonging to a union 8 points higher than workers in firms with fewer than twenty-five employees, and the sector and occupation effects are greater still. This pattern persists for all four block of results. The Time-since-immigration results, for example, reveal that Hispanics who migrated to the United States most recently have a probability of unionization 3 points lower than nonimmigrant whites. But the sector effect is seven times as large. Workers in the public sector have a unionization probability 21 points higher than private-sector workers. Sector, along with other key positional characteristics, trumps ethnicity and immigration status in predicting Hispanics' unionization rates.

Unionization has always been unevenly spread across the demographic landscape. The labor movement's upsurge between the Great Depression and World War II relied heavily on European immigrants and their children—immigrants like Sidney Hillman, a major player in the institutionalization of the labor movement in this country. During the labor movement's peak, unions helped provide a firm economic foundation for these otherwise disadvantaged populations. One bright spot for organized labor of late was its success organizing largely Hispanic janitors in Southern California, many of them immigrants. This campaign was exceptional because in recent decades top union leaders and many of their members had eyed immigrant workers warily. Many assumed immigrants were unorganizable, because of the precarious legal status of some recent arrivals, the lower labor standards immigrants were accustomed to in their home countries, and the resulting worry that employers would use immigrant labor to undercut existing wages and benefits of native-born workers. The Justice for Janitors campaign helped counter those claims and galvanized organizers across the nation who sought to capitalize on the class-based solidarity exhibited by many Hispanic immigrants.

The analyses of this chapter suggest that some of the rekindled enthusiasm on the part of labor organizers and supporters of the labor movement is warranted. Certain Hispanic subgroups, including immigrants who have lived in the United States for a number of years and immigrants who are citizens, have membership probabilities that exceed those of U.S.-born whites. Nonimmigrant Hispanics have some of the highest organization rates of all, echoing the historical pattern of immigrant groups and their children seeking unionized employment to assimilate upward into the middle class.[57]

Thus the version of solidarity theory positing that immigrants and their children are unorganizable is wrong, a finding that Eliseo Medina's

Table 6.2 Predicted probabilities from unionization regressions, 1994–2009

	Percentage-point difference*
1. Citizenship models	
Hisp. immigrant citizen	1.1
Hisp. immigrant noncitizen	–2.4
Firm size <25 vs. 1,000+	–8.1
Public vs. private	21.3
Production vs. professional/managerial	12.3
2. Nationality models	
Mexican nonimmigrant	0.5
Mexican immigrant	–1.6
Firm size <25 vs. 1,000+	–8.2
Public vs. private	21.4
Production vs. professional/managerial	12.3
3. Time-since-immigration models	
Hispanic nonimmigrant	0.9
Hisp. immigrant <5 years	–3.3
Firm size <25 vs. 1,000+	–8.1
Public vs. private	21.3
Production vs. professional/managerial	12.3
4. Generation models	
Mexican 2nd	0.8
Mexican immigrant	–1.6
Firm size <25 vs. 1,000+	–8.1
Public vs. private	21.3
Production vs. professional/managerial	12.3

Source: Author's compilations. Data come from the CPS-March files, 1994–2009.
Note: Sample restricted to employed workers, ages 16 to 64.
*Reference category: nonimmigrant, non-Hispanic white workers.

whole life attests to. But the results presented in this chapter do support researchers' claims—and past historical precedent—that the capacity for class-based mobilization among newcomers often takes time. Given that the Hispanic population has been growing for decades now, many Hispanic immigrants are acquiring important labor-market experience, and reorienting their expectations toward economic standards in the United States. Many of their children, meanwhile, are aging into their working years and, if the findings continue to hold, will make prime candidates for organizing campaigns. To the extent that union membership continues to provide a firm economic foundation for otherwise disadvantaged groups, the findings of the chapter portend economic gains over time and across generations for Hispanic immigrants and their offspring with jobs in labor-market positions still amenable to unions.

But those labor-market positions continue to shrink. And here the experience of recent Hispanic immigrants and their offspring diverges from that of immigrant populations who flooded into unions during the great upsurge in organizing during the 1930s and 1940s. Unlike then, immigrants now encounter labor markets largely hostile to unionization efforts. While Hispanics' and certain Hispanic subgroups' *relative* unionization rates are high, their *overall* unionization rates are low, along with nearly everyone else's. The results of Table 6.2 reveal that the substantive effects of immigrant status, ethnicity, and nationality pale in comparison to positional factors like sector, occupation, and firm size. In today's economy, in terms of your likelihood of belonging to a union, where you work and what kind of work you do matter much more than your ethnicity or whether you are an immigrant or not. That would be welcome news to immigrant workers eager for the benefits and protections a union offers if the labor-market positions amenable to unionization were plentiful. They are not. Lacking the organizational vehicle to lift immigrants and their offspring out of low-paying jobs offering few possibilities of advancement, many Hispanics stagnate economically in today's rather unprotected economy.

Justice for Janitors was not the first successful, high-profile organizing campaign involving Hispanics and Hispanic immigrants. During the mid-1960s Cesar Chavez painstakingly assembled a coalition of farmworkers, student activists, clergy, and politicians to pressure growers to recognize the National Farm Workers Association, later to become the Chavez-led UFW. The SEIU and other social movement unions have adopted and adapted key organizing strategies first championed by Chavez and his long-standing director of organizing, Marshall Ganz—strategies such as community outreach (especially to religious leaders), highly publicized protests, and other forms of direct action. Figures like Eliseo Medina and other veterans of the UFW provided a direct link between that historic campaign and the efforts of the SEIU and other unions today.

The UFW understood some forty years ago the myriad ways that existing labor law hindered the organization of new members. For a time, Chavez and his staff maneuvered successfully around these roadblocks, turning what ostensibly were legal obstacles into advantages for their campaigns. For example, Congress was able to pass the National Labor Relations Act (NLRA) only after exempting farm labor from the law's reach. This successful pressure from growers' associations meant that farmworkers had no legal right to organize. But it also meant that the UFW could legally generate "secondary boycotts," or the boycotting of a business that is not the direct site of a labor conflict. The NLRA deems secondary boycotts an unfair labor practice if orchestrated by a labor union protected by existing labor law, something the UFW was not. By turning its "exemption from the NLRA into an asset," Shaw recounted, the UFW organized boycotts against major grocery chains selling the products of farmworkers' labor.[58] This type of creativity and strategic thinking has served as a model for those unions still actively organizing new members. Stephen Lerner, one of the architects of Justice for Janitors, has remarked that he "was enormously influenced by the campaign tactics and strategies of the farmworkers movement."[59]

Membership in the UFW is currently down by over 60 percent from the union's heyday in the 1970s.[60] And while there are many causes of the UFW's decline—including dictatorial and erratic governance on the part of Chavez himself, especially in his later years—surely one of the main reasons relates to farmworkers' precarious labor-market position. During the 1980s, dozens of unionized produce companies in California began shutting down. Others that remained organized entered into joint ventures with nonunion firms, quickly shifting their operations to the unorganized workplaces. The results for the workers were predictable, but nonetheless dramatic. In the early 1980s, a union member working as a field irrigator averaged over $7 an hour, plus benefits. By the early 1990s, the nonunion worker doing the same job averaged $4.25 an hour and no benefits.[61] As author Frank Bardacke concluded, "Much of what the union had won was lost."[62] Organizing a highly competitive agricultural industry reliant on easily substitutable labor was never an easy task. In today's antiunion environment, with U.S. growers competing with firms in Central and South America, it is even harder.

Organizing highly competitive low-skill service industries has also proven exceedingly difficult. Despite the widely publicized organizing drives of the Justice for Janitors campaigns, the percentage of Hispanic janitors in labor unions has actually declined since 1990, along with the fraction of all janitors who claim union membership. This, of course, does not detract from the magnitude of SEIU's victory, nor should it dampen organizers' enthusiasms about replicating the tactics and lessons involved in Los Angeles, Houston, and elsewhere. The union won a series of dramatic victories that resulted in the organization of thousands of disproportionately Hispanic, disproportionately immigrant building cleaners who would not otherwise be unionized. But it ought to temper unions' and labor researchers' expectations about what the campaign means for labor's future, and for what role the labor movement may play in the upward assimilation of Hispanics. That these victories failed to reverse the broader trend of union decline simply highlights the challenging organizing environment all unions face in the twenty-first century. Today, only one in seven Hispanic janitors in the United States belongs to a union, down from one in five back in 1988, when Justice for Janitors began.[63]

7

The Ballot Box

Deunionization and Political Participation

The labor movement has been active in elections for well over half a century. The passage of pro-union legislation in the aftermath of the Great Depression, most notably the National Labor Relations Act of 1935, laid the legal foundation for labor's rapid growth and bonded the nation's emergent unions to the Democratic Party. Throughout the decades following the Depression, many unions emptied their coffers and exhausted their organizing muscle during election drives, providing a counterweight to the campaign efforts of the nation's business lobby. Labor leaders enjoyed privileged access to top Democratic officials and served as key advisers, helping to devise domestic policy throughout the New Deal era.

Organized labor's political clout became increasingly clear during the reelection drives of Franklin Roosevelt. *Time* reported that Roosevelt's 1944 campaign was marked in part by the "emergence of organized labor as an independent political power. Sidney Hillman's P.A.C. got the voters registered, and then delivered them to the polls."[1] In return for his efforts, Hillman, already a close confidant of the president, reportedly received veto power over the selection of the vice president, an issue the president's political enemies tried to use to their advantage. During the campaign, Republican state committees purchased a million dollars worth of radio advertising to spread the phrase "Clear everything with Sidney." Roosevelt's opponents charged the president with issuing the order to staff members tasked with vetting vice presidential nominees at the Democratic National Convention that August. Republicans and business leaders believed voters would recoil at the revelation of organized labor's tremendous power in politics. It didn't work. Sidney Hillman, at the time chairman of the Congress of Industrial Organizations' political action committee, "got the voters registered, and then delivered them to the polls," helping to ensure Roosevelt's fourth term. Roosevelt was deeply thankful, telling his friend, "One thing I want to make perfectly clear is my appreciation. It was a great campaign and nobody knows better than you how much you contributed to its success."[2]

We have met Sidney Hillman before, in Chapter 6. Hillman was a Lithuanian immigrant who founded and would serve as president of the Amalgamated Clothing Workers of America (now part of the UNITE half of the UNITE HERE trade union). In addition to being a close friend and obviously influential adviser to Roosevelt, Hillman served on various government boards, including the National Industry Recovery Board, and he helped Secretary of Labor Frances Perkins draft what would become the Fair Labor Standards Act.[3] Like the president he had worked so hard to elect, Hillman did not survive the fourth term Roosevelt had won. He died of a heart attack in the summer of 1946. President Harry Truman commemorated the labor leader's legacy by remarking that Hillman was "a great humanitarian and an outstanding statesman in the field of labor-management relations."[4]

Not only did union leaders like Hillman support Democrats, but the strong link between organized labor and the Democratic Party extended down to the union rank and file, where it would persist for decades. In 1964, for example, fully 86 percent of union members supported the Democratic candidate for president, Lyndon Johnson.[5] But organized labor was too large and politicized a constituency for Republican officeholders to ignore completely. The 1964 race represented the high water mark for labor's Democratic vote share. In more typical elections, many unionists voted Republican. And unlike today, it was not uncommon for a Republican officeholder to maintain strong alliances with labor leaders.

Given labor's strength, politicians from heavily industrialized locales with a strong union presence simply had no choice but to court labor's vote, regardless of their own party allegiances. For example, labor-backed legislative initiatives to raise the nation's minimum wage frequently gained the support of Republicans representing heavily unionized areas in the Northeast and Midwest. A House vote in 1966 to increase the minimum wage to $1.60 an hour garnered 165 Democratic and 18 Republican votes. Of those Republicans who broke party ranks, twelve came from just three states: New York, New Jersey, and Pennsylvania.[6] All three states had a strong union presence. Similarly, efforts to tilt the country's labor laws in a more pro-union direction, such as a fight in the mid-1960s to repeal section 14(b) of the Taft-Hartley Act—the section allowing for states to enact right-to-work legislation—relied on the support of non-southern Democrats and pro-labor Republicans like Senator Jacob Javits of New York.[7]

Organized labor's strength was such that even during periods of Republican ascendancy, elected officials could not afford to disregard union leaders' advice when devising policy. Take the case of W. J. Usery Jr. Usery was a longtime labor activist who got his start as a cofounder of a local branch of the International Association of Machinists (IAM) in Georgia. For years he rose through the ranks of the IAM before President Richard Nixon nominated him to be assistant secretary of labor in 1969.[8] While Nixon was no great supporter of the labor movement, he understood that labor's assistance was essential for his legislative program. As he put it, "No program works without Labor cooperation."[9] President Ford followed Nixon's precedent, promoting Usery to secretary of labor in 1976.[10]

That was nearly four decades ago. Do unions matter in politics anymore? In the aftermath of the 2008 elections, many labor leaders anxiously waited for the newly elected president to press for passage of the Employee Free Choice Act (EFCA). EFCA had been the signature legislative goal of the labor movement for years, and as a candidate Barack Obama had expressed his support for it on the campaign trail.[11] In its most robust form, the proposed legislation would radically recast how union elections are held in the United States, bypassing the traditional election campaign in favor of a "card check" policy in which a union is recognized after over half of workers sign up in support of collective bargaining. A compromise version of the bill would retain the secret-ballot election procedure, but would reduce election times, grant organizers greater access to employees on the work site, and institute binding arbitration if a contract had not been agreed upon after a specified period.[12] As Gerald McIntee, president of the American Federation of State,

County, and Municipal Employees (AFSCME) described it, quick passage of EFCA would be proper "payback" for all the efforts organized labor had expended on behalf of Obama and other Democrats during the campaign season.[13] Unions and their members had spent tens of millions of dollars and countless hours on the ground fighting to elect Democrats across the country during the 2008 contest, and they wanted legislative returns.

The "payback" AFSCME and other unions expected as a result of their 2008 campaign efforts never materialized. Once ensconced in the Oval Office, Obama expended no political capital on EFCA, and the legislation floundered during his first term. Unions were understandably frustrated by the lack of legislative gains from their election efforts.[14] But how significant were those efforts themselves? As I will explore in this chapter, the outcomes of other recent contests cast doubt on the organizing efficacy of unions during contemporary election drives and on the subsequent political clout of union leaders in shaping policy.

For example, early in the 2004 primary contest, ex-House leader Richard Gephardt secured the endorsements of over twenty labor unions, including the once-powerful Teamsters and Steelworkers. His campaign never took off, and he quit the contest prior to the first primary.[15] Howard Dean appeared set to lock up the Democratic nomination after two of the largest and most active unions, the Service Employees International Union and AFSCME, backed his candidacy. Dean lost the nomination to John Kerry. With the primary field cleared, organized labor backed Kerry, contributing manpower at the polls and tens of millions of dollars to unseat President George W. Bush. The election rested on the outcome in Ohio, a state with a disproportionately high share of union workers. Kerry lost.

During the protracted Democratic primary battle of 2008, labor unions diverged in their endorsements. Unions such as the International Association of Machinists and Aerospace Workers came out early to back Hillary Clinton, Barack Obama secured the support of the Correction Officers' Benevolent Association in the fall of 2007 (but not many others, at least early on), and John Edwards's populist campaign attracted the Steelworkers and the United Mine Workers of America (UMWA). It is unclear whether these endorsements affected the primary results; certainly the lack of big-name labor supporters did not doom Obama's primary campaign. The labor movement eventually rallied around the Democratic candidate once the primary field cleared, contributing millions of dollars in campaign funds and promising to send legions of union members to the polls to outvote the unorganized. The money undoubtedly helped, but with a unionization rate lower than it had been in nearly a century, did the manpower?

Answering this question requires an investigation into organized labor's impact on recent elections. Unions' organizing muscle may influence elections in various ways. For example, union election efforts carry weight if membership boosts voting rates (what I term the "direct effects" of unions on voting), and if these union votes skew toward a particular party or candidate.[16] In what follows I address these two potential influences, paying particular attention to organized labor's influence on voting rates. After all, the broad impact of union members' partisan cast depends on whether organized labor is able to influence turnout in the contemporary era of shrinking union rolls. As I will show, this ability of unions to increase turnout among its membership has been drastically curtailed.

The answer to the question of whether or not unions matter in politics anymore carries repercussions well beyond the relative fate of the Democratic Party. Political participation is strongly influenced by socioeconomic status (SES). The more education and income one has, the more likely one is to participate in politics. Unions are uncommon among organizations in that historically they helped equalize participation across SES divides. Indeed, other than unions, only churches mobilize the less-advantaged on a mass scale. In the immediate aftermath of the 2004 presidential election, story after story in the nation's newspapers credited Bush's victory to the mobilizing efforts of predominantly white Evangelical churches.[17] But unlike Evangelical churches, unions remain unique in that they are a set of associations with the potential to mobilize non-elite voters to support economically progressive policies. No political party will advocate on behalf of the economic interests of the working and middle class without a constituency pressing for pro-labor legislation. The question of unions' political impact therefore speaks to whether non-elites have a vital political voice in this contemporary era of nearly unprecedented economic inequality.

Whether unions continue to serve their historical role equalizing political participation depends not only on their ability to boost voting rates among members, but also on who these members are. As we have learned, most union members today are public-sector workers. And public-sector workers have, on average, higher education levels than workers in the private sector. The sectoral and educational shifts have implications for unions' ability to mobilize society's most vulnerable workers. After all, unions can mobilize the less-advantaged only to the extent that they represent the less-advantaged. Thus before turning to the analysis of union effects on voting, we first need to investigate the changing sectoral and educational makeup of today's labor movement.

A Changing Membership Base

Union members' education levels have increased in recent decades, as employers began demanding high school diplomas and even college experience for jobs that once required nothing more than a union card. Analyses of Current Population Survey (CPS) May and CPS-MORG data indicate that in 1973, over 40 percent of male, private-sector unionists had never completed high school. Of these members, over two-thirds worked in manufacturing and construction. Thirty-five years later, the percentage of union members lacking a high school diploma had fallen into the single digits. In the early 1970s, only a tiny fraction of male private-sector union members had completed college—roughly 2 percent. In 2009, fully one in seven had completed a four-year college degree.

An increase in the educational attainment of Americans in general does not fully explain these rising educational levels of unionists. In earlier decades, the fraction of union members lacking a high school diploma was larger than among nonmembers. By 2008, the percentage of nonunion workers without a high school diploma was nearly double the corresponding percentage of union members.

The increasing educational levels of unionists contributed to a change in the class makeup of the labor movement. According to the political scientists Jan Leighley and Jonathan Nagler, the fraction of union members in the top third of the country's income distribution increased by 24 percent between 1971 and 2004. As the proportion of high-income unionists increased, the proportion of members with income levels in the bottom third of the distribution decreased by nearly 45 percent.[18]

The changes in the composition of union members do not end there. Related to the education and income gains by union members over the past decades is the sectoral shift among the nation's trade unions. Today, the total number of public-sector union members exceeds their private-sector counterparts. This marks a dramatic break with decades past, when private-sector union rolls dwarfed those found in the public sector. Figure 7.1 displays the percentage of all union members who worked in the public and private sectors between 1973 and 2009. In the early 1970s, less than 20 percent all union members worked in the public sector. By 2009, the majority of union members worked for the government.

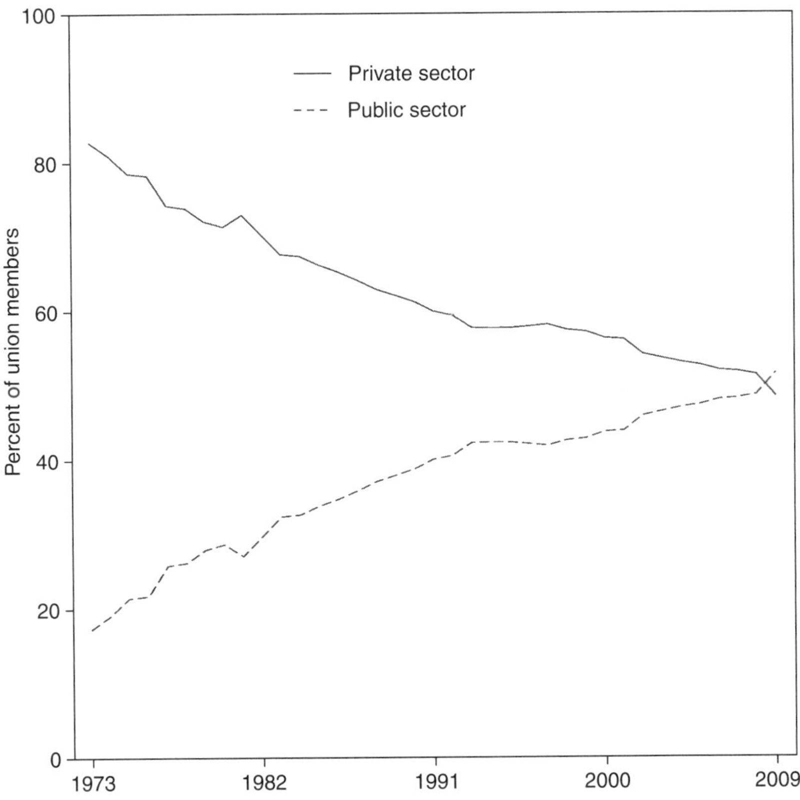

Figure 7.1. Union members in the public and private sectors, 1973–2009.
Source: Hirsch and Macpherson's Unionstats database, based on CPS-May data for 1973–1981 and CPS-MORG data for 1983–2009. See www.unionsats.com.

Why might the changing sectoral composition of the labor movement matter for politics? Public-sector workers, on average, have higher levels of education than private-sector employees. This is also true when restricting the analysis to union members. Figure 7.2 shows the fractions of public- and private-sector unionists who dropped out of high school, completed high school, and who had completed at least some college for three presidential election years: 1984, 1996, and 2008.[19] The figure highlights two noteworthy developments. First, *within* each sector, union members have made impressive educational gains, as noted earlier. For example, the percentage of private-sector unionists with at least some college experience more than doubled between 1984 and 2008. Meanwhile, the fraction of private-sector unionists who failed to complete high school plummeted. In 1984, over one in five union members in the private sector had not graduated from high school, half as many as in the early 1970s. By the election of 2008, that fraction had fallen to fewer than one in twenty. Educational gains among public-sector union members were not quite as steep, largely due to the already high proportion of government workers who

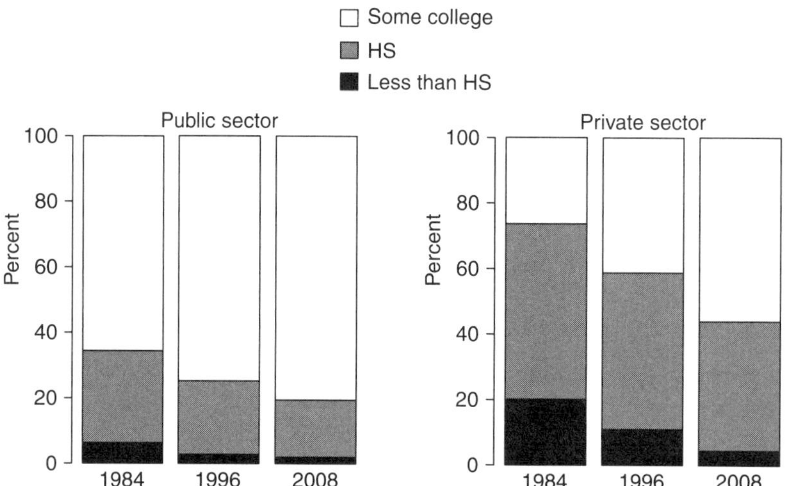

Figure 7.2. Educational attainment of U.S. union members by sector, 1984, 1996, and 2008. *Note:* Estimates limited to employed union members only, age eighteen and over, who are U.S. citizens. *Source:* Author's compilations, CPS-November data for 1984, 1996, and 2008.

had completed high school or more in 1984. But educational upgrading still occurred. Between 1984 and 2008, the proportion of public-sector unionists with at least some college experience increased by 23 percent.[20]

Second, *between* sector comparisons reveal large disparities in educational attainment. In 2008, for example, 40 percent of private-sector members had only completed high school—over twice the fraction of public-sector unionists. In 2008, the vast majority of public-sector members had attended college, with attendance rates 44 percent higher among governmental union members than among members in the private sector.

It is likely that unions' historical role in narrowing political participation gaps across income and educational divides was most pronounced in the private sector, where educational attainment—and political participation—was lower than in the public sector. Figure 7.3 presents voter turnout rates for public- and private-sector workers for all presidential and non-presidential (off-year) elections between 1984 and 2008. Even in those elections that galvanized the electorate, public-sector workers participated more than those in the private sector. The historic 2008 presidential contest witnessed elevated voter participation rates among both public- and private-sector workers, but public-sector employees outvoted those in the private sector by 13 percentage points. Sectoral differences are more pronounced during non-presidential election years, when overall turnout is depressed. In the off-year election of 1998, for example, public-sector workers outvoted private-sector employees by 23 percentage points. Overall, public-sector voter participation rates in non-presidential elections rivaled and often exceeded the presidential voting rates of private-sector employees.

The changing composition of organized labor limits unions' role in counteracting inequality in political participation. The majority of union members today are college educated, and the majority of union members today work in the public sector. The bond between education and civic participation is extremely strong. And the already high voter turnout rates and education levels among government workers, union and nonunion alike, leave little room for unions to raise turnout in the public sector. Thus, it is likely that the impact of unions on voting, and on equalizing the electorate, is even smaller than what is suggested by declining union rolls.

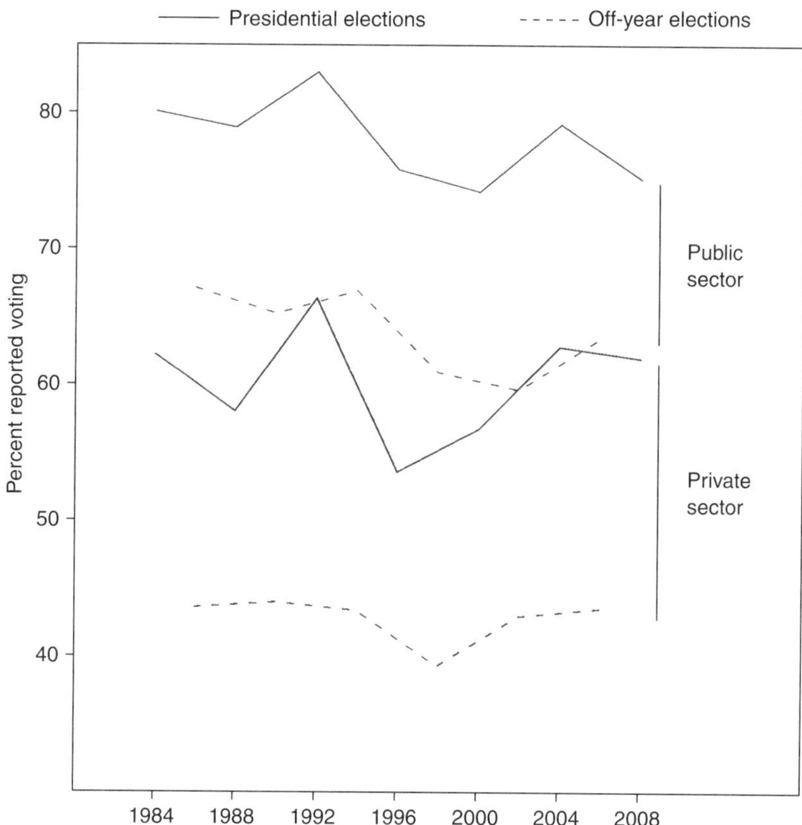

Figure 7.3. Voter turnout by economic sector, 1984–2008. *Note:* Estimates limited to employed U.S. citizens only, age eighteen and over. *Source:* Author's compilations, CPS-November data for 1984–2008.

Measuring Union Effects on Voting

> In this election as in so many others during the New Deal era, money was the least of the contributions labor offered the Democrats. Throughout the urban North the new unions recentered the party's electoral base, providing thousands of reliable precinct workers during each campaign season, and shifting to the Democratic column millions of new voters.
>
> —Nelson Lichtenstein, 2002[21]

The 1936 presidential election reversed Republican dominance in the nation's largest cities. Traditionally, Democratic strongholds included rural western areas and the states of the old Confederacy. As described above by labor historian Nelson Lichtenstein, the nation's fast-growing industrial unions—made up disproportionately of immigrants and their children—helped ensure Roosevelt's landslide reelection. The vote in cities with a strong manufacturing base swung toward the Democratic Party, tethering the rapidly unionizing urban masses to the New Deal political coalition.

The above quote also points to the myriad ways in which organized labor may affect electoral outcomes.[22] Money has always mattered in American politics, and unions have long used their money to support political allies. During the 1936 presidential campaign, for example, the powerful UMWA contributed a half million dollars to Roosevelt's reelection effort.[23] But as Lichtenstein suggests, it was through pathways other than financial contributions that unions historically had the greatest impact at the ballot box. Organized labor could never hope to match corporate coffers. In the hotly contested (and incredibly protracted) 2000 election cycle, business-related interests outspent organized labor by a ratio of fourteen to one.[24] Moreover, financial donations in and of themselves do little to counter inequality in political participation. Organized labor's role as an equalizing political institution rests on its ability to motivate members to volunteer their time and effort to politics. For this reason, social scientists who research organized labor and politics focus primarily on unions' abilities to affect voter behavior.

Measuring the direct effects of unions on voting is not straightforward. Ideally, one could randomly assign union membership to a group of workers, follow them over time, and compare their political behavior to the group of workers—the controls—who were not assigned union status. As I discuss in prior chapters, it is extremely difficult to replicate these laboratory conditions when dealing with the economic and political behavior of individuals. Another strategy would be to follow an individual over time through various election cycles as he or she enters or exits a trade union, and compare the person's political behavior while unionized to that when he or she was not unionized. Unfortunately, such time-series data do not exist. Instead, researchers interested in isolating direct union effects on voting must attempt to control for all the confounding factors thought to influence both membership in a union and voting behavior. The goal is to compare individuals who are observationally equivalent save for their union status and measure whether the union member votes more or less than the nonmember. The approach is similar to that of measuring union wage effects. The union vote premium, analogous to the union wage premium introduced previously, refers to the "difference in voting rates among persons with and without union attachment who have observationally similar characteristics," as the economist Richard Freeman has defined it.[25] Like the investigations of unionization (Chapters 5 and 6) and union wage effects (Chapters 2, 3, and 5), I use regression analysis to control statistically for the observed correlates of voting in order to isolate the impact of union membership.[26]

The Current Population Survey (CPS) November Voting and Registration files (CPS-November) and the National Election Study (NES) lend themselves to this analysis.[27] The CPS-November files are much larger than the NES and include a consistent measure for economic sector. They are most appropriate for the core analysis of unions and voting.[28]

Direct Effects of Unions on Voting, 1984–2008

Figure 7.4 displays the results of a cross-year investigation into the direct union effects on voting. The first set of columns shows raw turnout differentials between union members and nonmembers. They indicate that government employees outvote private-sector workers, a finding consistent with Figure 7.3. Averaged across nonmembers and union members, the sector voting differential is a full 18 percentage points. But these results fail to adjust for many of the dominant factors affecting one's probability of voting, such as education and income. The right-hand side of results do, and they reveal much narrower sector turnout differentials. After the adjustments, the sector difference in voting among union members is just 3.5 percentage points, while the gap among nonmembers is more than halved, from 18 to 8 points.

The results also indicate that unions continue to influence voter turnout in the contemporary United States, and that this influence varies by sector. First, the union vote premium: A weighted average of the sector-specific union vote premium (to account for the larger size of the private-sector workforce) indicates that union members' voting rates are approximately 5 percentage points higher than the rates of non-

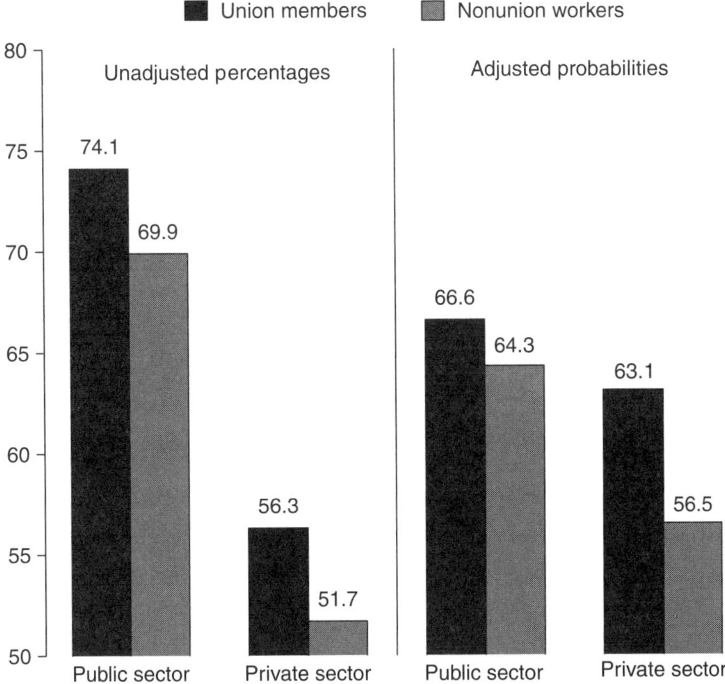

Figure 7.4. Probabilities of voting among union members and nonmembers by sector, 1984–2008. *Notes:* Unadjusted percentages represent voter turnout for various groups unadjusted for any other covariates. Adjusted probabilities generated from voter-turnout models that adjust for a range of demographic, economic, and geographic factors found to influence voting. Samples are restricted to employed citizens only, age eighteen and over. *Source:* Author's compilations, CPS-November data for 1984–2008.

members. This overall union vote premium is in line with what other research has found.[29] Second, sectoral differences in the premium: As shown, the ability of unions to influence political participation among their members is especially large in the private sector, where turnout rates run relatively low. The public-sector union vote premium is roughly a third as large as the private-sector union vote premium.[30]

These results reveal that the union vote premium is largest in the private sector, where unions have been receding for decades. As discussed earlier, today's organized workforce is increasingly an educated one. If organized labor's impact on voting is spread evenly among private-sector members, then the decreasing numbers of members at the bottom of the educational spectrum leaves less room for unions to narrow educational inequality in civic participation. But what if the ability of unions to influence their members to vote is concentrated among the least educated? If so, then the overall ability of organized labor to affect political inequality is even smaller than suggested by the shrinking numbers of unionized, private-sector workers. Not only are there fewer unionists among the least educated, but the impact of unions on voting might diminish as one climbs the educational ladder. In Figure 7.5 I test this hypothesis by estimating union vote premiums among private-sector workers for major education levels.

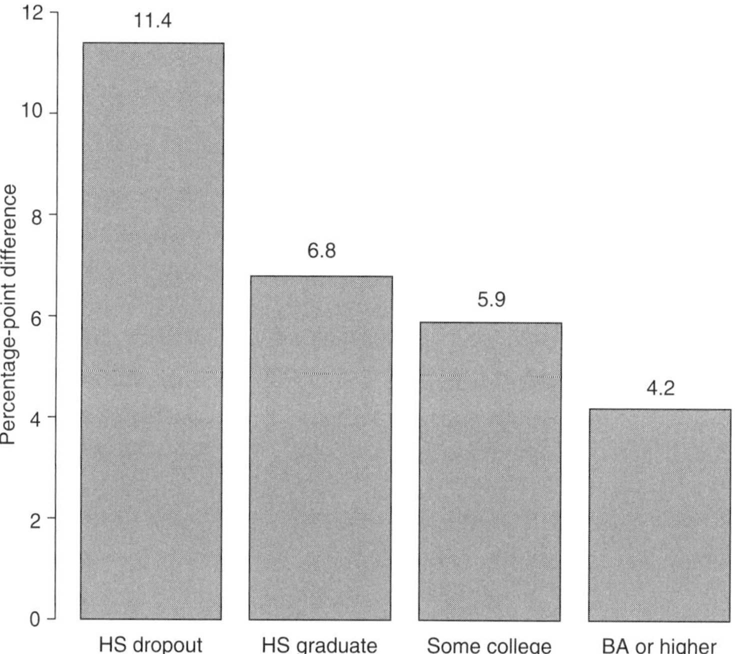

Figure 7.5. Differences in turnout probabilities between union members and nonmembers in the private sector by education level, 1984–2008. *Notes:* Point estimates represent the difference in voting probability between a union member of a given education level and an otherwise similar nonmember. Probabilities generated from voter-turnout models that adjust for a range of demographic, economic, and geographic factors found to influence voting. Samples are restricted to employed citizens only, age eighteen and over. *Source:* Author's compilations, CPS-November data from 1984–2008.

Union vote effects are largest for the least educated. Among high school dropouts in the private sector, union members' probability of voting is 11 percentage points higher than for otherwise similar non-members. Further up the educational spectrum, the gap in turnout differentials shrinks. Nonetheless, the union vote premium among private-sector college graduates is nearly twice the public-sector premium, displayed previously in Figure 7.4.[31]

Unions, Churches, and Elections, 1984–2008

The other major institution in the contemporary United States with the potential to equalize political participation across educational and income divides is the church. Research has consistently demonstrated that church attendance is associated with higher rates of voting, similar to the effect of union membership.[32] What is not clear is whether this relationship is stronger for low-SES churchgoers, mirroring the union membership pattern. For this analysis, the NES data set is more useful, as it includes measures of church attendance that the CPS-November files lack. In what follows I utilize the NES to estimate whether frequent church attenders (defined as those who attend at least once a month) were more likely to vote than infrequent and non-attenders during the 1984–2008 period. I then compare the results to an equivalent analysis on unions and turnout using the NES. However, unlike with the CPS analyses displayed above, because of data limitations in the NES I am unable to separate out the impact of unions on voting in the public and private sectors.

Figure 7.6 presents the results of an analysis similar to that displayed in Figure 7.5 but with a focus on the effects of church attendance on voting for various educational levels. Two results from this picture stand out. First, frequent church attenders are much more likely to vote than individuals who rarely or never attend. Among all respondents, those who attend church once a month or more outvoted those who rarely or never attend by an average of 11 percentage points across the 1984–2008 period.[33] Second, similar to the effect of union membership, the impact of church attendance on turnout is highest for those with the lowest levels of education. The effect of church attendance on voting for those with a college degree is just a third as large as it is among those with a high school diploma or less. Like unions, then, churches help

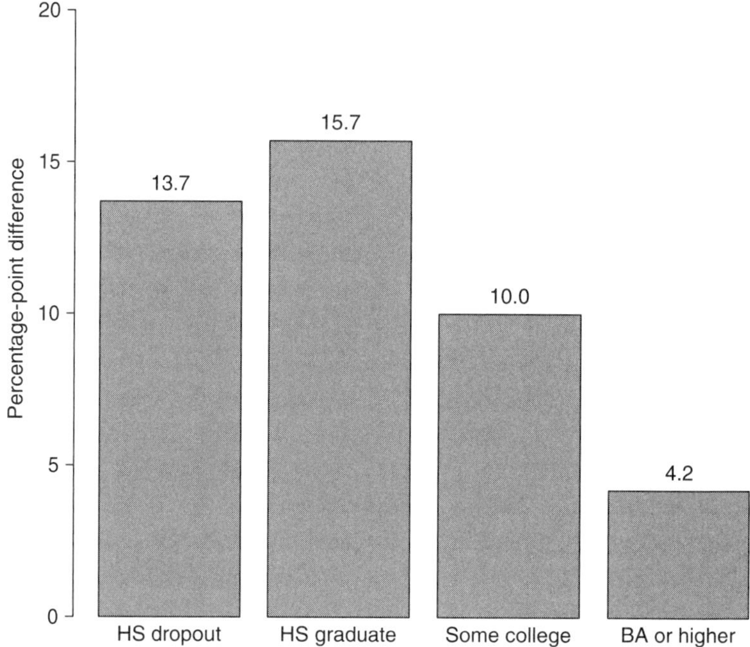

Figure 7.6. Differences in turnout probabilities between frequent and infrequent churchgoers by education level, 1984–2008. *Notes:* Point estimates represent the difference in voting probability between someone of a given educational level who attends church at least once a month and an otherwise similar respondent who attends church less than once a month or not at all. Probabilities generated from voter-turnout models that adjust for a range of demographic, economic, and geographic factors found to influence voting. Samples restricted to employed citizens only, age eighteen and over. *Source:* Author's compilations, NES Cumulative Data File for 1984–2008.

equalize political participation, although unlike the unionization differentials, the largest impact of church attendance on voting appears to be among those with just a high school diploma.[34]

How do these church attendance effects compare to that of union membership? The CPS results from Figure 7.5 show that the impact of union membership on voting is largest for individuals working in the private sector with less than a high school diploma. Among these respondents, union members had voting rates 11.4 points higher than otherwise similar nonmembers between 1984 and 2008. That effect is smaller than the largest vote differentials found between frequent churchgoers and those who never or rarely attend, although it is still substantial. The union and church attendance analyses are not directly comparable, however, given that they rely on different data sets, and the NES lacks key information on respondents' labor-market position.[35] An analysis of union vote effects in the NES that adjusts for church attendance along with the respondents' state of residence, year of the election, age, race, and marital status reveals voting differentials broadly comparable to the union analysis using the CPS. Once again, the impact of union membership on voting is strongest among high school dropouts, who are 10 percentage points more likely than nonmembers to vote. And once again, the smallest effect is among union members with a college degree or more, who had voting rates only 2.5 points higher than nonmembers with at least a college degree. While these differences in voter turnout are sizable, especially among the least educated, church membership *appears* to be a more powerful predictor of voting.[36]

But the union and church attendance analyses are not directly comparable for another reason—a reason that suggests these churchgoing effects may be slightly inflated. For the vast majority of unionists in the United States, membership is a compulsory feature of working a unionized job. Attending church, for adults anyway, is a voluntary activity. If an underlying characteristic jointly influences an individual both to join a church and participate in politics, then the voting differentials we see in Figure 7.6 will be biased upward. What appears to be the influence of churchgoing on voting may result from this other factor—let's call it a "participatory tendency." Selection of this sort is less of a concern with union members, who likely had little choice about their union membership.[37] A recent investigation that measured the effect of church attendance on voting before and after the repeal of so-called "blue laws"—laws that restrict commercial activity on Sunday—found that both church attendance and voting dropped in the aftermath of the laws' repeal.[38] That suggests that at least some of the effect of church attendance on voting is causal. However, without direct controls for an individual's "participatory tendency" it is impossible to tell what fraction of the church effect on voting is due to church membership, and what fraction is due to one's underlying inclination to participate in religious *and* civic life. Thus we should regard the results shown in Figure 7.6 as representing the upper bound of the true causal impact of churchgoing on voting.

I end this section with a brief examination into the party allegiances of politically active union members and frequent church attenders. While both church and union membership help raise voter turnout in the contemporary United States, the partisan cast of church and union members differs markedly. Figure 7.7 plots the fraction of frequent churchgoers and union members who voted for the Democratic presidential candidate during the elections between 1984 and 2008. Among all union members who voted for one of the major political party candidates, nearly two-thirds voted for the Democrat. Among all frequent churchgoers who voted for either a Republican or Democrat, less than half chose the Democrat. And, as the subsequent columns show, this

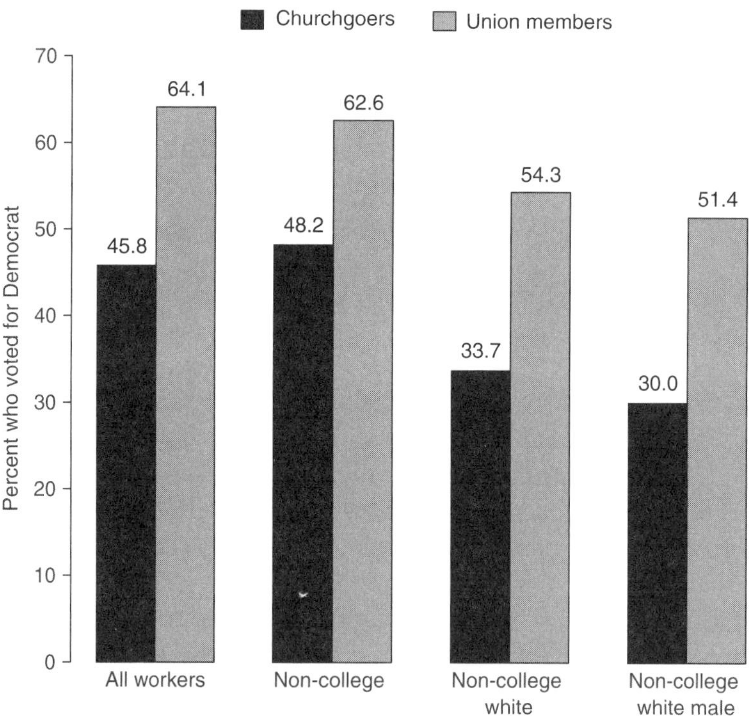

Figure 7.7. Partisan voting among union members and frequent churchgoers, 1984–2008, presidential races only. *Notes:* Point estimates represent the Democratic Party vote share for union members and frequent churchgoers for respondents who voted for either the Democratic or Republican presidential candidate. *Source:* Author's compilations, NES Cumulative Data File for 1984–2008.

partisan gap between union members and frequent churchgoers is especially large for whites and white male voters.

Whether pressing for increases in the minimum wage or fighting to alter the nation's labor laws to make organizing easier, Democrats have mostly been the ones in recent decades to champion the needs and policy desires of organized labor. The partisan behavior of union members reflects this alliance. The steep decline in unionization thus removes an important constituency for Democratic officeholders, forcing them to look for votes elsewhere. And as the dependence of Democrats on the labor movement decreases, so too does the movement's legislative impact. The policy desires of unions are not likely to sway officeholders no longer beholden to union members for their votes. Union decline therefore affects not only the relative electoral successes or failures of the Democrats, but also the type of legislation considered by our politicians.

Unlike union memberships, an analysis of the NES suggests that frequent church attendance has not declined appreciably over the past quarter century. This is especially true for white churchgoers, a constituency that leans heavily toward the Republican Party. White Evangelical churchgoers, in particular, have proven a durable electoral base for Republicans. And in recent decades it has been the Republican Party that has consistently blocked legislative efforts to narrow economic inequality, whether by contesting minimum wage increases, supporting tax cuts for top-end earners, or filibustering attempts to make labor organizing easier in the United States. Thus while unions and churches stand out as the major organizations that help narrow *participatory* inequality, the effects of unions and many churches on *economic* inequality are very different.[39]

2008 Reexamined

As the presidential fortunes of the Republican Party reversed in the 2008 election, stories emphasizing the GOP's success in motivating white Evangelicals to vote disappeared. A new election-related meme spread throughout the nation's press, this one focused on how a triumphant labor movement now expected legislative rewards for its campaign-related efforts.[40] Many reporters and editorialists simply declared that organized labor had played a pivotal role in expanding the Democratic House majority, and in delivering the Senate and White House to the

Democrats. Writing in the *Washington Times* shortly after the election, Gary Andres, a frequent conservative editorialist, observed: "No special interest group deserves more credit for electing and expanding a Democratic majority in Congress than organized labor. Unions infused Democrats with money, manpower and message support across America. Their resources are both concentrated and large, and they continue to provide electoral and legislative lifeblood."[41]

Prominent labor leaders shared this assumption of unions' outsize influence in helping Barack Obama defeat Senator John McCain in the presidential race, and in expanding Democratic majorities in Congress. John Sweeney, president of the American Federation of Labor-Congress of Industrial Organizations, applauded unions for powering "the engine of change" throughout the fall campaign. He went on to credit labor's "unprecedented" mobilization effort, and claimed that "union voters were the firewall that stopped John McCain" in heavily industrialized states like Ohio and Pennsylvania.[42]

Few within the labor movement or the media cited evidence proving that organized labor deserved credit for the Democrats' ascendancy. But some did, pointing to the millions of dollars unions poured into the campaign, and to exit poll results indicating that union members tilted toward the Democrats.[43] And indeed, an analysis of 2008 NES data buttresses the exit poll findings. Compared to nonmembers, respondents who belonged to a labor union favored the Democratic presidential candidate by 9 percentage points. Whereas 53 percent of unionized voters backed Obama, only 44 percent of nonunion voters supported the eventual president. Looking at the 2004 NES, however, suggests a more complicated story. In the presidential race of 2004, less than a third of nonunion voters backed the Democratic candidate, John Kerry, compared to just over half of union voters. The 20-percentage-point spread is over twice the difference in the union-nonunion voting rates of 2008. What seems to have happened in 2008 is not that union voters championed the Democratic candidate by any great margin—Obama's support among union members was only 2 percentage points higher than Kerry's—but that *nonunion* voters switched over to cast their votes for the Democrats in great numbers.

For any particular election year, the NES sample sizes are quite small, so the voting rates described above should be treated with some caution. In recent election cycles, CNN has provided results from its own surveys of voter characteristics, conducted as voters left their polling places.[44] The sample sizes of CNN's exit polls are substantial, averaging around seventeen thousand respondents per election, allowing for comparisons with the NES data. CNN's 2008 exit poll indicates that 60 percent of union members surveyed voted for Obama. Among nonunion voters, 52 percent backed Obama, for an 8 percentage point difference. In the 2004 race that returned President Bush to office for a second term, 61 percent of union voters supported Senator Kerry, compared to only 45 percent of nonunion respondents. Again, the fraction of the unionized electorate supporting the Democratic candidate remained relatively constant between 2004 and 2008. What changed was the voting behavior of nonunion Americans, and with it partisan control of the White House.

Another finding casts more doubt on the role of unions in the 2008 election. After all, the partisan behavior of unionized workers tells us little about organized labor's efforts to motivate members to turn out and vote on Election Day. If unions do not motivate their members to vote, then the overall impact on electoral outcomes will be small regardless of whether those voting all backed a particular candidate. To assess the direct effect of organized labor on voter turnout in 2008, Figure 7.8 replicates the earlier analysis of CPS-November data, restricting the time frame to 2008.[45]

The results indicate that the union vote premium in 2008 was slightly lower than its recent historical average. Union members had a voting probability about 3 percentage points higher than nonmembers. But unlike the results from the analysis that combined elections from 1984–2008, the union effect on voting in 2008 was limited entirely to private-sector members. By 2008, the labor movement's membership was nearly evenly split between public- and private-sector workers. Thus, in the 2008 presidential contest, union membership had no impact on the political participation of half the labor movement's base.

Historically, unions stood as the champion of the working class in the political sphere, encouraging members to vote and to campaign for labor-backed candidates and initiatives. As we have seen, unions continue to influence the participation of those who might not otherwise be motivated to vote. The union vote premium is highest among private-sector workers with low levels of education. Here too we see how important the labor movement is for vulnerable Americans, except in this case the focus is on low-educated workers, not racial and ethnic

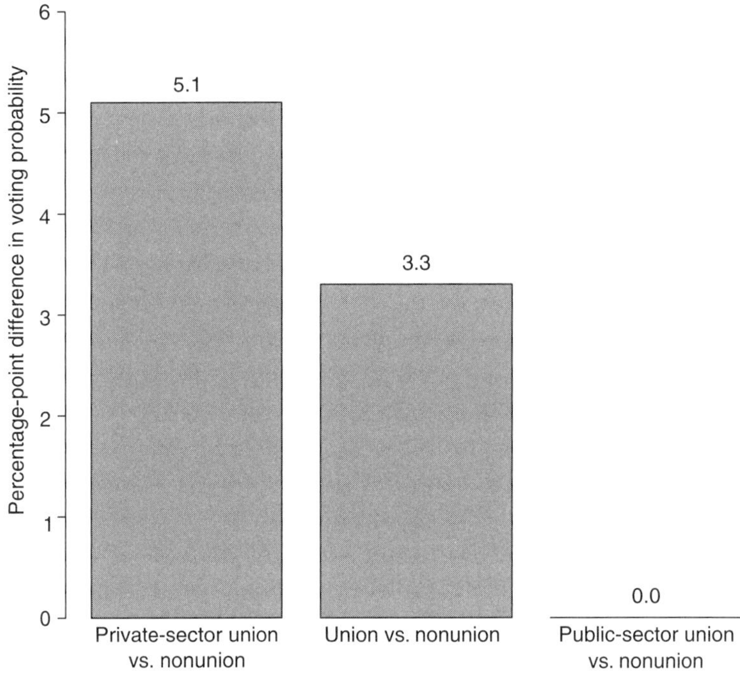

Figure 7.8. Union vote premium, 2008 presidential election. *Notes:* Union vote premiums generated from voter-turnout models that adjust for a range of demographic, economic, and geographic factors found to influence voting. Samples are restricted to employed citizens only, age eighteen and over. *Source:* Author's compilations, CPS-November data from 2008.

minorities or immigrants. Americans without college experience make up a segment of the electorate with comparatively low participation rates, partly due to the dearth of organizations that bother to target them. Unions and churches stand largely alone as buffers against greater inequality in political participation in the contemporary United States. Yet one of these buffers is rapidly eroding. Today, fewer and fewer unionists are drawn from the working class. Left behind are the millions of nonunion, working-class Americans lacking the organizational ties to lift them into the political realm.

While unions and churches both narrowed participatory inequality, only one of these sets of organizations has consistently championed measures to reduce economic inequality. For decades unions provided Democrats with a voting base and other resources in return for Democratic support of labor's legislative priorities. These priorities emphasized the economic needs of working-class and middle-class Americans. Many churches, especially Evangelical ones with predominantly white memberships, have similarly aligned themselves with a political philosophy, except their ties are to the Republicans, and their legislative agenda does not emphasize efforts to reduce economic inequality. And unlike unionization rates, church membership has held relatively steady over the past quarter century.

I should make clear what the preceding investigation does not find. My primary interest is on the role unions play in motivating Americans to vote. But labor unions also spend millions of dollars each election cycle on campaign-related activities, ranging from issue advertisements in the media, to increasing the coffers of candidates labor has endorsed. Unions clearly play a major role in our elections, even if their direct role in motivating members to vote has been drastically diminished. After all, money talks in contemporary American politics, and labor unions still have a lot of it.

Yet it is important to realize what the preceding findings mean for the civic inclusion of non-elites in our country. Unions do have a lot of money to spend on politics. The recent Supreme Court case *Citizens United v. Federal Election Commission* further erodes any impediments labor unions face in spending this money on campaigns. The case overturned prevailing law that had prohibited labor unions from running political advertisements mentioning a specific candidate's name within sixty days of a general election and thirty days of a primary. The ruling also allows corporations to spend freely on candidates and the causes they champion. For organized labor, competing with corporate donations will always be a losing battle. Organized labor was able to compensate for the financial power of the business lobby in the past through its advantage in manpower, motivating its millions of members and like-minded citizens to vote. In doing so, it boosted the political participation of non-elites, giving voice to the policy preferences of the working and middle class. As we have seen, this advantage, and with it the labor movement's ability to equalize civic participation, has been substantially weakened.

8

The Past as Prologue

The Labor Movement Pre–New Deal, Today, and Tomorrow

> We believe the time has come for the nation to reassess its implicit and explicit policies toward unionism, such as it has done several times in the past. And we hope that such a reassessment would lead to a new public posture toward the key worker institution under capitalism—a posture based on what unions actually do in the society and on what, under the best circumstances, they can do to improve the well-being of the free enterprise system, and of us all.
>
> —Richard Freeman and James Medoff, *What Do Unions Do?*[1]

By the close of the 1970s, innovative tactics adopted by management and used against organizing drives and existing unions shattered the relative labor peace that had predominated for decades. Traditionally protected U.S. industries, industries like auto manufacturing, opened up to competition from abroad, leading many firms to downsize and move to jurisdictions less labor friendly. The deregulation of other once heavily unionized industries brought on increasing competition from within, raising the costs of unionization for employers. The employers acted accordingly. Worried about the resultant drop in unionization rates in the private sector, the economists Richard Freeman and James Medoff ended their classic work, *What Do Unions Do?*, with a call to policymakers to redesign the legal apparatus governing management-union relations in the United States. The authors also exhorted employers to shed long-standing ideological antipathy toward the labor union and instead focus on ways to work with labor to ensure productivity growth and adequate worker compensation in the emerging global economy.

Nothing of the sort happened. Over a quarter of a century after Freeman and Medoff's work appeared, union declines continued, employer attacks on unions grew in sophistication and effectiveness, and policymakers failed to enact even one significant piece of pro-union legislation. As Freeman and Medoff warned and subsequent research confirmed, a withering labor movement widened income inequality in the United States.[2] And as this book demonstrates, the consequences did not end there. The collapse of private-sector unions eliminated a tested pathway to the middle class for millions of immigrants and their offspring, exacerbated racial inequality, reconfigured the electorate by reducing the political voice of those lacking a college education, engendered a radical shift in power in American workplaces away from average workers to their employers, and resulted in a labor movement dominated by government employees—employees who are, on average, more educated and better paid than the archetypical unionized factory workers of the past.

In certain ways, we have been here before. Often overlooked in the heady discussions about globalization and the new economy is that the state of organized labor and today's economic situation are not all that unique. During the 1920s employers and important state actors, especially in the judiciary, worked to arrest (often literally) further union expansion. "Yellow-dog" contracts barred potential employees from joining a union as a condition of employment. Many employers who eschewed this direct ban on organizing simply set up "company unions." Company unions remained under the direct control of the employer, had no affiliation with independent trade unions, and often interfered with the organizing efforts of independent unions. Meanwhile, the conservative judiciary of the period issued injunction after injunction during work stoppages, ordering striking workers to return to their jobs or face legal consequences.

The combined impact of these efforts paralyzed organizing activity and helped roll back union gains in prominent industries like mining and textiles. At the dawn of the decade, slightly over 5 million American workers belonged to a trade union. By the close of the 1920s, the number had shrunk to under 3.5 million: a 32 percent decline in just a decade.[3] As late as January 1932, *Harper's* ran a feature article titled "The Collapse of Organized Labor: Is the AFL on Its Deathbed?"—typical of 1920s and 1930s trade union news coverage. Labor's troubles in more recent years generated similar stories in the nation's popular press. During the 1980s, *Newsweek* published headlines such as "Labor Unions on the Ropes" and "Another Body Blow for Big Labor" as memberships fell and the political environment turned decisively antiunion. Media coverage would only get worse for unions as the twentieth century came to a close. The parallel press stories reflected organized labor's similar positions during the 1920s and today. Prior to the Great Depression, unionization rates in the United States stood at just over 10 percent, exactly their current level.

Weakened union power in the 1920s and early 1930s coincided with tremendous economic inequality. As the labor historian Irving Bernstein noted, "A striking feature of the American wage structure at the end of the twenties was the unusually wide spread that characterized differentials."[4] The economists Thomas Piketty and Emmanuel Saez's analysis of individual tax returns revealed that top-decile shares of wage income—in other words, the fraction of wage income captured by the top 10 percent of tax filers—peaked in 1928 before climbing again throughout the late 1970s and 1980s.[5] The prosperous economy of the 1920s ballooned corporate profits and swelled stockholders' pockets. It did not contribute much to the average worker's paycheck, especially for low-skilled workers in manufacturing. The economist (and later U.S. senator) Paul Howard Douglas suggested a connection between the two developments, arguing that the decline in labor's share of aggregate income may have contributed to the rise in corporate profits and stock market prices during the roaring 1920s.[6] Eighty years on, speaking of more recent developments, the chief investment officer of the giant banking conglomerate JPMorgan Chase echoed Douglas's argument, claiming that "profit margins have reached levels not seen in decades," due in large part to "reductions in wages and benefits" among U.S. workers.[7]

Figure 8.1 captures the dynamics of the rise and fall of the labor movement and economic inequality across the twentieth century. The picture plots the fraction of total income captured by the top 1 percent against the percentage of the nonagricultural labor force belonging to a union between 1920 and 2008. The top 1 percent income share series

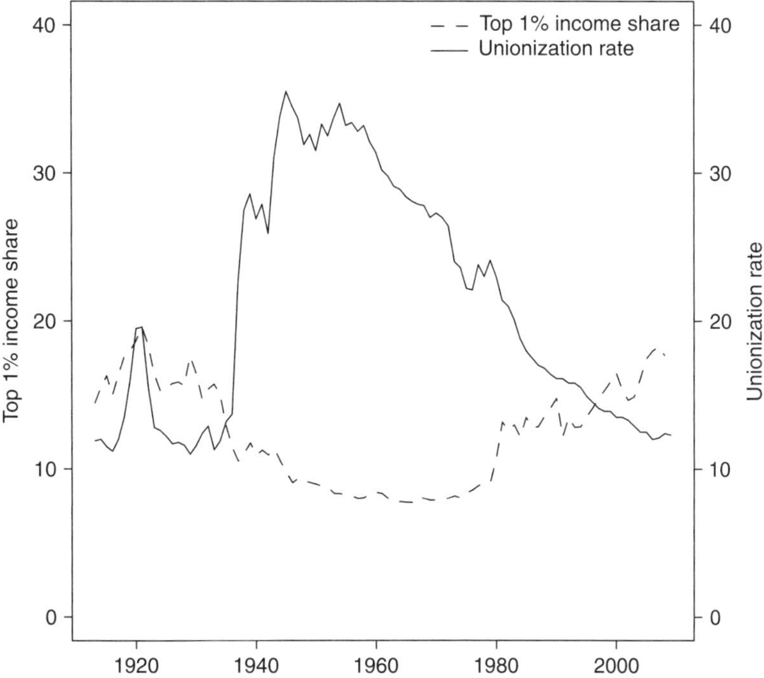

Figure 8.1. Unionization and inequality in the United States, 1913–2008. *Note:* Inequality estimates exclude capital gains. *Source:* Inequality data provided by Alvarado et al. 2011. For the database see http://g-mond.parisschoolofeconomics.eu/topincomes/. Unionization data for the years 1973–2008 provided by Hirsch and Macpherson's Unionstats database, based on the CPS-May and CPS-MORG files. See www.unionstats.com. Unionization data for the years 1930–1972 provided by the U.S. Department of Labor, Bureau of Labor Statistics, Division of Developments in Labor-Management Relations. For the years 1913–1929, total union membership estimates provided by Wolman 1936: Table 1, while total nonagricultural labor force estimates provided by Troy 1965: Table 2.

represents the portion of all income in the United States earned by those Americans richer than the bottom 99 percent.[8] In the early 1920s roughly a fifth of all income in the United States went to the top 1 percent. That fraction declined during the broad middle of the century—the period economic historians refer to as the "Great Compression." The series bottoms out in the mid-1960s, when the top percent captured less than 8 percent of total income. Over the next forty years, that share would more than double, reaching levels in the early years of the twenty-first century not seen since prior to the Great Depression. According to the Organisation for Economic Co-operation and Development, economic inequality in the United States in the mid-2000s surpassed levels found in twenty-eight of thirty other surveyed countries, including most of Europe, Canada, and Australia. Only Turkey and Mexico had inequality rates higher than our own.[9] Increasingly, the United States is a first-world economy with third-world inequality levels.

The unionization trend follows a nearly inverse pattern. While nearly a fifth of the nonagricultural workforce was organized at the beginning of the 1920s, unions' success was fragile, especially given the lack of a federal labor law to protect the rights of workers to organize. Unionization rates plummeted during the 1920s, but would rebound after that right was granted in 1935 with congressional passage of the National Labor Relations Act (NLRA). The unionization rate plateaued in the mid-1940s into the 1950s, when over a third of all nonagricultural workers belonged to a labor union, and then, as we have learned, commenced a long, steady decline—a decline that really accelerated starting in the late 1970s. The unionization rate today stands as low as it did when employers could legally bar their workers from collective bargaining.

How are the two trends related? Many factors account for the U-shaped inequality curve. No single explanation can account for such a complex economic phenomenon. Some of the contributing factors are largely unrelated to organized labor, ranging from drops in agricultural productivity (which widened inequality, especially in the early years of the twentieth century) to the onset of world wars (which lowered inequality by increasing labor demand). But this book has shown that when unions were strong, their impact on political and economic developments in the country ran wide and deep. One obvious linkage between weakened labor power and rising economic inequality is simply the reduction in the fraction of nonmanagerial, nonsupervisory employees who enjoy the union wage premium, an issue I explored in Chapter 3. That reduction widened wage gaps between average workers and managers. Other linkages are more indirect, but nevertheless powerful. Strikes, on the face of it, should result in income losses for all involved, both workers and management. But as I argued in Chapter 4, while the immediate impact of a strike is economically detrimental to all parties, the long-run impact once redounded to labor's benefit. The disappearance of strikes has removed another avenue through which average workers were able to capture a greater share of total income.

Other relationships between rising income differentials and the fortunes of organized labor are more distal, but nonetheless important. The increasing demand for skilled workers due to automation in the early decades of the twentieth century, and, in more recent periods, the computerization of occupations once reserved for unskilled and semiskilled workers exerted downward pressure on average workers' wages.[10] Take checkout clerks in retail stores today. Many establishments that once had human checkout clerks who rang up shoppers' purchases and bagged their goods have replaced these workers with computerized systems that let customers do much of the work. During the transition to the new technology many stores required checkout clerks to assist customers struggling to operate the new scanners. These workers were, in a very direct sense, contributing to their own obsolescence. This is a familiar story in capitalism's development. The successful quest for labor-saving technologies often displaces workers whose labor has been superseded.

It is not that a strong labor movement could, should, or would be able to forestall such forces. When unions were powerful, however, they moderated the impact of the introduction of new technologies in the workplace in various ways, as other research has demonstrated. For example, unions pushed for no-layoff guarantees or for the maintenance of wage floors after the restructuring at the workplace that occurs with technological upgrades.[11] These efforts lessened the disruptive effect on average workers' jobs and paychecks. Barring that, unions could bargain for retraining programs as a way to address the disemployment effects of labor-saving technologies.

Or take the demand for college-educated workers and the resulting "college wage premium." Policymakers and academics alike have converged on this development as the key to understanding inequality patterns since the nation's transition to a postindustrial economy. Accepting his party's nomination for reelection in 1996, President Bill Clinton declared, "By the year 2000 the single most critical thing we can do is to give every single American who wants it the chance to go to college."[12] The ambitious goal failed, and inequality continued to rise. President George W. Bush, while generally not remembered for his attention to economic inequality during his two terms, nonetheless identified it as a legitimate and long-standing issue, and offered a familiar solution to the problem. In an address on Wall Street late in his presidency, Bush remarked: "The fact is that income inequality is real—it's been rising for more than twenty-five years." He continued, "The reason is clear. We have an economy that increasingly rewards education."[13] The Princeton economist Ben Bernanke served terms as chairman of the Federal Reserve Board under both Presidents George W. Bush and Barack Obama. Bernanke, too, subscribed to the belief that education best explained growing economic disparities, remarking that "the larger return to education and skill is likely the single greatest source of the long-term increase in inequality."[14]

Generally, when researchers are interested in quantifying the effects of rising demand for educated workers, they calculate the difference in wages between the college-educated and those with a high school diploma or less, adjusted for the influence of other confounding factors such as union membership. This approach reveals a sizable education effect on growing inequality. Indeed, my work with Bruce Western demonstrates that growing demand for workers with college experience explains about a third of the recent rise in men's wage inequality—an effect similar in size to declining unionization. In our statistical analyses, we and others treat these two explanations for inequality—rising college premiums and declining unionization—as separate, competing phenomena. But they are likely more interconnected than that. A strong labor movement held wage differentials in check. The collapse of organized labor, then, opened up the possibility that earnings differentials based on educational credentials would widen. That is, the decline of one equalizing institution—organized labor—allowed for the disequalizing impact of education.

Here, too, the historical parallel is striking. In the 1920s, "the spread of differentials based upon skill was also unusually wide," according to the historian Irving Bernstein, with pay disparities between the skilled and unskilled increasing rapidly throughout the decade.[15] Douglas remarked that "the failure of the unskilled to share in the general advance" of the period was "startling."[16] Douglas's statement could easily describe the current situation, and indeed his sentiment has been expressed repeatedly by policymakers and the press when discussing trends in the income distribution from the 1980s onward.

The collapse of organized labor and rising returns to skill both in the 1920s and during more recent decades were influenced by broader developments in the nation's economy and polity. Both share common underlying explanations such as technological innovations and deregulation, along with other phenomena. But that is not to say that the relationship between unions and inequality, or that between the college wage premium and inequality, is spurious. The most sophisticated scholarly analyses reveal strong, independent effects of both deunionization and rising returns to education on inequality. And, as mentioned, organized labor, where and when it was powerful, cushioned the impact of many developments like technological upgrades on average workers in certain locales, and channeled them in different directions in others. Perfectly precise measurements of such complex, multifaceted politico-economic arrangements are likely beyond the reach of social science. But the basic pattern is clear: In our history, periods of rising inequality correspond with a weakened labor movement.

The decade leading up to the Great Depression was one such period. Inequality was high, and unions were on the defensive. Many assumed organized labor's demise was imminent, much as many do today. The swiftness of labor's turnaround during the late 1930s and 1940s was astonishing. While unionization in the United States peaked in the post–World War II era, the foundation for a revitalized labor movement was laid in the immediate aftermath of the Great Depression. President Franklin Roosevelt's election ushered in an administration eager to reverse the antiunion bias in federal law. Roosevelt, in fact, had taken an early lead on the issue when in 1930 as governor of New York he signed anti-injunction legislation. The 1935 passage of the NLRA established an oversight body—the National Labor Relations Board—charged with preventing unfair labor practices and overseeing union elections. In addition to changes in the law, competition within the labor movement combined with war-related production demands led to organizing drives in previously nonunion jurisdictions. Spurred on by a president who pressed for legal recognition of the right to collectively bargain, an economic calamity that had shaken Americans' faith in the free-market orthodoxy of prior decades, and an influx of foreign-born workers with past organizing experience, the rapidly expanding unions organized industry after industry in the run-up to World War II. Between 1933 and 1945, American Federation of Labor unions trebled in size, while the Congress of Industrial Organizations affiliates' membership doubled.[17]

The historical parallels traced above raise an obvious question: Does the past provide a precedent for labor today? Is another turnaround possible? After all, in late 2007 the nation fell into an economic collapse of a severity unseen since the Great Depression. The resulting political upheaval ushered in a reform-minded presidential candidate promising to restructure how American businesses, especially banking and finance, went about their business. It also produced Democratic Party control over all three branches of government, with the implicit promise of major legislative activity. Judging by the business lobby's frenzied spending in 2008 and 2009 on advertisements opposing organized labor's signature goal, one piece of legislation many employers were especially worried that the Democrats would pursue was the Employee Free Choice Act (EFCA).[18]

As we saw in the first chapter, EFCA went nowhere during Obama's first few years as president, and in 2010 Republicans narrowed the Democratic majority in the Senate and completely erased it in the House of Representatives, dooming EFCA's fortunes in the near future. Thus, in contrast to the flurry of pro-labor congressional activity of the 1930s, it does not appear that major legislative developments stemming from the economic breakdown will assist labor's rebirth today. A closer look at other factors that led to labor's rise in the past and collapse in the present likewise casts doubt on the likelihood that unions will repeat the rapid turnaround they enjoyed in the 1930s and 1940s.

Take "class warfare." It has become commonplace for politicians to accuse one another of engaging in the practice when arguing over tax policy or other efforts to reshape the income distribution. For example, in an ongoing debate over what to do about the nation's debt in the fall of 2011, Obama outlined a plan to roll back preexisting tax cuts on Americans earning $250,000 or more and to eliminate certain tax loopholes for wealthy Americans. The plan was quickly and widely derided by the president's opponents, with the Speaker of the House John Boehner declaring, "Class warfare isn't leadership."[19] This particular political trope has been seized upon by members of both major political parties in recent campaign cycles, with Vice President Al Gore describing presidential candidate George W. Bush's tax plan in 2000 as "class warfare on behalf of billionaires."[20] Eight years prior it was George W.

Bush's father who reproached his Democratic opponent, Bill Clinton, for what Bush viewed as Clinton's divisive approach to politics: "You know, Candidate Clinton is playing the old games that liberals love to play, class warfare, divide Americans rich from poor, one group from another."[21]

Despite the overheated political rhetoric, nothing approaching actual class warfare has threatened the country for generations. But it once did. As historian Beverly Gage recounted, "A century ago, the 'class question'—who would control industrial profits, who would set wages, whether capitalism was even compatible with democracy—was at the forefront of American politics."[22] And those who thought they had the answer to this question often resorted to violence to advance their preferred solution. The industrial titan John D. Rockefeller Jr. found himself embroiled in a nasty bit of class warfare in 1914 after guards at a company in which his family owned stock fired on striking workers and torched their makeshift tents, killing nearly two dozen, including eleven children. Soon thereafter, three anarchists accidentally blew themselves up while plotting a retaliation attack on Rockefeller.[23] A few years later, a bomb detonated near the headquarters of J. P. Morgan in downtown Manhattan, killing dozens in what was the largest domestic terrorist act until the Oklahoma City bombing in 1995. The perpetrators of the crime were never found, despite strong suspicion that the act had been carried out by socialists—or even directed by Russian agents.[24]

The specter of overseas developments haunted Americans worried about the stability of capitalism at home. Vladimir Lenin's successful victory in the Russian Revolution and then in the Russian Civil War brought forth and consolidated an avowedly communist world power. The United States' essentially open-borders policy prior to the quota system established in the 1920s meant that the foreign radicalism developing abroad could not be completely contained at home. As I discussed in Chapter 6, fully 20 percent of the U.S. workforce in 1910 was foreign born. Many of these immigrants brought with them political leanings decidedly to the left of those of the dominant political parties of the era. In 1912, the Socialist candidate for President, Eugene Debs, peaked in popularity, capturing 6 percent of total votes cast—nearly one million ballots overall. His support extended well beyond the immigrant ghettos of the northern cities, as he won more than 12 percent of the votes cast by Californians, and over 16 percent of the vote share in Oklahoma. Just over a decade later Robert La Follette, running as the Progressive candidate and promising pro-union reforms, won 17 percent of the popular vote, carrying his home state of Wisconsin. These leftist challenges to the establishment at home, combined with the growing power of communism abroad, motivated many American politicians—arguably none more so than Franklin Roosevelt—to seek a solution to the "labor question" that was avowedly pro-capitalist but would simultaneously ameliorate some of the very real economic problems experienced by average American workers.

The effort to solve the labor question peaceably gained urgency as the Great Depression eviscerated the nation's economy. And here another important difference between the 1930s and today emerges. According to numerous economic indicators the recession of 2007–2009 was more catastrophic than any the country had faced in three-quarters of a century, but the Great Depression still has no parallel. It shook the system to its core. At the close of the 1920s, the nation's overheated economy was running at full employment, with the unemployment rate in the mid-to-low single digits. The rate nearly tripled between 1929 and 1930, and then *nearly tripled again* between 1930 and 1933.[25] At its peak, unemployment in the United States during the Depression claimed one in every four workers; the rate was much higher among nonfarm employees. By contrast, the financial collapse of 2007–2009 doubled the unemployment rate, from approximately 5 percent to 10 percent. Redress for the victims of the 1930s calamity was scant, whereas a system of interconnected programs helped cushion the effects of the recent recession. Economists refer to programs that are automatically triggered by downturns as "automatic stabilizers," as they help stabilize the negative effects of recessions. Many of the automatic stabilizers—programs like food stamps and a national-level unemployment insurance system—did not exist in the early 1930s.

This confluence of a fundamental breakdown in the capitalist system across the globe and seemingly viable alternatives in the forms of communism and socialism compelled political leaders to act, and act quickly. Their actions provided the architecture for the American welfare state as we know it today. The more recent economic crisis was also global in nature. And while the suffering that ensued was real and widespread, the legacy of the Great Depression ensured that the misery would not be as severe as experienced in the 1930s. Moreover, the collapse of the Soviet Union and other communist regimes at the tail end of the twentieth century left no alternative vision of an economic order to replace the preexisting arrangement of a largely unfettered postindustrial capitalism. As a result, the spectrum of policies seriously considered to deal with the recent financial crisis ranged from standard Keynesian responses to radical right-wing austerity measures.[26] And aside from an exceedingly brief political moment when passage of EFCA looked possible, policymakers proposed no other comprehensive pro-union measures.

Finally, the nature of capitalism has also changed, and in a way that likely precludes a renaissance for organized labor in the near term. As I discussed in Chapter 1, mass industrialization of the U.S. economy really commenced with the run-up to World War II. In the 1940s, over a third of the total nonfarm workforce was employed in manufacturing. The giant smokestack factories that dotted the upper Midwest and northeastern states churned out American-made goods in industries often protected from overseas competition—and often protected from much domestic competition as well. The regulation of other industries where unions would establish a stronghold, such as trucking, helped prevent the entry of new nonunion firms that could underbid existing organized companies. And the war itself created labor shortages and huge production demands that benefited unions. Companies desperate for workers and eager to keep production humming were more amenable to workers' desires than they would be in tougher economic times.

Today, only about one in ten workers is employed in manufacturing. Not only has the fraction of workers in goods-producing enterprises dropped, but the very nature of manufacturing has changed as well. Gone are the days of heavily protected industries that could afford to pass on union wage premiums through higher price tags. The value of imports as a fraction of the nation's gross domestic product nearly tripled between the early 1970s and 2008.[27] The rise of Chinese manufacturing is especially relevant here. Recent research from the economists David Autor, David Dorn, and Gordon Hanson found that between 1990 and 2007, import competition from China lowered wages for American workers in local labor markets and increased unemployment.[28] Unionized firms would feel these pressures especially acutely, as the union wage premium meant that productivity increases had to offset the higher labor costs associated with organization or else the organized firm would face a strong competitive disadvantage. According to the labor economist Barry Hirsch, this is exactly the situation in which scores of unionized manufacturing plants have found themselves in recent years.[29] The available research suggests that many unions have positive, although quite modest and variable, effects on productivity. But in highly competitive industries, these positive effects fail to outweigh the higher labor costs associated with unionization, resulting in lower profit margins in organized firms.[30]

Other major industries that unions in the 1930s and 1940s had successfully organized also experienced significant changes. A series of legal decisions in the 1970s freed construction firms to shed their unions through a number of practices, most notably "double-breasting." Double-breasting is a tactic whereby an employer with a unionized enterprise opens another, nonunion one—with the employer often endeavoring to move most operations to the nonunion enterprise. This practice is especially easy in construction, given that construction projects tend to be relatively brief. As a result, construction companies could move from operating a unionized establishment on one project to a nonunion one on another, and over time shift more and more work to the nonunion subsidiaries.[31] In transportation, meanwhile, deregulation of much of the industry raised competitive pressures, resulting in lower wages. Many unionized companies simply could not compete.

Thus while the basic trends in unionization and inequality were similar in the 1920s and today, the conditions that paved the way for union renewal in the past are missing in the present. Then again, virtually no one surveying the economic and political climate in the 1920s could have predicted the rebirth of organized labor. And there is no reason that the factors sparking labor's ascent in the pre–World War II period must be replicated in order for labor to experience resurgence in the future. So could a turnaround occur? Absolutely. But there is little in the historical record for labor to guide its recovery.

From organized labor's perspective, it is hard to imagine the situation getting much worse. So what direction should unions take in this bleak environment? Recent research in labor studies by pro-union academics and activists has offered dozens of tactical guides, reappraisals, and broad strategies to reverse labor's decline.[32] Much of this research emphasized organizing strategies that have proven effective in today's incredibly challenging organizing environment. Unions that embraced these strategies have found some success, although not enough to arrest steady declines in the overall unionization rate.

Aside from a few high-profile victories that relied on innovative organizing strategies, such as the Justice for Janitors campaign I described in Chapter 6, a couple of other recent developments should give labor sympathizers some grounds for cautious optimism. First are recent polls indicating high levels of support for unions among younger Americans. For example, in a March 2011 Gallup poll that asked respondents whom they supported in the ongoing disputes between several Republican governors and public-sector unions, eighteen-to-thirty-four-year-olds supported the unions by a 61 percent to 27 percent margin (among those fifty-five and older, support was split, 45 percent to 45 percent).[33] If support for unions remains strong among younger cohorts as they age, then the labor movement might expect steady gains in popularity in the future.

But as I explored in Chapter 1, support alone among a wide swath of the population will not reverse current unionization trends. The plight of the labor movement has to command a heightened saliency in the public's mind. Only then can general support translate to the pressure necessary to push lawmakers to alter the organizing context and enact other changes that would benefit unions. Achieving this will not be easy. But the current era of low wage growth and high inequality might provide an opening. Inequality has entered the country's lexicon largely as a result of the Occupy Wall Street protests that began in the fall of 2011. This new focus on issues of economic fairness needs an institutional carrier to sustain the message. Stagnant earnings despite increasing productivity, as well as, most recently, the return of big bonuses for bailed-out Wall Street firms highlight an economic game that in many Americans' eyes has become rigged against average workers. Many now see rising inequality as a symptom of a system that denies a fair share to working people, and a visible sign of thwarted opportunity. A frontal attack on the problem of inequality by the labor movement might help address obstacles to the future of worker representation and reveal how past union successes helped sustain the broad-based prosperity of the twentieth century's middle decades.[34] After all, if this book demonstrates anything, it is the central role organized labor's demise has played in exacerbating inequality of various kinds. And historically, successful efforts to reduce inequality in the United States and elsewhere have relied on a strong labor movement.

As of this writing, the likelihood that a union-led movement against inequality could reverse current organizing trends remains small. And even should a broad-based movement emerge with backing from organized labor, the obstacles to achieving durable change remain formidable. In recent decades, U.S. firms have waged a battle on numerous fronts to shift power away from workers and toward employers. Many of these employers are eager to press their current advantage. For example, in the summer of 2012 the manufacturer Caterpillar squared off against its unionized workforce. The company had enjoyed a record profit of nearly $5 billion in 2011, and was on pace to break that achievement in 2012, yet still, according to the *New York Times*, it was "insisting on a six-year wage freeze and a pension freeze."[35] As unions recede from the private sector, the costs of unionization for any particular employer rises—further entrenching employer opposition to organizing. Indeed, Caterpillar's rationale for its aggressive stance was that it needed to maintain competitiveness with nonunion firms.

Moreover, politicians, no longer so reliant on labor for electoral support, now have little incentive to cross organized business by supporting pro-labor legislation. And as the management professor Peter Cappelli has argued, union revitalization is unlikely "unless the political climate in the U.S. changes quite radically."[36] Meanwhile, the economic factors that destabilized the labor movement initially—factors like the continuing decline of manufacturing coupled with increasingly open markets—show no signs of abating.

Thus it is worth contemplating whether there are prospects for wage growth and employment security for average workers in the absence of unions. The comparative picture is not welcoming. Looking across the developed world, low unionization correlates with higher poverty.[37] Yet in recent years scholars have begun paying attention to the variation in employment practices in the United States, even in those sectors usually associated with low unionization and low wages. Though retail, for example, is dominated by Walmart, other nonunion companies like Costco have succeeded despite radically different managerial practices. Costco's wages are comparatively high, benefits comparatively generous, and—partly as a result—turnover is significantly lower relative to its peers.[38] Costco remains an outlier amid an industry eagerly adopting the "low-road" organizational approach. Yet Costco shows that companies can survive taking the high road, and a public sufficiently exercised about growing inequality and wage stagnation could push Costco's peers toward a more worker-friendly organizational model, even without pressure from unions.

In addition to making work pay through high wages and decent benefits, another strategy to help average employees leaves the actual conditions of work much as they are and operates through the tax and transfer system to ensure a decent living for all working Americans. Most recent policy initiatives aimed at the working and middle class have followed this pathway, such as the Earned Income Tax Credit (EITC) for lower-income working Americans, and lower tax rates for middle-income Americans. Many of these policies attempt to ensure that post-tax, post-transfer pay is decent even if earnings are not. Further expansion of the EITC, job retraining credits, and other policy initiatives could cushion the shocks inherent in today's economy. Often the political push for this type of legislation came from unions. It remains to be seen which political power brokers will fill the void in their absence.

❁ ❁ ❁

> Many people watching tonight can probably remember a time when finding a good job meant showing up at a nearby factory or a business downtown. You didn't always need a degree, and your competition was pretty much limited to your neighbors. If you worked hard, chances are you'd have a job for life, with a decent paycheck and good benefits and the occasional promotion. Maybe you'd even have the pride of seeing your kids work at the same company. That world has changed. And for many, the change has been painful.
>
> —Barack Obama, 2011[39]

In his 2011 State of the Union address, President Obama invoked a vision of what we might call "the American way of life." It is a familiar and comfortable vision, one that once was—and to a significant degree, remains—deeply ingrained in the collective psyche of Americans. The notion of a steady job that pays well, that offers security and stability for a family, and that doesn't require more than a dozen years of schooling: This is the implicit promise many Americans came to expect in the decades surrounding World War II. And fulfilling this particular manifestation of the American Dream remains a goal for millions of Americans who grew up the children of men and women of modest backgrounds who nonetheless managed to achieve a stable, middle-class existence.

What is paradoxical about this version of the American Dream is that despite its ubiquity, persistence, and power, it rested on a particular set of political and economic arrangements that were historically anomalous. For only a few decades was the actualization of this vision a reasonable expectation for Americans. Persistently high inequality combined with wage stagnation for the bottom end of the distribution characterized much of the economic landscape prior to the Great Depression. Since the end of the 1970s, similar conditions have returned. Yet this vision's hold over our collective imagination remains strong. And it remains strong in spite of the fact that Obama's warning in his 2011 State of the Union speech has become familiar. For years now politicians, members of the nation's press, and many academics have warned us of the increasing unattainability of this dream. We hear that the "world has changed" in a manner that has rendered the vision increasingly unreachable, especially for those who fail to secure a college education. And it has changed in a way to make the economic lives of many Americans more precarious and "painful," while rewarding those at the top to an extent unseen since the early decades of the last century.

Yet when our nation's politicians warn us that the world has changed, rarely do they tell us that one major change has been the destruction of private-sector labor unions. Unions' starring role in creating this vision of American economic life has been largely forgotten, along with its historically anomalous character. But unions were absolutely central to undergirding the period of the "Great Compression" when inequality was low, and productivity increases were coupled to rising wages for average American workers. The influence of unions was especially important for society's most vulnerable and historically disadvantaged workers, who otherwise lacked the resources, wealth, and connections necessary to secure a strong economic foothold. We simply cannot understand many developments today—such as the lack of economic assimilation of many immigrants, trends in racial wage disparities, or rising political inequality in our elections—without accounting for the dramatic decline of the labor movement and how this decline has radically reshaped our system of economic rewards.

The world conjured up by the familiar vision of the American Dream has indeed changed. At the very least, we need to be clear about what we have lost, and why we have lost it. Understanding the consequences of the decline of the labor movement helps us to make sense of this altered landscape. It is also worth emphasizing that there is nothing inevitable about the disappearance of labor unions in the United States. As I emphasize in Chapter 1, political actors intervened at various times to reinforce the effects of economic developments, employer onslaughts, and an institutional framework all tilted against the interests of unions. There are ways in which unions can be strengthened—such as the ones described earlier in the chapter—that may be politically unfeasible at the moment, but that are not in any way unnatural or impossible. Many academics, business leaders, and politicians seem enamored with the notion that recent technological changes and everything that falls under the rubric of "globalization" imply one and only one pathway for us to take, despite the enormous variation we see among the advanced nations in terms of the role of unions in the economy and polity. Many benefit from such a narrow frame of reference, and work very hard to convince us that the only way forward is without the equalizing force that unions have provided. That does not make them right.

Appendix

Data and Methods

Data Sources

The analyses in this book rely on data from the Current Population Survey (CPS), the National Election Studies (NES), and the Federal Mediation and Conciliation Service (FMCS). Below I describe the key features of each set of surveys, paying particular attention to the CPS, which is the core data source used in the empirical chapters.

CPS

The CPS is conducted by the Bureau of Labor Statistics.[1] It is a monthly survey that samples fifty thousand to sixty thousand households drawn from the civilian, noninstitutional population of the United States. The CPS contains a wealth of measures related to labor-market outcomes and demographic indicators, making it an invaluable resource for research on the labor force. Although the CPS is a monthly survey, it does not survey completely new households each month. Rather, the sample is divided into eight "rotation groups." Each rotation group is interviewed for four consecutive months, dropped from the observation sample for eight months, and then returned to the survey for an additional four consecutive months. Thus, surveyed households are measured for eight months in total: four consecutive months in one year, followed by four consecutive months one year later.

For the analyses in this book I utilize the CPS-May, CPS-March, CPS-November Voting Supplements, periodic CPS Benefit Supplements (conducted in May 1988, April 1993, February 1995, and February 1997), and the CPS-MORG. No CPS series included questions on union membership until 1973, when the item was first introduced on the CPS-May survey. Unless otherwise indicated, all the original analyses in the book that extend back to 1973 rely on the CPS-May for the years 1973–1981 (see, for example, Figure 2.4). No CPS survey included a unionization item in 1982, and therefore all of the analyses that rely on 1973–2009 CPS data exclude 1982 data. I generate estimates for 1982 by averaging 1981 and 1983 results. For example, the Hispanic unionization rate displayed in Figure 6.3 is the average of the 1981 and 1983 rates. I replicate this procedure to generate estimates for 1994 (averaging 1993 and 1995 rates), since I exclude 1994 CPS data from all analyses for reasons detailed below.

For the years 1983–2009 (excluding 1994) I mostly rely on the CPS-MORG data sets, given their larger sample sizes. Households in the fourth and eighth month of observation (the CPS refers to this as "month in sample") are designated "merged outgoing rotation groups" (MORGs) because they are either leaving the sample for the eight-month hiatus, or they are leaving the sample permanently. Thus the CPS-MORG data is composed of those observations in the fourth or eighth month of the observation sample. The CPS-MORG surveys have included union membership items since 1983. In supplementary analyses in Chapters 2, 5, and 6 I use the CPS-March data sets. Unlike the CPS-MORG data sets, the March files include a variable on firm size, a variable on residential tenure, and items on fringe benefits.

Questions about fringe benefits are also available in the CPS Benefit Supplements. Along with the CPS-March data sets, for analyses in Chapter 2 I utilize these periodic CPS Supplements that ask respondents various questions about whether their employer provides health care and pension plans, and, if so, whether the respondent is eligible and enrolled in the plans. In Chapter 7 I investigate how union membership affects voter turnout. For many of the analyses in the chapter I use the CPS-November Voting Supplements. The supplements contain information on union membership and ask respondents whether or not they had participated in that November's election, along with standard CPS demographic, geographic, and labor-market information.

Most of the CPS files, including all the CPS-MORG data sets, all the CPS-November data sets, all the CPS-March files, and nearly all the CPS-May files, come from the Unicon Research Corporation's CPS Utilities program (http://www.unicon.com/). In the 1980 Unicon May file, the earnings information is invalid. For that year, I use the CPS-May from ICPSR: http://www.icpsr.umich.edu/icpsrweb/ICPSR/series/00024. ICPSR also provides the four CPS Benefit Supplements I analyze in Chapter 7.

NES

In Chapter 7 I utilize election data from the NES. The NES began in 1948 and contains information on a range of election-related characteristics, such as whether respondents voted, what party they voted for, questions about religious affiliation and church membership, and background demographic and labor-market variables. The survey is based at the University of Michigan. More information about the surveys can be found at http://electionstudies.org/.

FMCS

In Chapter 4 I explore strike activity in the contemporary United States utilizing data from the FMCS. With the exception of the airline industry (which falls under the jurisdiction of the National Mediation Board—see my discussion in Chapter 1), parties unable to resolve contract differences must file with the FMCS prior to any work stoppage, as specified in section 8d of the National Labor Relations Act. The FMCS strike data contain detailed measures on the number of workers involved in a dispute, duration, location, date, employer name, union name, and company product. I obtained the data set after filing a Freedom of Information Act request with the agency. The FMCS series is limited to 1984–2002.[2]

Sample Construction

For the models of union membership and log wage models in Chapters 2, 3, 5, and 6, I limit the sample to employed respondents with valid data on union membership and earnings who are between the ages of sixteen and sixty-four. (In the CPS, only employed respondents are asked about their union membership). For the analyses of voter turnout in Chapter 7, I restrict the sample to citizens between the ages of eighteen and over with valid information on whether or not they voted and whether or not they belong to a labor union. Changes in the CPS over the nearly forty years in my series present several significant challenges for data analysis. Below I discuss the most serious of these challenges.

1. Allocated Earners in the CPS

Beginning in 1979, respondents missing on wage items in the CPS had their wages imputed. The CPS's wage imputation algorithm did not include unionization as one of the matching variables. Inequality research has found that the inclusion of imputed earners results in biased regression coefficients on non-match criteria such as union membership. In recent years, inclusion of imputed earners leads to a reduction of union wage gaps of approximately 0.05, and, as sociologists Ted Mouw and Arne Kalleberg have found, the inclusion of imputed earners may result in biased estimates of other related trends, such as within- and between-occupation wage dispersion.[3] For these reasons I exclude imputed earners from the unionization and wage models.

The process of dropping imputed earners is not straightforward. I follow the strategy of economists Barry Hirsch and Edward Schumacher and estimate the proportion of wage and salary earners with allocated earnings for each survey year.[4] I was able to match their proportions designated as allocated for the entirety of the series by following these steps:

1. 1973–1978: For these years, the CPS did not allocate earnings to respondents missing on earnings. I retain all respondents with valid wage and union information.
2. 1979–1988, excluding 1982: The allocation flag accurately identifies all allocated earners, which I drop from the sample.
3. 1989–1993: For these years, the allocation flag identifies only a fraction of allocated earners. However, one can correctly identify respondents with imputed earnings by comparing the unedited weekly earnings item with the edited variable. I drop those not

missing on the edited earnings variable but missing on the unedited variable.

4. 1994: Respondents missing on earnings items have their wages imputed; however, there is no valid allocation flag for this year. I exclude 1994 data.
5. 1995: I retain those respondents with non-imputed earnings for those months in which the allocation flag identifies imputed earners. This results in a sample size in 1995 approximately one-fourth as large as the preceding and following years' samples.
6. 1996–2009: For these years, the allocation flag correctly identifies imputed earners, which I drop. This results in a final data set spanning the years 1973–2009 (excluding 1982, 1994, and three-quarters of 1995) where allocated earners are treated consistently.

2. Wage Topcodes and Outliers

The CPS raised its topcode values in 1989 and 1998. For the years directly preceding the resets, the fraction of CPS respondents who report topcoded earnings is nontrivial. Analysts utilizing the CPS files must make some assumption regarding mean wages for topcoded respondents. Unless I note otherwise, I follow the strategy of economist Thomas Lemieux in his 2006 *American Economic Review* article and adjust topcoded earnings by 1.4. Other strategies, such as trimming top earners, produce similar results for the core analyses in the book, and are available upon request. I also follow Lemieux and limit the sample to workers reporting hourly wages between $1 and $100 in 1979 dollars.[5]

3. Industry Coding

Changes in the CPS industry codes over time—specifically, between the 1981 May and 1983 MORG, the 1991 and 1992 MORG, and the 2002 and 2003 MORG data sets—complicate the creation of a consistent industry classification. A consistent industry recode must balance issues of sample size, changes in the CPS codes, and a desire for as detailed a set of industry measures as possible. I create two industry measures, both of which span the 1973–2009 period. The first is a set of fifteen industries; the second a slightly expanded set of eighteen industries. A few industries, such as mining and construction, are Standard Industrial Classification (SIC) one-digit industry classifications and are consistently coded as such in the CPS over time. Others such as "personal services" were extensively revised. I believe that the changes to the industry codes are not so great as to prevent a time-consistent recode. Below I describe the most significant recodes, focusing on the eighteen-industry variable. A full set of STATA code used to create both industry measures is available upon request.

1. 1973–2002: The early industry code changes (between 1981 and 1983 and 1991 and 1992) are quite minor with respect to the eighteen-industry classification. For example, "grocery retailing" (CPS industry code 628 in 1981) was simply reassigned to code 601 in 1983. FIRE industries were coded 707–719 in the early years. They were reassigned to values 700–712 in later years without much realignment of the underlying industries (the major exception being savings and loan associations, added to the FIRE industries beginning with the 1983 MORG file). Other code changes were similarly superficial, and involved assigning a new range of values to broad-based industries (SIC 1- and 2-digits) of the type that I utilize. While some 2- and 3-digit classifications shifted or changed, my industry groupings rely on stable 1- and 2-digit categories for these years.
2. 2003–2009: Industry codes significantly changed in later years, even affecting aggregated industry sectors. Matching "business/repair services," "personal services," "entertainment/recreation services," and "professional/other services" between 2002 and 2003 involved unavoidable inconsistencies, as these categories were eliminated and their underlying industries allocated to existing or new categories (e.g., "accommodation and food services" includes some industries previously listed under "personal services"). Some 3-digit industries, such as "internet service provider," were introduced in the redesigned codes in 2003. Certain coding choices (for example, how to classify "internet service providers") involved subjective judgment. My bridging strategy avoids major discontinuities,

so the 2003 industry distribution is similar to the distribution in 2002.

The industries in the fifteen-industry classification are (1) agriculture/forestry/fisheries, (2) mining, (3) construction, (4) manufacturing durables, (5) manufacturing nondurables, (6) transportation, (7) communications, (8) utilities / sanitary services, (9) wholesale trade, (10) retail trade, (11) FIRE, (12) business repair services, (13) repair services (14) recreation/entertainment services, (15) professional services, and a residual category, (16) unclassified.

The industries in the eighteen-industry classification are (1) agriculture/forestry/fisheries, (2) mining, (3) construction, (4) manufacturing durables, (5) manufacturing nondurables, (6) transportation, (7) communications, (8) utilities / sanitary services, (9) wholesale trade, (10) retail trade, (11) FIRE, (12) business repair services, (13) repair services, (14) recreation/entertainment services, (15) professional services, (16) grocery store retailing, (17) auto manufacturing, (18) printing/publishing, and a residual category, (19) unclassified.

For analyses that include public-sector workers, such as those explored in Chapter 3, I add a final "government" classification to the industry variables.

The Union Wage Premium

In Chapters 2, 3, and 5 I estimate union wage premiums. In this section I briefly describe the limitations in accurately estimating premiums, and the strategies I employ to overcome these limitations.

First and foremost is the drawback that comes with using individual-level data to estimate establishment or unit-level processes. After all, unionization occurs when a bargaining unit in an establishment votes to organize, not when any given worker decides he or she would like to be in a union. The reliance on individual-level data may obscure important establishment-level differences that jointly influence wage rates and unionization probabilities. For example, larger firms, on average, have higher wage scales than smaller ones, although the effect seems to have declined over time.[6] And unions tend to concentrate in larger firms. Thus some of the apparent union wage effect may be attributable to the influence of firm size. Workers in larger firms are more likely to be unionized, and workers in larger firms outearn otherwise similar workers in smaller firms.

The CPS-May and CPS-MORG data sets do not include a question about firm size. The much smaller CPS-March series does for a subset of years. As a check on the private-sector premium estimates shown in Figure 3.1, I reestimate union wage premiums using CPS-March data sets. First I simply replicate the model specification used to generate the premiums shown in the figure using CPS-March data. Next, I add the firm-size control to gauge its influence on union wage premiums. Because of the smaller samples of the March series, I pool across survey years and estimate average private-sector premiums for the final decade of the data (2001–2009), broken down by gender.

The results indicate that firm size is indeed a confounding influence on union wage premiums. But they also demonstrate that only a small portion of the union premium is attributable to organized labor's concentration in larger firms. Among men, the inclusion of firm-size indicators reduces the wage premium by about 4 percentage points over the period, from 23 percent to 19 percent. Among women, the reduction was a slightly more substantial 6 points. In sum, firm size does affect the estimation of union wage premiums, but not dramatically.

Other firm-level variables that may affect union wage premiums are unavailable in nearly all individual-level data sources of the type I utilize, including the CPS-March series. But it is hard to think of omitted variables whose impact on union wage premiums would be of similar magnitudes and operate in the same direction as firm size. For example, unions may target more-profitable firms—firms that are able to reward their employees comparatively well. On the other hand, workers in struggling, unprofitable firms may be more receptive to an organizing effort, offsetting any positive relationship between profitability and unionization. Other potential confounding influences are similarly ambiguous in terms of their effect (if any) on union wage premiums.

Recent analyses using data on union certification elections within establishments represent another strategy for estimating union wage effects. The labor economists John DiNardo and David Lee focused on close election results within manufacturing establishments between 1984 and 1999, and their findings suggested negligible wage gains from unionization, at least in the short-to-medium term. Their focus on close elections raises questions about how generalizable these results are to all unionization campaigns, as unions will often wait to call for an election until they have achieved a great deal of employee support. And in a follow-up article that employs different estimation techniques on data from a broader set of firms, David Lee and Alexandre Mas argued that the costs of unionization to companies (measured by declining equity value) are sometimes rather substantial, providing indirect evidence that unions *do* raise wage rates higher than at otherwise similar nonunion establishments.[7] What both these studies lack is information on establishments that unions were able to organize outside the traditional NLRB election process—an increasingly desirable route taken by many unions today.[8]

Other studies on union wage effects in the United States that utilize non-CPS data find substantial premiums. For example, using a unique data set on workers in the hotel, gaming, and recreation industries in Reno and Las Vegas, Nevada, economist Jeffrey Waddoups found significantly higher wages for the unionized workforce in Las Vegas compared to an otherwise similar set of workers in nonunion Reno.[9] Another recent study by the economists Maury Gittleman and Brooks Pierce that used unique establishment-level data on jobs classified by skill requirements found a union wage premium "within the range of typical estimates," and most of these typical estimates stem from the CPS.[10]

Aside from the relative lack of firm-level information, the other major drawback with the reliance on annual series of the CPS is that it is hard to rule out individual-level, stable characteristics that may jointly determine union membership and wages. For example, higher demand for unionized employment among workers could enable employers to select only the most productive workers for union jobs. If so, the comparatively high wages we see among union members may partly reflect their higher levels of productivity. The CPS includes core proxies of productivity, such as education. But employers may see things that surveyors do not measure—soft skills such as assertiveness, or further details on the employees' relevant work experience. The positive selection of more-productive workers into union jobs, then, could bias estimates of union wage premiums.

The design of the CPS allows researchers to match a subset of respondents across single-year periods.[11] In my recent research with Meredith Kleykamp, we capitalized on this aspect of the survey design and created a mini-panel data set with information on respondents from consecutive survey years. We then estimated union wage premiums in analyses that allow us to rule out fixed person-level characteristics, and to target only those individuals who gain union membership across the panel. These results yielded lower, although still sizable, union wage premiums. For example, in models of private-sector men, the cross-sectional coefficient for unionization was 0.25, compared to 0.16 in the panel models.[12] On the one hand, these results may suggest that union wage premiums generated from cross-sectional data are overstated because of positive selection. On the other hand, some researchers have argued that premiums estimated using CPS longitudinal data are understated because of greater measurement error.[13]

A potential issue that arises when estimating union wage premiums through standard regression equations is that union members are concentrated in certain industries and geographical locations and are almost entirely absent from others. If there are areas in the distribution of covariates in which no overlap exists between union and nonunion respondents, regression results may be biased. Researchers use propensity score matching (PSM) techniques to overcome this issue. The advantages of PSM relative to traditional linear regressions are actually twofold. First, PSM does not rely on the assumption of linearity; and second, as mentioned, PSM explicitly deals with the problem of common support by comparing wage (or voting—as I test in Chapter 7) outcomes for union members and nonmembers matched on their propensity to belong to a union.

There has been only one U.S.-based PSM analysis of union wage premiums. In it, economist Ozkan Eren estimates a slightly *larger* union effect compared to standard regression models. However, his two sets of estimates—PSM and linear regression—are roughly comparable, indicating that selection on observables is of modest concern when estimating union wage premiums in the United States.[14]

I obtain further evidence that regression-based and PSM union wage premiums in the United States are similar through an analysis of private-sector union wage premiums for men in 1985, 1995, and 2005. For this investigation, I match respondents on the following covariates: race/ethnicity, marital status, experience and experience^2, metropolitan residency, education, major occupation, hours worked, state of residence, and the eighteen-category industry measure. After I match on these characteristics, less than a percentage point of the sample falls outside the range of common support. These observations are dropped. In 1985, a standard OLS regression model estimates a union wage premium of 0.26 (or a 30 percent wage advantage for union members). The PSM estimate using nearest neighbor with replacement produces a slightly higher premium of 0.27. In 1995, the standard OLS regression model estimates a union wage premium of 0.24, exactly the result obtained using PSM. A similar lack of discrepancy was found in 2005, and in supplemental analyses of female union wage premiums. The results also do not differ based on my specification of PSM. Nearest neighbor with and without replacement and kernel estimations produce similar premiums. This exercise lends confidence that the regression results presented in the book are unbiased when it comes to selection on observable characteristics.

Where does the preceding discussion leave us? No data set or estimation technique is perfect, and researchers interested in this topic must choose one set of limitations over others. The advantages that come with using the CPS-May and CPS-MORG series are substantial. Large sample sizes allow for the inclusion of numerous controls while retaining enough statistical power to analyze results annually, the series are representative of the entire labor force, and they extend back decades. Moreover, for my purposes what is most important about what I show in Figures 2.4 and 3.1 is not so much the size of the union wage premiums—after all, numerous studies over the years have established sizable wage premiums—but the trend lines, especially the resiliency of the private-sector union wage premium for men. Biases of constant magnitude in my analyses will not affect the trends, and theoretically there is little to suggest that the effect of, say, unmeasured soft skills on jointly determining union membership and wages has changed over time.

Details on the Analyses in Individual Chapters

Chapter 1

Figure 1.2 presents unionization rates for eight advanced industrial democracies. Depending on the extent to which collective bargaining coverage extends to nonunion workers, a country's unionization rate may fall well below its coverage rate. Figure A.1 presents the corresponding coverage rates for the eight countries. As shown, the greatest disparity between unionization and coverage rates is in France. In countries like the United States and Canada, the coverage rate only slightly exceeds the overall unionization rate.

Chapter 2

Part of Chapter 2 focuses on how union wage effects differ in the public and private sectors. To produce the union wage premium series shown in Figure 2.4, I estimate annual union wage premiums for public- and private-sector workers separately using CPS-May and CPS-MORG data from 1973–2009. I regress log weekly wages on a set of covariates, including the respondent's union status, for each survey year excluding 1982 and 1994. For individual *i*,

$$Y_i = \alpha + U_i \beta + X_i \gamma + \varepsilon_i$$

where U_i indicates being a union member, X_i is a set of demographic, geographic, and socioeconomic covariates, including year and state-grouping fixed effects, and ε_i is residual individual-level variation.

The covariates included in the regressions (and captured in the X_i) are as follows: four mutually exclusive race/ethnicity measures (non-Hispanic white, non-Hispanic African American, non-Hispanic other race, and Hispanic); sex; marital status (not married or married); a set of four mutually exclusive education indicators (less than high school, high school diploma, some college, four or more years of college); potential experience and potential experience^2; a set of four broad occupational indicators (professional/managerial, farm/forestry/fisheries, service, production/craft/repair); a set of fifteen industry dummies (see the section above for a listing of the industries); hours worked per week; a variable measuring whether the resident lives in a metropolitan area; and a series of twenty-three state-grouping dummies.[15] Sample sizes for the CPS-May years (1973–1981) average approximately 50,000, while sample sizes for the CPS-MORG years (1983–2009) average around 170,000. I estimate nearly seventy models to produce the public- and private-sector series in Figure 2.4, so space considerations preclude a full set of results here, although they are available upon request.

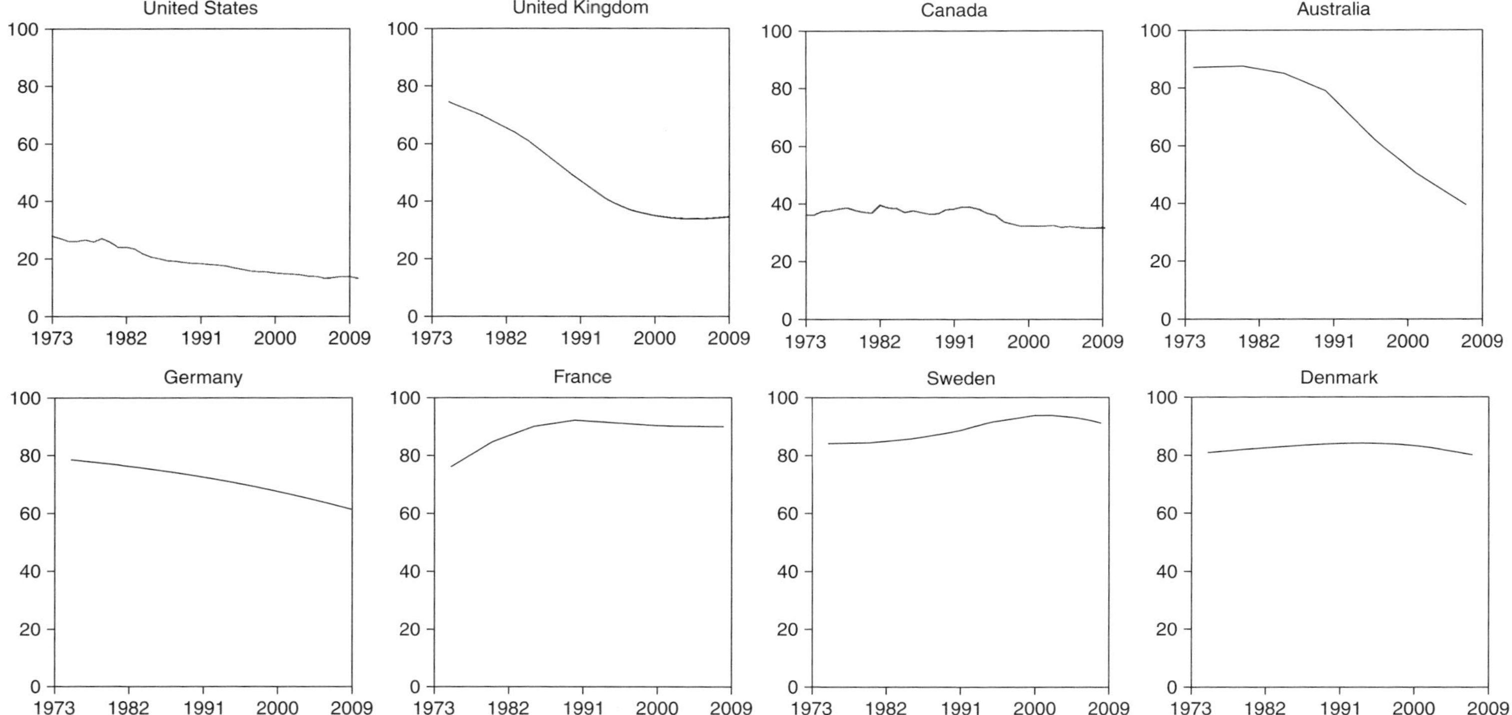

Figure A.1. Union contract coverage rates by country, 1973–2009. *Notes:* Samples restricted to employed wage and salary earners, excluding sectors and occupations legally excluded from the right to bargain collectively. Annual coverage rates are available for the United States and Canada. For the other six countries, the coverage trend lines represent a loess fit. *Source:* Visser 2009.

In Table 2.1 I limit the sample to public-sector workers and pool across the years 1983–2009. Model 1 includes all public-sector workers; Model 2 is limited to nonfederal public-sector workers; and Model 3 is limited to nonfederal public-sector workers in states with comprehensive bargaining laws. These states are WA, OR, CA, AK, NM, ND, SD, NE, KS, MN, IA, IL, MI, WI, OH, FL, WV, PA, NY, NJ, ME, NH, VT, MA, RI, MT, and CT. All three models include state and year fixed effects; otherwise, the specification is the same as in the cross-sectional models used to produce Figure 2.4.

To produce the wage predictions shown in Table 2.2, I estimate a union wage premium model with all the standard covariates described previously. I again pool across the 1983–2009 period. The predictions in the table were estimated using the levpredict command in STATA 11.

The second half of the chapter focuses on how unions influence the fringe benefits of workers. I use CPS-March data and data from the periodic CPS Benefit Supplements for these analyses. In Figure 2.6 I present the health insurance coverage and take-up rates for union and nonunion workers in the public and private sectors. The adjusted difference series are based on models predicting coverage and take-up using 1993 CPS-Benefit Supplement data (1993 is the only Benefit Supplement year that contains all the variables necessary for this analysis). The covariates in these models are as follows: union membership (the key predictor of interest); tenure at the firm (measured in months); the four-category race/ethnicity measure; the four-category education measure; potential experience and potential experience^2; the four-category occupation measure; a nine-category industry measure; region fixed effects; an indicator measuring whether the respondent lives in a metropolitan area; sex; a marriage indicator; a sex × marriage interaction term; and a six-category measure of the respondent's firm size. The nine industries are (1) manufacturing, (2) mining, (3) construction, (4) communications/utilities, (5) trade (wholesale and retail), (6) service/FIRE, (7) government, (8) agriculture/forestry/fisheries, (9) unclassified. The firm-size categories are (1) <10, (2) 10–24, (3) 25–99, (4) 100–499, (5) 500–999, (6) 1,000 or more.

The outcome variables for these models are dichotomous, so the use of linear probability models violates standard OLS assumptions. However, comparisons with logit probability models reveal substantively similar results, and so for ease of interpretation Figure 2.6 is based on linear regression results. In Table A.1 I provide results from the linear regression model predicting health care coverage supplemented with a logit specification for comparison. Results from similar models predicting take-up are available upon request.

The models used to generate the predicted probabilities shown in Tables 2.3 and 2.4 rely on CPS-March data from 1988–2009. The March series has two key drawbacks relative to the CPS's Benefit Supplements. First, over the years, both the sampling universe for the health care questions, and the questions themselves, change. It is possible to generate a consistent series capturing whether individuals receive health insurance from their employer and, if so, whether the employer pays for part or all of the insurance costs, but little other information is available beyond these two questions. Second, the March questions about health care coverage refer to the last survey year. For example, a question about health insurance in the 1996 survey asks about coverage in 1995. The union question asks about membership *last week*. Using unionization last survey week as a proxy for unionization last survey year introduces measurement error into estimates of union effects on health care provision.[16] Still, other research has found that respondents interpret the health insurance questions as referring to a point in time between the survey and last calendar year, thereby likely reducing error on the union variable.[17]

Unlike the much smaller benefit supplements, the larger sample sizes of the March files allow for the inclusion of key covariates, such as controls for individual states, in models estimating union effects on health care coverage. State controls are especially important in estimating union effects among government workers, given the wide range of state-level laws governing public-sector collective bargaining.

To predict whether or not a respondent's employer pays for all or some of his or her health insurance, I restrict the sample to workers who receive health insurance from their employer. I then estimate a logistic regression model with the following controls (for details of the control variables' categories, see above): union membership (the key predictor of interest); the four-category race/ethnicity measure; the four-category education measure; potential experience and potential experience^2; the four-category occupation measure; the nine-category industry measure; an indicator measuring whether the respondent lives in a metropolitan area; sex; a marriage indicator; a logged measure of the

Table A.1 Estimates of the union effect on health care coverage, 1993

Public sector	Linear estimates		Odds ratios from logistic model	
Union	**0.14**	(0.12, 0.17)	**3.02**	(2.37, 3.85)
Demographic and labor-market position controls:				
African American	0.00	(−0.04, 0.05)	0.99	(0.68, 1.43)
Hispanic	0.00	(−0.06, 0.06)	1.06	(0.67, 1.68)
Other race	−0.02	(−0.11, 0.07)	0.71	(0.38, 1.32)
Married	**−0.13**	(−0.17, −0.09)	**0.37**	(0.28, 0.50)
Male	0.02	(−0.03, 0.07)	1.40	(0.96, 2.03)
Male × married	**0.13**	(0.07, 0.19)	**2.44**	(1.52, 3.89)
Potential experience	**0.01**	(0.01, 0.02)	**1.08**	(1.04, 1.12)
Potential experience^2	**−0.00**	(−0.00, −0.00)	**0.99**	(0.99, 0.99)
HS (reference is <HS)	−0.01	(−0.09, 0.07)	0.94	(0.56, 1.60)
Some college	−0.02	(−0.10, 0.06)	0.95	(0.55, 1.63)
College degree or higher	0.02	(−0.06, 0.11)	1.29	(0.72, 2.32)
Tenure at firm (× 100)	**0.08**	(0.07, 0.10)	**1.01**	(1.01, 1.01)
Major industry and occupation effects		Yes		Yes
Region effects		Yes		Yes
Metro effects		Yes		Yes
Firm size effects		Yes		Yes
N		3,764		3,764
Number of parameters		33		33
R^2	0.18		0.22	

Private sector				
Union	**0.11**	(0.08, 0.13)	**2.28**	(1.88, 2.76)
Demographic and labor-market position controls:				
African American	**–0.05**	(–0.08, –0.02)	**0.75**	(0.63, 0.90)
Hispanic	**–0.07**	(–0.10, –0.04)	**0.66**	(0.55, 0.78)
Other race	0.02	(–0.02, 0.06)	1.12	(0.86, 1.46)
Married	**–0.14**	(–0.16, –0.12)	**0.44**	(0.39, 0.50)
Male	–0.01	(–0.03, 0.02)	1.01	(0.87, 1.17)
Male × married	**0.16**	(0.13, 0.19)	**2.54**	(2.12, 3.05)
Potential experience	**0.02**	(0.01, 0.02)	**1.08**	(1.06, 1.09)
Potential experience^2	**–0.00**	(–0.00, –0.00)	**0.99**	(0.99, 0.99)
HS (reference is <HS)	**0.14**	(0.11, 0.16)	**2.09**	(1.80, 2.42)
Some college	**0.15**	(0.12, 0.18)	**2.24**	(1.92, 2.61)
College degree or higher	**0.24**	(0.20, 0.27)	**3.66**	(3.05, 4.39)
Tenure at firm (× 100)	**0.10**	(0.09, 0.11)	**1.01**	(1.01, 1.01)
Major industry and occupation effects		Yes		Yes
Region effects		Yes		Yes
Metro effects		Yes		Yes
Firm size effects		Yes		Yes
N		15,490		15,490
Number of parameters		33		33
R^2	0.28		0.26	

Note: 95% confidence intervals in parentheses. Data come from the CPS-April Benefits Supplement. All models weighted with the appropriate supplement weights. All coefficients from suppressed covariates available upon request. Coefficients in bold are significant at the 0.05 level.

respondent's total earnings from the prior survey year; year and state fixed-effects; hours worked per week; and a five-category firm-size measure. The five-category firm-size measure is similar to the six-category measure described above, except here I collapse those working in firms with fewer than twenty-five employees and fewer than ten employees into one category because of changes in firm-size variable codes in the CPS-March over time. I run these models separately on private- and public-sector workers. Core results are presented in Table A.2.

Based on the above model, I predict the probabilities that a respondent's employer pays for all his or her health care for union and nonunion workers, for workers in firms of difference sizes, for different years, and for workers in the 25th and 75th income percentiles using the prvalue command in STATA 11. I display these results in Table 2.3.

To generate the results displayed in Table 2.4 I perform the same set of procedures, except here I am predicting whether or not the respondent receives an employer-provided pension. The model specification is the same, but the sample is larger because I am not restricting it to those who receive health insurance from their employer. I present the core results from these models in Table A.3.

Chapter 3

In Chapter 3 I estimate union wage effects for private-sector workers and the effect of industry-region unionization rates on the weekly wages of private-sector nonmembers. The union wage premium series shown in Figure 3.1 is based on annual regressions of log weekly wages (in constant 2007 dollars). The models rely on CPS-May and CPS-MORG data from 1973–2009. The key predictor of interest is a dichotomous union membership indicator; the other controls in the models replicate those used in Chapter 2.

To generate Figure 3.2 I estimate the effect of industry-region unionization rates on private-sector workers who do not belong to a union. As a result, the models used to predict the figure are restricted to nonunion workers only. These models also rely on CPS-May and CPS-MORG data from 1973–2009. Here the key predictor of interest is a continuous measure of the respondent's industry-region unionization rate. To create an industry-region unionization rate, I divide the sample into

Table A.2 Odds ratios from models of whether respondents' employer pays for all health care, 1988–2009

	Public-sector		Private-sector	
Union	**1.16**	(1.09, 1.23)	**2.23**	(2.13, 2.32)
Other demographic and labor-market position controls:				
African American	**0.83**	(0.76, 0.91)	**0.82**	(0.78, 0.87)
Hispanic	**0.78**	(0.68, 0.88)	**0.86**	(0.80, 0.91)
Other race	1.07	(0.93, 1.24)	0.96	(0.89, 1.04)
Married	**0.84**	(0.79, 0.90)	**0.90**	(0.87, 0.93)
Potential experience	**0.97**	(0.96, 0.98)	**0.98**	(0.98, 0.99)
Potential experience^2	**1.00**	(1.00, 1.00)	**1.00**	(1.00, 1.00)
HS (reference is <HS)	0.89	(0.75, 1.06)	**1.11**	(1.04, 1.18)
Some college	0.91	(0.77, 1.08)	**1.18**	(1.11, 1.26)
College degree or higher	0.94	(0.78, 1.12)	**1.23**	(1.15, 1.32)
Weekly hours	1.00	(0.99, 1.01)	**1.00**	(1.00, 1.00)
Log annual earnings	0.99	(0.94, 1.06)	**1.12**	(1.09, 1.15)
Firm size 1,000+ (reference is <25)	**0.63**	(0.53, 0.74)	**0.36**	(0.34, 0.37)
Selected major industry controls (reference is manufacturing):				
Construction	**2.25**	(1.39, 3.65)	**1.23**	(1.14, 1.32)
Retail and wholesale trade	1.30	(0.65, 2.59)	**0.89**	(0.85, 0.94)
Selected occ. controls (reference is professional/ managerial):				
Production/craft/repair	1.10	(0.96, 1.25)	**0.95**	(0.90, 0.99)
Service occupations	1.03	(0.95, 1.11)	0.99	(0.96, 1.03)
State fixed effects		Yes		Yes
Metro effects		Yes		Yes
Year effects		Yes		Yes
N		37,654		135,290
Years covered		1988–2009		1988–2009
Number of parameters		100		100
R^2	0.08		0.07	

Notes: 95% confidence intervals in parentheses. Data come from the CPS-March files, 1988–2009. Models weighted with the appropriate CPS weights. Odds ratios from suppressed control variables available upon request. Odds ratios in bold are significant at the 0.05 level. Sample restricted to respondents who receive health insurance from their employer.

Table A.3 Odds ratios from models of employer pension offers, 1988–2009

	Public		Private	
Union	**2.21**	(2.06, 2.38)	**2.32**	(2.23, 2.42)
Other demographic and labor-market position controls:				
African American	**0.75**	(0.69, 0.82)	**0.87**	(0.84, 0.91)
Hispanic	**0.82**	(0.73, 0.92)	**0.75**	(0.71, 0.78)
Other race	**0.56**	(0.49, 0.64)	**0.72**	(0.68, 0.76)
Married	**1.20**	(1.12, 1.27)	**1.17**	(1.14, 1.20)
Potential experience	**1.08**	(1.07, 1.09)	**1.05**	(1.05, 1.06)
Potential experience^2	**0.99**	(0.99, 0.99)	**0.99**	(0.99, 0.99)
HS (reference is <HS)	**1.34**	(1.17, 1.53)	**1.65**	(1.58, 1.72)
Some college	**1.40**	(1.22, 1.61)	**1.78**	(1.70, 1.86)
College degree or higher	**1.54**	(1.33, 1.78)	**2.05**	(1.94, 2.15)
Weekly hours	**1.03**	(1.02, 1.03)	**1.01**	(1.00, 1.01)
Log annual earnings	**2.75**	(2.59, 2.93)	**2.86**	(2.79, 2.93)
Firm size 1,000+ (reference is <25)	**1.86**	(1.61, 2.15)	**5.54**	(5.36, 5.73)
Selected major industry controls (reference is manufacturing):				
Construction	**1.80**	(1.22, 2.65)	**0.61**	(0.58, 0.64)
Retail and wholesale trade	1.02	(0.64, 1.62)	**0.57**	(0.85, 0.94)
Selected occ. controls (reference is professional/managerial):				
Production/craft/repair	1.07	(0.95, 1.21)	**0.90**	(0.86, 0.93)
Service occupations	1.06	(0.98, 1.14)	**0.95**	(0.92, 0.98)
State fixed effects		Yes		Yes
Metro effects		Yes		Yes
Year effects		Yes		Yes
N		54,384		254,119
Years covered		1988–2009		1988–2009
Number of parameters		100		100
R^2	0.26		0.28	

Notes: 95% confidence intervals in parentheses. Data come from the CPS-March files, 1988–2009. Models weighted with the appropriate CPS weights. Odds ratios from suppressed control variables available upon request. Odds ratios in bold are significant at the 0.05 level.

seventy-two industry-regions: four regions × eighteen industries. The industries are the eighteen-industry classification listed earlier. The other controls included in these reduced-form regressions are as follows: a dichotomous measure of whether the respondent works in manufacturing; region fixed effects; a four-category race/ethnicity measure; potential experience and potential experience^2; indicators for whether the respondent works in a metropolitan area; average weekly hours worked; a four-category education measure; and a four-category occupation measure.

Ideally I would measure the union effect on nonunion wages adjusted for the influence of stable industrial characteristics that pattern wage rates. For example, if wages in transportation run higher than, say, communications for reasons unrelated to the presence or absence of unions, then analyses that fail to account for these industry-specific features will produce biased estimates of union effects. In statistical terms, one solution would be to include industry fixed effects to eliminate stable industry characteristics that may be related to wages. The problem is that much of the variation in unionization rates at the industry level is between industries, rather than within industries over time. For example, differences in unionization rates between retail trade workers and those in durable manufacturing are large regardless of what year you are examining.

As an imperfect corrective, my analyses include region fixed effects, plus a simple control for whether or not the respondent works in manufacturing, the traditional redoubt of union strength. Caution then should be taken with these findings, since some of the industry-region unionization effect is likely picking up influences more related to stable, industry-specific features rather than union strength.

Chapter 4

In Chapter 4 I discuss my prior research on strike activity and industry-region wage levels.[18] I compare my findings with the sociologist Beth Rubin's earlier work.[19] Formally extending my own methodology backward to match Rubin's is not possible for two main reasons. First, gaps within the strike series itself, in particular between 1977 and 1983, prevent one from constructing a seamless series. Second, even if I wanted to replicate my analysis only using pre-1978 strike data, CPS-union data extend back only to 1973.

If the literature on strike effects was contradictory, a replication of historical data using a version of the methodology employed in Rubin's study would certainly be warranted. However, prior research uncovering a positive wage-strike relationship has been sufficiently varied in level of analysis and time period covered that I remain confident an extension backward of my own methods—were one possible—would corroborate the general pattern previously discovered. For example, the economist Orley Ashenfelter and his colleagues found evidence of a strike-union-wage link in the U.S. manufacturing sector between 1914 and 1963.[20] As another example, using cross-industry micro-data from a 1979 telephone survey, the sociologist Michael Wallace and his colleagues discovered in some of their models that workers who had participated in a strike during their past had higher wages than otherwise similar non-strikers.[21] Finally, the economist Martin Paldam provided evidence of a reciprocal wage-strike relationship using cross-national Organisation for Economic Co-operation and Development data between 1948 and 1975.[22]

Chapter 5

The analyses for Chapter 5 estimate African American unionization probabilities and the wage effects of unionization for whites and African Americans. For the unionization models I use to create Figure 5.3 I estimate a series of logistic regressions given that the outcome—whether or not the respondent belongs to a union—is binary. I run these models separately on males and females, as indicated by the two panels in Figure 5.3. I use data from the CPS-May and CPS-MORG for the period 1973–2009. For the series of race/ethnicity models I simply regress union membership on a set of race/ethnicity dummy variables: non-Hispanic white, non-Hispanic African American, non-Hispanic other race, and Hispanic. The positional model is written as follows: For individual *i*,

$$n_i = \log\frac{\pi(union_i)}{1-\pi(union)_i} = \alpha + R_i\beta + X_i\gamma$$

where R_i captures the respondent's race, and X_i is a set of demographic, geographic, and socioeconomic covariates, including a state-grouping fixed effect.

The covariates I include in the positional models are as follows: race/ethnicity (as just described); sex; marital status; the four mutually exclusive education indicators; potential experience and potential experience^2; the four broad occupational indicators; the set of fifteen industry dummies; a dichotomous economic-sector variable (public or private); a full-time/part-time indicator; the measure of whether the resident lives in a metropolitan area; and a series of twenty-three state-grouping dummies. Again I estimate nearly seventy models to produce the race/ethnicity and positional series in Figure 5.3, so space considerations preclude a full set of results. They are available upon request, and interested readers should see my 2012 *American Journal of Sociology* article with Meredith Kleykamp for further details on a similar estimation strategy.[23]

To produce the results displayed in Table 5.1, I regress log weekly wages on a set of covariates, including the respondent's race/ethnicity and union status. The models rely on CPS-May and CPS-MORG data from 1973–2009. I estimate an OLS regression model. My outcome variable of interest, *Yi,* is logged weekly wages. For individual *i,*

$$Y_i = \alpha + R_i\beta + U_i\theta + (RU)_i\zeta + X_i\gamma + \varepsilon_i$$

where R_i captures the respondent's race, U_i indicates being a union member, $(RU)_i$ is the interaction of race/ethnicity × union, X_i is a set of demographic, geographic, and socioeconomic covariates, including year and state-grouping fixed effects, and ε_i is residual individual-level variation. The covariates I include in the model approximate those in the unionization models described above, except that now union membership is a key predictor instead of the outcome variable of interest, and I include in these models a full slate of race/ethnicity and union interactions. The interaction terms reveal whether and to what extent the union wage premium varies by race. I present results for a select group of covariates in Table A.4. A full set of results, including coefficients for the state-grouping and year dummies, are available upon request.

Table A.4 Estimates of union wage effects for private-sector workers, 1973–2009

	Females		Males	
Union main effect	**0.21**	(0.21, 0.22)	**0.25**	(0.24, 0.25)
African American main effect (reference is white)	**−0.07**	(−0.08, −0.07)	**−0.16**	(−0.16, −0.16)
Union × African American	**−0.01**	(−0.02, −0.00)	**0.02**	(0.01, 0.02)
Other demographic and labor market position controls:				
Hispanic main effect	**−0.13**	(−0.13, −0.12)	**−0.19**	(−0.19, −0.18)
Other race main effect	**−0.06**	(−0.06, −0.05)	**−0.10**	(−0.11, −0.10)
Married	**0.03**	(0.03, 0.03)	**0.14**	(0.14, 0.14)
Potential experience	**0.02**	(0.02, 0.02)	**0.04**	(0.04, 0.04)
Potential experience^2	**−0.00**	(−0.00, −0.00)	**−0.00**	(−0.00, −0.00)
HS (reference is <HS)	**0.15**	(0.15, 0.15)	**0.19**	(0.19, 0.19)
Some college	**0.26**	(0.26, 0.27)	**0.29**	(0.29, 0.30)
College degree or higher	**0.47**	(0.47, 0.48)	**0.57**	(0.57, 0.57)

Selected industry controls (reference is agriculture/forestry/fisheries):				
Transportation	**0.19**	(0.18, 0.20)	**0.17**	(0.16, 0.18)
Manufacturing durables	**0.25**	(0.24, 0.26)	**0.25**	(0.24, 0.25)
FIRE	**0.20**	(0.19, 0.21)	**0.26**	(0.25, 0.26)
Selected occ. controls (reference is professional/managerial):				
Production/craft/repair	**−0.32**	(−0.32, −0.32)	**−0.27**	(−0.28, −0.27)
Service occupations	**−0.23**	(−0.23, −0.23)	**−0.26**	(−0.26, −0.26)
Weekly hours	**0.04**	(0.04, 0.04)	**0.03**	(0.03, 0.03)
State grouping effects		Yes		Yes
Metro effects		Yes		Yes
Year effects		Yes		Yes
N		1,366,860		1,540,254
Years covered		1973–2009		1973–2009
Number of parameters		90		90
R^2	0.70		0.67	

Notes: 95% confidence intervals in parentheses. Data come from the CPS-May/MORG files, 1973–2009. Models weighted with the appropriate CPS weights. Coefficients from suppressed control variables available upon request. Coefficients in bold are significant at the 0.05 level. Estimates restricted to private-sector workers ages 16 to 64 with positive earnings and hours worked. Dependent variable in both models is logged weekly wages.

The lack of a substantively large (and positive) union × African American interaction effect is a bit puzzling. African American overrepresentation in unionized jobs would seem to imply that many blacks receive a larger relative return from unionization than similarly situated whites. After all, if African American workers seek union jobs in part to escape discriminatory employers in the nonunion sector, then the relative benefits of union employment for blacks should exceed those enjoyed by their organized white counterparts. How so? Assume Worker A is African American, nonunion, and takes home $200 a week. An otherwise similar white employee (Worker B) at the same firm makes $210 a week, the differential attributable to discrimination. Now say a union successfully organizes their plant, or the two workers transfer to a neighboring plant that is organized. Both workers see their wages increase to $250 a week. While the wage rate is the same, the relative benefit of unionization is higher for the black worker, as the standardized and transparent pay scales—due to collective bargaining—eliminate the discriminatory element of the wage. As Table A.4 makes clear, I don't find much evidence to support this scenario. Indeed, in the analyses of female private-sector workers, African Americans' relative wage gains from unionization run slightly *lower* than whites'. In my prior work with Meredith Kleykamp, we advance two possible explanations for this unexpected finding: African Americans could be concentrated in unions less effective at securing wage increases for their members compared to others, or unions may not be able to blunt all discriminatory processes at the work site.[24]

I conclude the analytical section of Chapter 5 with a set of counterfactual estimates, presented in Figures 5.5 and 5.6. They are based on the weekly wage regressions presented in the table above. I briefly describe the process used to estimate these results in the chapter; see also my 2012 article with Meredith Kleykamp for further details.[25]

Chapter 6

For my investigation of unionization among Hispanics and Hispanic subpopulations, I again estimate a series of logistic regressions. For the estimates presented in Figure 6.3 I use data from the CPS-May and CPS-MORG for the period 1973–2009. The analysis is similar to that in

Chapter 5. For the series of race/ethnicity models I regress union membership on a set of race/ethnicity dummy variables: non-Hispanic white, non-Hispanic African American, non-Hispanic other race, and Hispanic. The positional model is the same as described above, except now the predictor of interest is whether or not the respondent is Hispanic. All covariates are the same as those included in Chapter 5's analysis of African American unionization probabilities. For further details on a similar estimation strategy, readers should see my 2009 *American Sociological Review* article with Meredith Kleykamp.[26]

To generate the results on display in Table 6.1 I estimate a set of logistic models predicting unionization for Hispanic subpopulations using CPS-March data pooled across the 1995–2009 period. The outcome variable depends on the set of subpopulations under examination. For example, to generate the block of results for the nationality model, I regress union membership on a set of race/ethnicity and immigrant status indicators. I divide respondents into ten mutually exclusive categories: white nonimmigrant, black nonimmigrant, non-Mexican Hispanic nonimmigrant, other race nonimmigrant, white immigrant, black immigrant, non-Mexican Hispanic immigrant, other race immigrant, Mexican nonimmigrant, and Mexican immigrant. White nonimmigrants are the reference category for this block of estimates. For the citizenship model, I regress union membership on a set of twelve indicators of a respondent's race/ethnicity, whether the respondent is an immigrant, and citizenship status. For this model, white nonimmigrant citizens are the reference category. For the time-since-emigration models, I divide the sample according to race/ethnicity, immigrant status, and time since emigration (for the immigrants in the sample). Nonimmigrant whites are again the reference category. For the generation models, I divide the sample according to race/ethnicity, immigrant status, and generation of immigrant. Nonimmigrant whites, third generation or above, are the reference category.

Controls used in these models replicate those used to produce Figure 6.3, except for the addition of a variable capturing respondents' firm size, a variable measuring whether the respondent moved in the prior survey year, and a year fixed effect. The sample size for the "all workers" set of results is 238,336, while the sample size for the "private-sector workers" set of results is 197,169. Space considerations again prevent the inclusion of a full set of coefficients from these models; results for all the suppressed coefficients not shown in Table 6.1 are available upon request. The predicted probabilities that I display in Table 6.2 rely on Table 6.1's regressions; I generate them using the prchange and prvalue commands in STATA 11.

Chapter 7

In Chapter 7 I first estimate the effect of union membership on self-reported turnout using CPS-November files from 1984–2008. The outcome variable is a binary measure of turnout in that November's election. Similar to the investigations of union membership in Chapters 5 and 6, since the outcome variable is dichotomous, the use of linear probability models violates standard OLS assumptions. I fit a series of logistic regression models for these analyses. Supplemental PSM models produce similar results. Below I present the baseline main effects model estimating separate union and sector coefficients. For individual *i* the probability of voting is estimated as,

$$n_i = \log\frac{\pi(vote_i)}{1-\pi(vote)_i} = \alpha + U_i\beta + P_i\gamma + X_i\zeta$$

where U_i captures whether the respondent is a member of a union, P_i indicates whether the respondent is employed in the public sector, and X_i is a set of demographic, geographic, and socioeconomic covariates, including state fixed effects.

Aside from union membership and sector, the remaining predictors for the main effects model are as follows: a dichotomous marriage indicator; age and age^2; the four-category race/ethnicity measure; the four-category occupation measure; sex; the four-category education measure; weekly earnings (in constant 2007 dollars); a full-time indicator; a measure of whether the respondent owns or rents his/her home; year and state fixed effects; the metropolitan status indicator; state-level unionization rates; and the nine-category industry measure. Models including an expanded set of industry controls reveal substantively similar results.[27]

Following estimation of the main union and sector effects, I specify a model that interacts union and sector in order to isolate union influ-

Table A.5 Odds ratios from models of voter turnout, 1984–2008

	Interaction model	
Union main effect	**1.32**	(1.25, 1.39)
Public sector main effect	**1.39**	(1.29, 1.49)
Union × public sector	**0.84**	(0.77, 0.91)
Age	**1.05**	(1.04, 1.06)
Age^2	**0.99**	(0.99, 0.99)
Male	**0.96**	(0.93, 0.99)
Af. Am. (reference is white)	**1.25**	(1.15, 1.36)
Hispanic	**0.85**	(0.80, 0.91)
Other race	**0.50**	(0.46, 0.54)
Married	**1.23**	(1.19, 1.27)
HS (reference is HS dropout)	**1.95**	(1.81, 2.10)
Some college	**3.30**	(3.06, 3.56)
College degree or higher	**4.80**	(4.41, 5.24)
Weekly earnings (× 100)	**1.00**	(1.00, 1.00)
Full time	**0.74**	(0.71, 0.77)
Rent (reference is own)	**0.60**	(0.57, 0.63)
State unionization rate	0.99	(0.96, 1.01)
State and metro effects		Yes
Year effects		Yes
Occupation and industry effects		Yes
N		169,899
Number of parameters		92
R^2	0.15	

Note: 95% confidence intervals in parentheses. Data come from the November files of the CPS, 1984–2008. All models weighted with the appropriate CPS weights. Odds ratios from suppressed covariates available upon request. Odds ratios in bold are significant at the 0.05 level. Standard errors adjusted for clustering in state.

ences on voting for public-sector workers and private-sector workers separately. In Table A.5 I present the results for selected covariates from this model; a full set of odds ratios is available upon request.

Based on the model above, I predict the voting probabilities for union and nonunion workers in the public and private sectors and display them in Figure 7.4 using the prvalue command in STATA 11.

I also test to see whether the union effect on voting varies by educational level. The highly educated already turn out to vote more than

Table A.6 Odds ratios from NES models of voter turnout, 1984–2008

	Church×education interaction model	
Non-frequent churchgoer, HS (reference is non-frequent churchgoer, <HS)	**2.12**	(1.67, 2.71)
Non-frequent churchgoer, some college	**4.24**	(3.40, 5.29)
Non-frequent churchgoer, BA or higher	**10.00**	(7.58, 13.18)
Frequent churchgoer, <HS	**1.77**	(1.25, 2.51)
Frequent churchgoer, HS	**4.14**	(3.36, 5.14)
Frequent churchgoer, some college	**7.16**	(5.62, 9.12)
Frequent churchgoer, BA or higher	**14.20**	(10.37, 19.43)
Union	**1.26**	(1.10, 1.44)
Age	**1.05**	(1.02, 1.07)
Age^2	0.99	(0.99, 1.00)
Male	1.00	(0.88, 1.14)
African American	**1.32**	(1.10, 1.60)
Hispanic	0.84	(0.68, 1.05)
Other race	**0.57**	(0.45, 0.72)
Married	**1.13**	(1.03, 1.23)
Family income: middle third (reference is bottom third)	**1.24**	(1.10, 1.41)
Family income: top third	**1.42**	(1.27, 1.59)
Home owner (reference is renter)	**1.66**	(1.46, 1.88)
State fixed effects	Yes	
Year effects	Yes	
N	12,481	
Number of parameters	78	
R^2	0.21	

Notes: 95% confidence intervals in parentheses. Data come from the NES cumulative file, 1984–2008. Odds ratios from suppressed control variables available upon request. Odds ratios in bold are significant at the 0.05 level.

others. It is fair to assume, then, that the ability of unions to affect voting is constrained among highly educated individuals. The predicted probabilities in Figure 7.5 are based on a model similar to the one above, except this one includes a full set of union × education interactions and is limited to private-sector workers only. To generate Figure 7.8 I run the same model but limit the sample to 2008 data.[28]

To generate Figures 7.6 and 7.7, I use the NES cumulative file, restricted to the years 1984–2008. Figure 7.6 is based on a logistic regression model predicting self-reported turnout where the key independent variables are a series of church attendance × education interactions. Here frequent churchgoers are defined as those who attend at least once a month. Other controls used in the model are as follows: a dichotomous marriage indicator; age and age^2; the four-category race/ethnicity measure; a three-category family income indicator that captures whether the respondent's family income falls in the bottom third, middle third, or top third of the distribution; a home-ownership indicator; an indicator of whether the respondent belongs to a union; and year and state fixed effects. The sample size for this model is 12,481. In Table A.6 I present core results from this model. A full set of results is available upon request.

Running a similar model using the NES cumulative file except with union × education interactions and controlling for frequent church attendance results in a unionization-education gradient comparable with the one shown in Figure 7.5. The NES model produces slightly smaller union effects, however. For example, Figure 7.5 indicates that union members with a high school diploma outvote otherwise similar nonmembers by 7 points. The corresponding result from the NES model is 5 points. Among those with a BA degree or higher, Figure 7.5 reveals a union-nonunion differential of 4 points, while the NES model estimates a 2-point difference. Key controls missing from the NES—including occupation, industry, and especially economic sector—do not allow for direct comparisons between the two sets of estimates.

Notes

Introduction

1. For more on these broad trends in unionization rates, see Rosenfeld 2010b.

2. Yeselson 2012.

3. Matusow 1998: 160.

4. For union membership data prior to the early 1970s, see Mayer 2004.

5. Yeselson 2012.

6. For more on the racism endemic in the labor movement, see Hill 1996. For more on union ties to the Mafia, see Jacobs 2006.

7. Joe Tex's song "A Woman's Hands" appeared as the A-side of the 1967 single released by Dial Records. "C.C. Rider" was the B-side.

8. For trends in female labor-force participation rates throughout much of the twentieth century, see Smith and Ward 1985.

9. Quoted in Mishel 2011.

10. Frank 2008.

11. Weber 1947.

1. The Collapse of Organized Labor in the United States

1. Quoted in *U.S. News & World Report* 1972.

2. Kotz 1977 interviewing then-president of the American Federation of State, County, and Municipal Employees Jerry Wurf.

3. Fantasia and Voss 2004: 84.

4. For an early example of this argument, see Moody 1988.

5. See Milkman and Voss's 2004 edited collection.

6. The fraction of France's workforce covered by a union contract actually increased during the 1970s and remained steady through the 1990s and early 2000s. In many European nations, contracts negotiated between employers

and unions are extended to nonunion workers. The scope and extent of mandatory extension varies. See Figure A.1 in the Data and Methods Appendix for a version of Figure 1.2 that displays union contract coverage rates over time. Of the nations shown in Figure 1.2, contract coverage rates declined in the United States, Australia, Great Britain, Germany, and Canada.

7. Surowiecki 2011.

8. Freeman 2007.

9. Peter D. Hart Research Associates, February 2005, Study #7518.

10. Freeman 2007: table 4.

11. Ibid.: 2.

12. For example, see the March 2011 Gallup poll at http://www.gallup.com/poll/146921/americans-back-unions-governors-state-disputes.aspx. Nearly two-thirds of polled Republicans expressed support for governors in their confrontations with public-employee unions compared to less than one in five Democrats.

13. Mak 2011.

14. Fones-Wolf 1995.

15. Swenson 2002: 299.

16. Fones-Wolf 1995: 24.

17. Lichtenstein 2002: 99.

18. Yeselson 2012.

19. For evidence of union effects on firm productivity, see Hirsch 2008.

20. Farber and Western 2001: 481.

21. Godard 2009: 99.

22. See Figure A.1 in the Data and Methods Appendix for examples of nations like France where the collective bargaining coverage rate far exceeds the unionization rate.

23. Western 1994: 501. See also Western 1993.

24. Western 1993; 1995: table 1.

25. See Wyatt and Greenhouse 2011 for more on the dispute.

26. Bronfenbrenner 2009.

27. For more on the 2000 unionization drive involving Delta's baggage and cargo handlers, see Thurston 2000. For background on the 2002 drive involving flight attendants at Delta, see Cleeland 2002.

28. A 2010 report by the Communication Workers of America highlighted that under the old NMB union election standard, not one member of the House of Representatives would have won his or her prior election. See http://files.cwa-union.org/national/issues/CollectiveBargaining/IfCongressionalElectionsWereLikeProposedNMBUnionElections.pdf.

29. For just a few examples, see Cowie 2010; Freeman and Kleiner 1990; Goldfield 1987; Hacker and Pierson 2010.

30. Prior to the institutionalization of organized labor in the United States, both sides in many labor disputes "skirted the law," often violently. By the

postwar period, however, unionization drives tended to be more scripted and restricted to the broad confines of what prevailing law allowed.

31. Hacker and Pierson 2010: 129.

32. Farber 1999; Farber and Western 2002: Figure 2.

33. Raynor 2006.

34. Hacker and Pierson 2010: 129–131.

35. Cowie 2010: 296.

36. Logan 2008: 185–186.

37. Trottman 2008.

38. Lofaso 2011: 66.

39. Geoghegan 1991: 252.

40. Frymer 2008:1.

41. Swenson 2002.

42. Brady 2007.

43. Hall and Soskice 2001: 19.

44. Esping-Andersen 1990.

45. Towers 1989: 167–173.

46. Cooper and Ellem 2008.

47. See Lichtenstein 2005 for more on the parallels—and stark differences—between GM during the mid-twentieth century and Walmart today.

48. Lichtenstein 2005: 22.

2. Government Is Not the Answer

1. Quoted in Greenhouse 1999.

2. Boris and Klein 2010.

3. Meany 1955: 38.

4. In 2003, California voters "recalled" Gray Davis in the middle of his term, opening up the governorship to action-movie star Arnold Schwarzenegger. Impeachment befell Blagojevich after federal prosecutors arrested him on corruption charges in 2008. Spitzer avoided the possibility of a similar spectacle and resigned after reports surfaced of his role in a prostitution ring. The downfalls of all three—while interesting political footnotes—bear no relation to their role in assisting public-sector unionization. Governors who issued similar executive orders or signed similar pieces of legislation, such as Iowa's Tom Vilsack, remain scandal-free and active in politics.

5. See McCartin 2011 for a discussion of Reagan's relationship with public-sector unions while he was governor of California.

6. Freeman and Kleiner 1990; Kleiner 2001.

7. Freeman 1988: 75. See pp. 70–72 for a discussion of the organization process in the United States.

8. For a map and discussion of public-sector bargaining legislation throughout the states, see Kearney 2001 (especially chap. 3 and figure 3.1). While

collective bargaining between unions and state agencies is barred in Virginia and North Carolina, a small percentage of each state's workforce is unionized (see Figure 2.1 of this chapter). Take, for example, the State Employees Association of North Carolina (SEANC): SEANC is an SEIU affiliate that boasts of over fifty thousand members. While it cannot collectively bargain with the state, it actively lobbies the state for legislation that would benefit its members. Similar organizations exist in Virginia. Indeed, in North Carolina and Virginia—states that expressly forbid collective bargaining among state workers—the public-sector unionization rate among state and local government workers is equivalent to the nation's private-sector unionization rate.

9. Kinnard 2012.

10. Quoted in Greenhouse 2011.

11. Wisconsin's 2009 private-sector unionization rate was 8 percent, slightly higher than the national average at the time. Its public-sector organization rate of 53 percent far surpassed the national average in 2009.

12. See Kelleher 2011 for a summary of the political fights leading up to the passage of Wisconsin's antiunion bill. As of this writing, the Wisconsin Supreme Court has ruled that the passage of the law was constitutional, and the state has begun implementation.

13. Many observers suggest that Walker's exclusion of police and firefighters from the law's reach was a political ploy to sow divisions within the ranks of public-sector unionists, and to reward the few public-sector unions that had endorsed his candidacy. (A handful of protective service unions provided Walker with what little union support he received in the race). Walker's own explanation stressed his fear that including protective-service unions might trigger a potentially devastating strike by police or firefighters. See Schaper 2011.

14. See unionstats.com for 2010 and 2011 data on public-sector memberships in Wisconsin.

15. Belkin and Maher 2012.

16. Franklin 2005.

17. This electoral feat is especially impressive given that the Democratic presidential candidate, Barack Obama, received nearly 50 percent of the vote in Indiana.

18. Smith and Haberman 2010.

19. Quoted in Fields 2011.

20. *Wall Street Journal* 2010.

21. Quoted in Walsh 2011.

22. Author's compilations, based on 2008 CPS-MORG data.

23. Herbst 2010.

24. Reagan's famous formulation of government as the problem came in his first inaugural address. For the complete text see http://www.reaganfounda

tion.org/pdf/Inaugural_Address_012081.pdf. His less famous formulation of government as an unwelcome bedmate stems from campaign appearances during the late 1970s. See Endicott 1978.

25. Remarks from Dole's convention address can be found in the *New York Times* 1976: 11. The text of Goldwater's 1964 address can be found in the *New York Times* 1964: 14.

26. Clinton's summation of his political era can be found at http://clinton4.nara.gov/WH/New/other/sotu.html.

27. The passage of the Patient Protection and Affordable Care Act of 2010 is a perfect example. While easily one of the most far-reaching and transformative pieces of domestic legislation passed in decades, it keeps the basic health care infrastructure in place. The majority of Americans will continue to be insured through their employer (instead of the government), and the major insurance companies that structure the system will for the most part remain privately owned.

28. OECD 2009 provides public-sector employment shares; Visser 2006 provides cross-national unionization rates for twenty-four countries.

29. Blanchflower 2006: table 2.

30. For details on the statistical analyses, see the "Union Wage Premium" section of the Data and Methods Appendix.

31. Blanchflower and Bryson 2004: table 3.

32. Specifically, I use the CPS-May and CPS-MORG data on the civilian workforce. See the Data and Methods Appendix for further details.

33. Researchers frequently log dependent variables such as wages that are positively skewed. Logging helps make the skewed distribution more normal. And given that the dependent variable is in log form, the coefficients can be transformed to represent percent higher wages for union versus nonunion workers. For example, a union coefficient of 0.11 can be interpreted as a union wage premium of 12%, since $e^{.11} = 1.12$. In the figure I present the percent wage differences only. See the Data and Methods Appendix for model details.

34. Blanchflower and Bryson 2004: table 3.

35. Ibid.: 411.

36. Beginning in 1983, the CPS-MORG files include a variable asking all respondents who indicate they work in the public sector whether they work for the local, state, or federal government.

37. See Kearney 2001: figure 3.1.

38. These models are equivalent to the models run on individual survey years except that they include year fixed-effects. Disaggregating the data by type of government worker and limiting the sample to certain states reduce the sample sizes, making it more difficult to estimate public-sector premiums accurately for each individual year. Also, the lack of clear time trends in

public-sector wage premiums evident in Figure 2.4 lessens the need for another time-series investigation. See the Data and Methods Appendix for further details.

39. Boris and Klein 2012: 174.

40. Ibid.: 175.

41. Cox and Oaxaca 1982.

42. Pencavel 2005: 75.

43. Kotz 1977: 146.

44. To predict the wages used for the comparisons, I again limit the sample to nonfederal workers and to the 1983–2009 period, when the data contain indicators for all fifty states and indicators for type of public-sector employment. The model replicates the one used to measure the wage premiums shown in Table 2.1.

45. Why potential experience? Unfortunately, the CPS-MORG files lack measures of tenure at the job. Analysts who use the data sets must then create proxy measures for job experience, often done by subtracting the respondents' ages from their education levels minus six to create a measure of time out of school.

46. Jones 2011.

47. For an early example of this research, see Freeman 1981.

48. Freeman and Medoff 1984: chap. 4.

49. Budd 2005 uses establishment-level data, while Buchmueller, DiNardo, and Valletta's 2002 and 2004 analyses rely on employee data as well as surveys of establishments.

50. Buchmueller, DiNardo, and Valletta 2002.

51. Zimmerman 2004.

52. Greenhouse and Abelson 2011.

53. Farber and Levy 2000: table 1.

54. Buchmueller, DiNardo, and Valletta 2002: table 3.

55. Please see the Data and Methods Appendix for a discussion of the relative advantages and drawbacks of the CPS-March and Benefit Supplements data sets.

56. I exclude other benefit supplements because they either do not include questions on union membership or use a sampling frame that is designed to ask the benefit questions of contingent employees only.

57. Buchmueller, DiNardo, and Valletta 2002.

58. The controls used in this analysis largely mirror past research on the topic, and include demographic characteristics such as sex, marital status, and race, economic characteristics like industry and occupation, and the geographic characteristics of metropolitan status and region (the small sample sizes of the supplements prevent me from including state fixed effects). I provide details on the model in the Data and Methods Appendix. Similar to Buchmueller, DiNardo, and Valletta 2002 I estimate linear probability models for ease of interpretation, and the ad-

justment represents the union coefficient on models predicting insurance take-up and coverage. Logit models provide similar substantive results, as I show in Table A1 of the Data and Methods Appendix. In addition to a measure of firm size, I also include an indicator of tenure at the firm, as many companies and agencies have a waiting period until one can qualify for benefits.

59. Given the larger sample sizes and years covered by the March series, I am able to include state fixed effects, as well as many of the other controls used in the prior investigations.

60. I generate the predictions by specifying a value on a key variable and setting all other variables at their means.

61. Unlike the CPS-Supplements investigation, these models do not include a control for firm tenure (unavailable in the CPS-March series). Tenure had a strong effect on take-up and coverage rates in the private sector, and thus the private-sector union effect on premium costs may be exaggerated, assuming that unionization is positively correlated with tenure at a firm. On the other hand, the premium costs analysis is limited to those already covered by their employer's health insurance. While many firms require waiting periods before a worker is deemed eligible for insurance, it is likely less common to require waiting periods to qualify for lower premium costs once an employee is enrolled in his or her firm's plan.

62. Quoted in Preston 2011.

63. The table and the models that provide the basis for it mirror Table 2.4 except that here I model whether the respondent is enrolled in an employer-provided pension plan. The controls used in the analysis are the same ones used to model premium costs. See the Data and Methods Appendix for details.

64. Blanchflower 2006: tables 4 and 5.

65. Unionization rates in Table 2.5 exceed those displayed in Figure 2.2 by a few percentage points because of slight differences in sample restrictions between my own data and those provided by Hirsch and Macpherson's unionstats.com database.

66. Blanchflower 2006. Controls include state fixed effects, industry and occupation indicators, and a range of demographic and labor-market factors found to pattern unionization rates.

3. Wages and Inequality

1. A small fraction of nonunion workers in the private sector are covered by a union contract. In 2009, for example, 0.8 percent of the private-sector workforce reported that they were covered by a union contract but remained nonunion (see Hirsch and Macpherson's http://unionstats.com/). This can occur when an employee joins a union firm and has yet to sign up for membership, or when an employee in a union firm in a right-to-work state refuses membership.

2. For a recent example, see my work with Bruce Western, Western and Rosenfeld 2011.

3. Maynard 2008.

4. See www.fordahead.com for the company's bargaining position entering the fall 2011 rounds of negotiations. I retrieved the above quote from the "Labor Cost Gap" section of the website.

5. Both the foreign transplants and the "Big Three" have included profit-sharing clauses in contracts for decades now. These clauses increasingly take the place of automatic wage increases.

6. Quoted in Lichtenstein 1995: 270; Serrin 1983.

7. Based on my analysis of CPS-May data.

8. Ramsey 2011.

9. I provide full details on the premium models in the Data and Methods Appendix. I tested numerous alternative specifications, including a model with an expanded set of eighteen industry controls, and one with a control for industry-region unionization rates. I also estimated propensity score matching (PSM) models. The results of these and other estimation strategies are similar to what I display in Figure 3.1, rarely deviating by more than a percentage point or two. For example, the union coefficient from a standard OLS model of men's wages using 1985 CPS-MORG data is 0.26. The ATT from a PSM model on the same data with nearest-neighbor matching with replacement is 0.27. Further details on the PSM models are provided in the Data and Methods Appendix's "Union Wage Premiums" subsection.

10. To generate the premiums, I regress respondents' log weekly wages on a range of independent variables, the key one being union membership. I calculate the premiums in the figure by exponentiating the union coefficients, since they represent log weekly wages. For example, a union coefficient of 0.22 translates to a union wage advantage of 25%, since $e^{.22} = 1.25$.

11. These premium estimates are broadly comparable with prior research that uses the CPS to establish cross-sectional union wage premiums. For example, in their table 4, Hirsch and Schumacher 2004 estimate an average premium of 0.20 (or a 22% wage advantage) between 1973 and 2001 for both men and women. In their table 2, Blanchflower and Bryson 2004 report a female union wage premium of 0.22 between 1974 and 1979, and 0.13 between 1996 and 2001. Their models lack occupation controls, which leads to a depressed premium estimate. For a discussion of choice of controls when modeling union wage premiums, see Hirsch 2004: 239–241.

12. The measurement of union wage premiums has produced a voluminous literature. In the Data and Methods Appendix's "The Union Wage Premium" subsection I describe some of the limitations that arise in accurately estimating union wage premiums and explore how various researchers, including myself, have approached the issue.

13. Foulkes 1980: 153.

14. Rosenfeld 2006b.

15. Leicht 1989.

16. Quoted in *Knowledge@Wharton* 2012a.

17. Neumark and Wachter 1995.

18. Waddoups 1999.

19. Catron 2013: appendix A.

20. Western and Rosenfeld 2011.

21. I calculate industry-regional unionization rates for nonunion workers using the CPS-May and CPS-MORG data sets from 1973 to 2009. I disaggregate industries into eighteen categories, balancing sample-size considerations with the need to maintain relatively homogeneous industry groups. The models estimating union wage premiums shown earlier in the chapter include a slightly coarser set of fifteen industry categories to maintain consistency with model specifications in other chapters, especially Chapter 2. As a robustness check, I reestimated premiums including the eighteen industry dummies. The expanded set of industry controls reduced union wage advantages in the early years of the series by roughly 1 percentage point. By the end of the series there were no differences.

22. See Western and Rosenfeld 2011 for further details on this particular analytical strategy. Capturing the effect of industry-regional variation in unionization on nonunion wages involves numerous modeling decisions. I expand on these in the Data and Methods Appendix.

23. Assuming the effects of industry-regional unionization rates on nonunion wages are linear.

24. And in any case the point estimates are likely confounded by industry features uncaptured by the models. Please see the discussion in the Data and Methods Appendix for more.

25. *Knowledge@Wharton* 2012a.

26. Yeselson 2012.

27. The measure is less sensitive to dynamics occurring at the very top of the wage distribution than other possible inequality indicators, such as Gini coefficients. Changes in CPS topcodes over time render wage estimates at the very top of the wage distribution imprecise.

28. Fernandez 2001: 316–317.

29. Lemieux, MacLeod, and Parent 2009: 22.

30. Stetson 1958.

4. Strikes

1. Quoted in *New York Times* 1981.

2. McCartin 2011: 241.

3. Ibid.: 242. McCartin's book provides a comprehensive history of PATCO's rise and demise.

4. Kennedy 1960.

5. McCartin 2011: 243.

6. Ibid.: 284.

7. Ibid.: 285.

8. McCartin 2011:285.

9. President Clinton would later lift the ban prohibiting PATCO strikers from reapplying for the former jobs. See Early 2006 for key facts about the PATCO strike, and Shostak and Skocik 1986 for a historical perspective.

10. Geoghegan 1991: 5.

11. Rosenblum 1995: 10.

12. Cramton and Tracy 1998.

13. For more on the strike, see Clark 1992 and LeRoy 1995: 433.

14. For more on the strike, see Greenhouse 2003.

15. Neither the BLS nor the FMCS work stoppage data sets distinguish between strikes and employer-instigated lockouts. I use the terms "strikes" and "work stoppages" synonymously, but it should be noted that the work stoppage series in Figure 4.1 includes both strikes and a much smaller number of lockouts. The BLS and FMCS data exclude unauthorized (so-called wildcat) strikes, which make up a small proportion of all work stoppages. See Byrne and King 1986 for a discussion of wildcat strikes.

16. For a discussion of the limitations of relying on the BLS's large-strike database, see Skeels, McGrath, and Arshanapalli 1988.

17. For an early statement on the relationship between strike activity and the business cycle, see Rees 1952. See Kaufman 1982: 475 for details on the strike waves of the post–World War II years and the late 1960s.

18. See Korpi and Shalev 1979, 1980, and Hibbs 1978: 175 for more on strike rates over time in Europe.

19. McCammon 2001.

20. See Kaufman 1992 for a review of strike research in labor economics.

21. Fantasia 1989; Lambert 2005.

22. Brecher 2009: 73.

23. *New York Times* 1907.

24. Ibid.

25. Lambert 2005: 115.

26. Kaufman 1982: 475.

27. Brecher 2009: 74.

28. Wallace, Leicht, and Grant 1993.

29. Kalleberg, Wallace, and Raffalovich 1984; Rubin 1986.

30. *Wall Street Journal* 1967.

31. Hormel, the maker of low-cost meat products like Spam and Dinty Moore stews, tends to operate countercyclically, as demand for its products picks up in economic downturns. See Genoways 2011 for more.

32. For a comprehensive history of the 1933 Hormel plant strike, see Engelmann 1974.

33. Associated Press 1986.

34. Genoways 2011.

35. Rosenfeld 2006a.

36. For more details on the data and methods of this investigation, see Rosenfeld 2006a.

37. Rosenfeld 2006a: tables 7 and 8.

38. Wallace 1989.

39. Brecher 2009: 75.

5. The Timing Was Terrible

1. See Olzak 1989.

2. Ibid.: 1239.

3. Ibid.: 1304.

4. Tuttle 1969: 414.

5. Ibid.: 415.

6. For more on the incident see the contemporaneous account in the January 21, 1922, edition of the *Chicago Defender.*

7. For example, Arnesen argued that native whites and European immigrants made up the majority of strikebreakers during the late nineteenth and early twentieth centuries. See Arnesen 2003: 320.

8. Frymer 2008: 28–29; Katznelson, Geiger, and Kryder 1993.

9. Statistic cited in Frymer 2008.

10. And the early advantages among African Americans displayed here should be treated with some caution, given small sample sizes among black public-sector workers in the May-CPS files used to construct the rates for 1973–1981.

11. In my sample, the overall unionization rate among transportation workers fell by 60 percent between the early 1970s and the early years of the twenty-first century. Meanwhile manufacturing's total employment share declined from about a third of all employed workers to just 15 percent.

12. Aldridge 1999.

13. Western 1994.

14. Hirsch and Addison 1986: 61. For more on these and other positional characteristics and how they affect unionization, see my prior work with Meredith Kleykamp, Rosenfeld and Kleykamp 2009.

15. Freeman and Medoff 1984.

16. Ibid.: chap. 2.

17. Anderson 1982: 82.

18. Ibid.: 83.

19. Korstad and Lichtenstein 1988: 793.

20. Frymer 2008: 48.

21. Arnesen 1998: 152.

22. Korstad and Lichtenstein 1988: 794.

23. Beck 1980.

24. Lichtenstein 2002: 78.

25. Smith 1999.

26. Quoted in Honey 1999: 98. Branch belonged to the United Rubber Workers.

27. Goldfield 1993: 5.

28. Stepan-Norris and Zeitlin 2003: chap. 9.

29. Brueggemann and Boswell 1998.

30. Hill 1996: 199.

31. Anderson 1982: 86.

32. Frymer 2008.

33. Honey 1999. See chap. 3 for a comprehensive account of Irene Branch's remarkable career.

34. Stein 1998: 151.

35. Ibid.: 356–357.

36. Minchin 1999: 243.

37. Lichtenstein 2002: 83.

38. See Honey 1999; Korstad and Lichtenstein 1988; and Lichtenstein 2002.

39. Freeman and Rogers 1999.

40. Ibid.: 111.

41. I present details on the modeling, including a listing of the control variables, in the Data and Methods Appendix.

42. The African American effect is significant at the 0.05 level for both sexes for every year of the investigation. Among females, models run on some of the CPS-May years fail to converge. For those years, I ran a reduced-form model with a manufacturing dummy instead of the full slate of industry indicators.

43. Rosenfeld and Kleykamp 2012: table A3.

44. Ibid.: table 2.

45. I level out the series by adding locally weighted smoothing lines, which highlight the dominant trends in the two series.

46. Trends in racial wage inequality are highly sensitive to the inclusion of tail-end, high earners in the sample, who are measured imprecisely because of changes in CPS topcodes over time. In supplemental analyses, I trimmed top earners, and the results indicate more-muted racial wage gaps, especially among private-sector men. The basic patterns, especially the dramatic rise in racial wage inequality among women, remain similar regardless of how one handles top-end earners.

47. Sugrue 2005: table 5.2.

48. Korstad and Lichtenstein 1988: 807.

49. The research on black-white wage inequality among private-sector males is extensive. See Bound and Freeman 1992; Bound and Holzer 2000; and McCall 2001: 536 for some of the best quantitative work on the topic. For

more on the "spatial mismatch" between employment in the postindustrial economy and inner-city African Americans, see Wilson 1987.

50. Grodsky and Pager 2001.

51. See also Pettit and Ewert 2009: figure 1.

52. Zipp 1994. For a brief discussion of the historical importance of public-sector employment for minorities, see Grodsky and Pager 2001: 549.

53. Bound and Dresser 1999: 61.

54. McCall 2001: 536.

55. Bound and Freeman 1992: 216–217.

56. For the major exception, see Bound and Dresser 1999.

57. For recent examples of this approach to measuring the union wage premium, see Blanchflower and Bryson 2004; Hirsch 2004.

58. Supplemental analyses substituting an hourly wage variable in place of weekly wages result in substantively similar findings. I prefer weekly wages because of changes in the hours-worked-per-week question in the CPS. (The hours-worked-per-week variable is used to construct hourly wages for non-hourly workers).

59. Wages increase for a time over one's working career, and then level off before diminishing at the far end of the career curve. It is important to capture this curvilinear nature of the age-wage relationship. In statistical models, this entails entering a control for potential work experience and potential work experience^2.

60. But of course the process is not foolproof. Potentially relevant variables missing from the CPS-May and CPS-MORG files include a measure of industrial concentration, firm size, and firm tenure. The much smaller CPS-March files do include measures of firm size and tenure for some of the years covered by my analyses. Robustness checks using the CPS-March data sets indicate slightly smaller union wage premiums than those that I uncover using the CPS-May and CPS-MORG files, and similar black-white wage disparities. See the Data and Methods Appendix for more on the CPS-March series and its use in estimating union wage premiums and for a discussion of the race×union interactions I include in the wage models in this chapter.

61. Rosenfeld and Kleykamp 2012.

62. In previous work I explored alternative ways of estimating union wage premiums, such as utilizing the limited panel nature of the CPS to track whether those survey respondents who gain union membership across a one-year period had higher wages than those who remained nonunion. See Rosenfeld and Kleykamp 2012 for further details.

63. Calculated by taking the difference between the counterfactual-predicted wage gap (4.8) and the model-predicted wage gap (6.3) and dividing by the counterfactual-predicted gap (4.8).

64. Korstad 1993: 42.

65. Glenn 1985.

66. Anderson 1982: 83.

67. Ibid.: 95.

68. Ibid.: 96.

69. Northrup and Larson 1979. See the tables in their chap. 3 for the racial and gender employment distributions at the company during the years of the decree.

70. Ibid.: table III-1.

71. Honey 1999: 345.

72. Quoted in ibid.: 347.

6. Justice for Janitors?

1. For information on Medina's remarkable biography, see Pawel 2006; Pawel 2009.

2. Shaw 2007.

3. Shaw 2008: 211.

4. See Chap. 2 for a discussion of the organizing drive.

5. For more on immigrants and unions, especially during the early decades of the U.S. labor movement, see Montgomery 1987 and Yellowitz 1977.

6. See Fraser 1991 for a comprehensive biography of Hillman's life.

7. Mills and Atkinson 1945: 160.

8. For the role of European immigrants in forging the nation's nascent labor movement, see Hourwich 1912; Lieberson 1980: 351–353. For the role unions played in incorporating European arrivals and their offspring, see Cohen 1990; Milkman 2006: 118–121.

9. See Newburger and Gryn 2009 for historic trends in the percentage foreign born of the U.S. workforce.

10. Perlman 1928: Chap. 5.

11. Saxton 1975; Mink 1986.

12. Montgomery 1987: 335.

13. Freeman and Rogers 1999.

14. Yellowitz 1977: 139–140.

15. *New York Times* 1912.

16. *New York Times* 1919.

17. *New York Times* 1908.

18. Montgomery 1984: 109.

19. Montgomery 1987: 235–236.

20. Ibid.: 174.

21. Ibid.: 83.

22. Milkman 2006: 114.

23. Levenstein 1968: 207.

24. For the AFL's stance toward Mexican immigration in the early twentieth century, see Levenstein 1968: 207–208.

25. For the full statement, see http://www.aflcio.org/About/Exec-Council/EC-Statements/Immigration2.

26. Newburger and Gryn 2009.

27. An estimated eleven million immigrants were living in the United States illegally as of 2005, including seven million illegal migrants from Mexico. The number today is undoubtedly higher. For more on immigration trends and the changing composition of the immigrant workforce, see Martin and Midgley 2006.

28. According to my analyses of the CPS-MORG, the Philippines, India, and China are the other top contributors to American's immigrant population. However, the total fraction of all immigrants in the United States who were born in any one of these countries doesn't exceed 5 percent. Very recently the rate of in-migration from Latin America has stalled dramatically, with net migration from Mexico now at zero.

29. For competing treatments of these issues, see Alba and Nee 2003; Telles and Ortiz 2008.

30. Lichtenstein 2002: 267; Milkman 2006: 133.

31. Fisk, Mitchell, and Erickson 2000: 202.

32. Montgomery 1984: 202.

33. Shaw 2008: 216.

34. The literature on the Justice for Janitors campaign is extensive. See Ruth Milkman's 2000 edited collection for a primer on the campaign, as well as the challenges of organizing immigrants in the twenty-first century. The contribution by Fisk, Mitchell, and Erickson provided valuable background information for this chapter.

35. The campaign would also serve as the backdrop for director Ken Loach's 2000 film *Bread and Roses,* starring the Academy-Award winning actor Adrian Brody as a labor organizer.

36. Quoted in Greenhouse 2000.

37. Allen 1994; Waldinger et al. 1998.

38. Milkman 2006.

39. Lee 2005: table 2 finds that a percentage-point increase in the net migration rate is associated with approximately a half-percentage-point decrease in unionization. Brady 2007: table 4 finds a positive effect of a country's net migration rate on its level of union membership.

40. Cohen 1990: 324–325; Piore 1979.

41. Morawska 1985: 273.

42. Waldinger and Der-Martirosian 2000.

43. Milkman 2006.

44. Milkman 2006: 137; Waldinger et al. 1998: 117.

45. Sites and Parks 2011: 56–57.

46. The basic framework for the analyses to follow comes from my prior work with Meredith Kleykamp. See Rosenfeld and Kleykamp 2009 for more.

47. The total number of these factors exceeds fifty in the annual models I present in Figure 6.3 below; other models that I discuss later in the chapter have over one hundred independent variables. I present details on the modeling, including a listing of the control variables, in the Data and Methods Appendix.

48. This exercise is analogous to the results shown in Figure 5.3 of the prior chapter, except here I do not disaggregate by sex or sector.

49. Again, workforce experience is not directly observed in the CPS-May or CPS-MORG series—there are no questions that capture time in the labor force. I follow standard practice in the literature and define potential experience as age minus years of education minus six, approximating the potential time spent out of school.

50. Waldinger and Der-Martirosian 2000: 54.

51. To account for time-specific developments affecting unionization probabilities, all of the underlying models include year indicators.

52. Aguilera and Massey 2003; Alba and Nee 2003: 163–166.

53. Aldrich and Waldinger 1990.

54. In my prior work with Meredith Kleykamp we investigated whether Hispanics and Hispanic subpopulations were more likely to join a union over a one-year period, using a subset of the CPS-MORG series. Results are broadly consistent with what I display in this chapter. See Rosenfeld and Kleykamp 2009 for more.

55. In past work, Rosenfeld and Kleykamp 2009: table 5, I conducted analyses limited to immigrants only, finding that non-Mexican immigrants had the highest odds of unionization and of joining a union over a one-year period.

56. I generated the predictions by setting all other covariates at their mean values, using the prchange and prvalue commands in Stata 11.

57. What explains these elevated probabilities? Similar to other quantitative research on this topic, the data I utilize cannot adjudicate between various hypotheses stemming from solidaristic theories of group mobilization. For example, we cannot tell precisely whether the elevated odds of unionization for non-Mexican Hispanic immigrants and their children derive from past experiences of labor organization or from organizers' ability to capitalize on ethnic-based solidarities.

58. Shaw 2008: 43. Shaw's book provides a comprehensive overview of Chavez's life and his leadership of the UFW.

59. Quoted in Shaw 2008: 100.

60. Wozniacka 2011.

61. Brazil 1991.

62. Bardacke 2011: 724.

63. Based on my analysis of the 1988 and 2009 CPS-MORG files.

7. The Ballot Box

1. *Time* 1944.

2. Quoted in Renshaw 1986: 18.

3. See Fraser 1991 for a discussion of Hillman's political roles during the New Deal.

4. Quoted in *Los Angeles Times* 1946.

5. Chang 2001: 380.

6. For the complete roll call, see *New York Times* 1966.

7. The repeal effort ultimately failed. See the *New York Times* 1965 for more.

8. Levine 1969.

9. Quoted in Matusow 1998: 160.

10. *Los Angeles Times* 1976.

11. Newton-Small 2008.

12. See my discussion of EFCA in Rosenfeld 2010b: 6.

13. Sands 2008.

14. The president did appoint pro-labor members to the NLRB and signed the Lilly Ledbetter Fair Pay Act into law in 2009, both of which benefited labor unions. However, unlike EFCA, neither move restructured the basic organizing framework that had stunted union growth for decades.

15. Gephardt would soon leave politics altogether and begin a new career as president of Gephardt Group, a lobbying firm. Prominent unions have accused one of the firm's major clients, Sodexo, of poor worker treatment, including substandard pay and dangerous working conditions. See Bogardus 2010.

16. Unions may also boost turnout by motivating nonmembers to vote (the "indirect effects" of unions on voting). In my prior work I find no evidence of indirect effects in recent elections. See Rosenfeld 2010a for more.

17. For just a few examples, see Galloway 2004 and Milbank 2004. Recent research (Claasen and Povtak 2010: table 7) has found that the much-heralded Evangelical effect was attributable largely to rising education and income levels among white Evangelicals. White Evangelicals flocked to the polls in unprecedented numbers in 2004, as the nation's newspapers and magazines suggested. But they did so largely because they were richer and more educated than in past election cycles. Still, as I will demonstrate, church attendance remains a powerful predictor of voter turnout.

18. See Leighley and Nagler 2007: 430.

19. This series begins in 1984 because that is the first election year in which the CPS-November files included questions about both voting and union membership.

20. Calculated by taking the difference between the 2008 level (80.6 percent) and the 1984 level (65.6 percent) and dividing by the 1984 level.

21. Lichtenstein 2002: 46.

22. And of course unions' political efforts do not end at the close of every election cycle. The discussion in Chapter 2 of labor's lobbying efforts to reclassify home-care aides as public-sector employees makes clear that unions engage in a range of political activities, some of which are only tangentially related to elections, and some of which are completely unconnected to elections. This chapter focuses on labor's election-related efforts.

23. Dray 2010: 488.

24. Masters 2004: table 12.

25. Freeman 2003: 16.

26. For a discussion of the variables included in the models, see the Data and Methods Appendix.

27. The CPS-November series and NES rely on respondents' self-reports. If union members or public-sector employees systematically exaggerate their electoral participation relative to others, the results of this analysis may be biased. Existing research demonstrates that differences in voting behavior between union members and nonmembers and public-sector and private-sector workers remain similar in magnitude regardless of whether one examines self-reports or validated voter data. See Freeman 2003: appendix table B; Garand, Parkhurst, and Seoud 1991: 196.

28. Most of the estimates I provide are of union effects averaged across the 1984 to 2008 time frame. I include year fixed effects in the cross-year analyses in order to control for the influence of election-specific factors, such as the higher turnout rates during presidential contests.

29. See, for example, Freeman 2003: table 5.

30. The results displayed in the figure are derived from logistic regression models that include a sector × union interaction term. Propensity score matching models run on public-sector and private-sector workers separately produce substantively similar results.

31. I calculate the public-sector union vote premium by taking the difference in adjusted probabilities for union and nonunion government workers ($66.6-64.3=2.3$ percentage points).

32. For a classic investigation, see Olsen 1972. For more recent treatments, see Cassel 1999; McKenzie 2001.

33. Calculated by taking a weighted average of the four differentials shown in the figure, where the weights correspond to each educational category's fraction of the total sample.

34. These analyses control for union membership along with a set of demographic and geographic covariates available in the NES. See the Data and Methods Appendix for details.

35. Key correlates that I am unable to adjust for in the NES analyses include sector, occupation, industry, and metropolitan status.

36. In supplementary analyses I include controls for religiosity and religion. The size of the church attendance effects remain comparative to those displayed in the figure.

37. The exception being union members in "right-to-work" states, where unionization rates are comparatively low.

38. Gerber, Gruber, and Hungerman 2008.

39. Here too I am focusing mostly on the effects of churches with predominantly white memberships. African Americans tend to vote Democratic, whether frequent churchgoers or not.

40. For just a few examples, see Fletcher 2008 and Greenhouse 2008.

41. Andres 2008.

42. Sweeney's remarks during his postelection press briefing can be found at http://edit.aflcio.org/Press-Room/Press-Releases/ Remarks-by-AFL-CIO-President-John-Sweeney-AFL-CIO.

43. See, for example, Mullins and Maher's 2008 insightful investigative report in the *Wall Street Journal* on unions' election-related activities.

44. CNN's 2008 exit poll data can be found at http://www.cnn.com/ELECTION/2008/results/polls.main/, and its 2004 exit poll results can be found at http://www.cnn.com/ELECTION/2004/pages/results/states/US/P/00/epolls.0.html.

45. The only difference in the 2008 regression specification is the lack of year fixed effects, since I am focusing only on one election year's worth of data.

8. The Past as Prologue

1. Freeman and Medoff 1984: 251.

2. I explored this issue in greater detail in Chapter 3 and in my prior work with Bruce Western, Western and Rosenfeld 2011.

3. Bernstein 1960: 84.

4. Ibid.: 67.

5. Piketty and Saez 2003: Figure 9.

6. Douglas 1930: 546.

7. Quoted in Meyerson 2011.

8. The series excludes money earned from capital gains; including capital gains would result in a similar trend line with higher levels of inequality. Other measures of inequality would likewise produce a comparable trend line.

9. As indicated by country-level Gini coefficients, a commonly used inequality metric. See www.stats.oecd.org for more country-level comparisons of inequality and poverty. For this particular query, see http://stats.oecd.org/Index.aspx?QueryId=26067.

10. See Goldin and Katz 2008 for a historical analysis of the relationship between technological changes, education, and worker compensation in the United States.

11. Fernandez 2001.

12. For the full transcript of the speech, see http://www.pbs.org/newshour/convention96/floor_speeches/clinton_8-29.html.

13. Quoted in Abramowitz and Montgomery 2007.

14. Bernanke delivered this 2007 speech, "The Level and Distribution of Economic Well-Being," to the Greater Omaha Chamber of Commerce on February 6. For the complete transcript see http://www.federalreserve.gov/newsevents/speech/bernanke20070206a.htm.

15. Bernstein 1960: 68.

16. Douglas 1930: 179.

17. Tomlins 1979: table 1.

18. See, for example, this ominous advertisement warning that "if you think the economy is bad now, it could get worse" should EFCA pass: http://laborpains.org/2008/11/21/efac-launches-anti-efca-campaign-with-national-tv-ad/. The Employee Freedom Action Committee, an organization founded to attack politicians who supported EFCA, sponsored the ad in 2008.

19. Quoted in Kuhnhenn 2011.

20. Quoted in Seelye 2000.

21. Quoted in Reuters 1992.

22. Gage 2007.

23. Ibid.

24. See Gage 2009 for an in-depth investigation into the Morgan building bombing.

25. See Romer 1986: table 9; VanGiezen and Schwenk 2001.

26. For more on the intellectual edifice of the neoclassical revolt, and its lasting legacy, see Blyth 2002.

27. U.S. Council of Economic Advisers 2010: table B1.

28. Autor, Dorn, and Hanson 2012.

29. Hirsch 2008.

30. Hirsch 2007.

31. Belman and Voos 2006: 68.

32. Notable examples include Clawson 2003 and Ruth Milkman and Kim Voss's 2004 edited collection,.

33. Gallup poll. March 2011. For further details see http://www.gallup.com/poll/146921/americans-back-unions-governors-state-disputes.aspx.

34. For a more detailed discussion of this possible route to revitalization, see Western and Rosenfeld 2012.

35. Greenhouse 2012.

36. Quoted in *Knowledge@Wharton* 2012b.

37. Brady, Fullerton, and Cross 2010.

38. See Pfeffer 2007 for a discussion of the heterogeneity in managerial practices in the United States.

39. A full transcript of Obama's 2011 State of the Union address can be found at http://www.whitehouse.gov/the-press-office/2011/01/25/remarks-president-state-union-address.

Appendix

1. Portions of the following discussion are based on the online supplemental Data Appendix of my 2011 article with Bruce Western: Western and Rosenfeld 2011. See http://asr.sagepub.com/content/suppl/2011/08/01/76.4.513.DC1/western_online_supplement.pdf for a copy of the article's appendix.

2. See Rosenfeld 2006a for more details on the FMCS data and my procedure for merging it with the CPS-MORG series.

3. For estimates of union wage effects with and without imputed earners, see Hirsch and Schumacher 2004: table 6. For an analysis of how including imputed earners biases occupational wage inequality estimates, see Mouw and Kalleberg 2010: 413.

4. Hirsch and Schumacher 2004: table 2.

5. Lemieux 2006.

6. Hollister 2004.

7. DiNardo and Lee 2004; Lee and Mas 2009.

8. Eaton and Kriesky 2001.

9. Waddoups 1999.

10. Gittleman and Pierce 2007: 201.

11. See the Data and Methods Appendix of Rosenfeld and Kleykamp 2012 for further details.

12. Rosenfeld and Kleykamp 2012: table 2.

13. Freeman 1984; Hirsch and Schumacher 1998: 207.

14. Eren 2007.

15. Prior to 1977 the CPS-May series lacks a full set of state measures, identifying only twelve states and the District of Columbia, along with ten multistate groupings.

16. Specifically, the measurement error on the unionization variable will bias the union coefficient toward zero in models investigating health insurance outcomes. See Schmitt 2008: 9.

17. Shore-Sheppard 1996.

18. Rosenfeld 2006a.

19. Rubin 1986.

20. Ashenfelter, Johnson, and Pencavel 1972.

21. Wallace, Leicht, and Grant 1993.

22. Paldam 1983.

23. Rosenfeld and Kleykamp 2012: table 2.

24. Ibid.: 1488–1489.

25. Ibid.: 1484–1486.

26. Rosenfeld and Kleykamp 2009: figure 2, table 2.

27. In supplemental analyses I added a control for respondents' state-level unionization rate. The addition of a state-level variable to individual-level data introduces the potential for biased estimates in models that do not deal with the clustering of observations. For this reason, these models are adjusted for clustering by state. In no model was the state-level unionization coefficient significant.

28. See Rosenfeld 2010a for a similar estimation procedure of union vote premiums, except limited to elections between 1984 and 2006.

References

Abramowitz, Michael, and Lori Montgomery. 2007. "Bush Addresses Income Inequality." *Washington Post.* February 1.

Aguilera, Michael B., and Douglas S. Massey. 2003. "Social Capital and the Wages of Mexican Migrants: New Hypotheses and Tests." *Social Forces* 82:671–701.

Alba, Richard, and Victor Nee. 2003. *Remaking the American Mainstream: Assimilation and Contemporary Immigration.* Cambridge, MA: Harvard University Press.

Aldrich, Howard E., and Roger Waldinger. 1990. "Ethnicity and Entrepreneurship." *Annual Review of Sociology* 16:111–135.

Aldridge, Delores P. 1999. "Black Women and the New World Order: Toward a Fit in the Economic Marketplace." In *Latinas and African-American Women at Work,* edited by Irene Browne, 357–379. New York: Russell Sage Foundation.

Allen, Stephen G. 1994. "Developments in Collective Bargaining in Construction in the 1980s and 1990s." In *Contemporary Collective Bargaining in the Private Sector,* edited by Paula B. Voos, 411–445. Madison, WI: Industrial Relations Research Association.

Alvarado, Facundo, Anthony B. Atkinson, Thomas Piketty, and Emmanuel Saez. 2011. *The World Top Incomes Database,* http://topincomes.g-mond.parisschoolofeconomics.eu/.

Anderson, Karen Tucker. 1982. "Last Hired, First Fired: Black Women Workers during World War II." *Journal of American History* 69:82–97.

Andres, Gary. 2008. "Union Power: How to Navigate Political Potholes." *Washington Times.* December 18.

Arnesen, Eric. 1998. "Up from Exclusion: Black and White Workers, Race, and the State of Labor History." *Reviews in American History* 26:146–174.

———. 2003. "Specter of the Black Strikebreaker: Race, Employment, and Labor Activism in the Industrial Era." *Labor History* 44:319–335.

Ashenfelter, Orley, George E. Johnson, and John H. Pencavel. 1972. "Trade Unions and the Rate of Change of Money Wages in United States Manufacturing Industry." *Review of Economic Studies* 39:27–54.

Associated Press. 1986. "Troops Block Road; Strikers Are Replaced." February 4.

Autor, David H., David Dorn, and Gordon H. Hanson. 2012. "The China Syndrome: Local Labor Market Effects of Import Competition in the United States." National Bureau of Economic Research Working Paper 18054, National Bureau of Economic Research, Cambridge, MA.

Bardacke, Frank. 2011. *Trampling Out the Vintage: Cesar Chavez and the Two Souls of the United Farm Workers.* London: Verso.

Beck, E.M. 1980. "Labor Unionism and Racial Income Inequality: A Time-Series Analysis of the Post–World War II Period." *American Journal of Sociology* 85:791–814.

Belkin, Douglas, and Kris Maher. 2012. "Wisconsin Unions See Ranks Drop ahead of Recall Vote." *Wall Street Journal.* May 30.

Belman, Dale, and Paula B. Voos. 2006. "Union Wages and Union Decline: Evidence from the Construction Industry." *Industrial and Labor Relations Review* 60:67–87.

Bernstein, Irving. 1960. *The Lean Years: A History of the American Worker, 1920–1933.* Boston: Houghton Mifflin.

Blanchflower, David G. 2006. "International Patterns of Union Membership." *British Journal of Industrial Relations* 45:1–28.

Blanchflower, David G., and Alex Bryson. 2004. "What Effect Do Unions Have on Wages Now and Would Freeman and Medoff Be Surprised?" *Journal of Labor Research* 25:383–414.

Blyth, Mark. 2002. *Great Transformations: Economic Ideas and Institutional Change in the Twentieth Century.* New York: Cambridge University Press.

Bogardus, Kevin. 2010. "Former House Dem Leader Gephardt Hired as Lobbyist by Firm Battling SEIU." *The Hill.* June 15.

Boris, Eileen, and Jennifer Klein. 2010. "'Not Really a Worker': Home-Based Unions Challenged in Court." *Labor Notes.* October 19.

———. 2012. *Caring for America: Home Health Workers in the Shadow of the Welfare State.* New York: Oxford University Press.

Bound, John, and Laura Dresser. 1999. "Losing Ground: The Erosion of the Relative Earnings of African American Women during the 1980s." In *Latinas and African American Women at Work,* edited by Irene Browne, 61–104. New York: Russell Sage Foundation.

Bound, John, and Richard B. Freeman. 1992. "What Went Wrong? The Erosion of Relative Earnings and Employment among Young Black Men in the 1980s." *Quarterly Journal of Economics* 107:201–232.

Bound, John, and Harry Holzer. 2000. "Demand Shifts, Population Adjustments, and Labor Market Outcomes during the 1980s." *Journal of Labor Economics* 18:20–54.

Brady, David. 2007. "Institutional, Economic, or Solidaristic? Assessing Explanations for Unionization across Affluent Democracies." *Work and Occupations* 34:67–101.

Brady, David, Andrew S. Fullerton, and Jennifer Moren Cross. 2010. "More Than Just Nickels and Dimes: A Cross-National Analysis of Working Poverty in Affluent Democracies." *Social Problems* 57:559–585.

Brazil, Eric. 1991. "Fewer Jobs for Farm Workers: Lean Days for Salinas Valley Laborers." *San Francisco Examiner.* June 30.

Brecher, Jeremy. 2009. "The Decline of Strikes." In *Encyclopedia of Strikes in American History,* edited by Aaron Brenner, Benjamin Day, and Immanuel Ness, 72–80. Armonk, NY: M.E. Sharpe.

Bronfenbrenner, Kate. 2009. "Prepared Statement for the National Mediation Board." Technical report, national mediation board rule change hearing, National Mediation Board, Washington, DC.

Brueggemann, John, and Terry Boswell. 1998. "Realizing Solidarity: Sources of Interracial Unionism during the Great Depression." *Work and Occupations* 25:436–482.

Buchmueller, Thomas C., John DiNardo, and Robert G. Valletta. 2002. "Union Effects on Health Insurance Provision and Coverage in the United States." *Industrial and Labor Relations Review* 55:610–627.

———. 2004. "A Submerging Labor Market Institution? Unions and the Nonwage Aspects of Work." In *Emerging Labor Market Institutions for the Twenty-First Century,* edited by Richard B. Freeman, Joni Hersch, and Lawrence Mishel, 231–264. Chicago: University of Chicago Press.

Budd, John W. 2005. "The Effect of Unions on Employee Benefits: Updated Employer Expenditure Results." *Journal of Labor Research* 26:669–676.

Byrne, Dennis M., and Randall H. King. 1986. "Wildcat Strikes in U.S. Manufacturing, 1960–1977." *Journal of Labor Research* 7:387–401.

Cassel, Carol A. 1999. "Voluntary Associations, Churches, and Social Participation Theories of Turnout." *Social Science Quarterly* 80:504–517.

Catron, Peter. 2013. "Comment on Rosenfeld and Kleykamp, *ASR,* December 2009: Immigrant Unionization through the Great Recession." *American Sociological Review* 78:315–332.

Chang, Tracy F. 2001. "The Labour Vote in US National Elections, 1948–2000." *Political Quarterly* 72:375–385.

Claasen, Ryan L., and Andrew Povtak. 2010. "The Christian Right Thesis: Explaining Longitudinal Change in Participation among Evangelical Christians." *Journal of Politics* 72:2–15.

Clark, Kim. 1992. "Using the Replacement-Worker Weapon: Caterpillar." *Baltimore Sun.* April 19.

Clawson, Dan. 2003. *The Next Upsurge: Labor and the New Social Movements.* Ithaca, NY: Cornell University Press.

Cleeland, Nancy. 2002. "Flight Attendants Union Defeated at Delta." *Los Angeles Times.* February 2.

Cohen, Lizabeth. 1990. *Making a New Deal: Industrial Workers in Chicago, 1919–1939.* New York: Cambridge University Press.

Cooper, Rae, and Bradon Ellem. 2008. "The Neoliberal State, Trade Unions and Collective Bargaining in Australia." *British Journal of Industrial Relations* 46:532–554.

Cowie, Jefferson. 2010. *Stayin' Alive: The 1970s and the Last Days of the Working Class.* New York: New Press.

Cox, James C., and Ronald L. Oaxaca. 1982. "The Political Economy of Minimum Wage Legislation." *Economic Inquiry* 20:533–555.

Cramton, Peter, and Joseph Tracy. 1998. "The Use of Replacement Workers in Union Contract Negotiations: The U.S. Experience, 1980–1989." *Journal of Labor Economics* 16:667–701.

DiNardo, John, and David S. Lee. 2004. "Economic Impacts of New Unionization on Private Sector Employers: 1984–2001." *Quarterly Journal of Economics* 119:1383–1441.

Douglas, Paul H. 1930. *Real Wages in the United States, 1890–1926.* Boston: Houghton Mifflin.

Dray, Philip. 2010. *There Is Power in a Union: The Epic Story of Labor in America.* New York: Doubleday.

Early, Steve. 2006. "An Old Lesson Still Holds for Unions." *Boston Globe.* July 31.

Eaton, Adrienne E., and Jill Kriesky. 2001. "Union Organizing under Neutrality and Card Check Agreements." *Industrial and Labor Relations Review* 55:42–59.

Endicott, William. 1978. "Reagan Still Has Crowds with Him." *New York Times.* January 19.

Engelmann, Larry D. 1974. "'We Were the Poor People'—the Hormel Strike of 1933." *Labor History* 15:483–510.

Eren, Ozkan. 2007. "Measuring the Union-Nonunion Wage Gap Using Propensity Score Matching." *Industrial Relations* 46:766–780.

Esping-Andersen, Gosta. 1990. *The Three Worlds of Welfare Capitalism.* Princeton, NJ: Princeton University Press.

Fantasia, Rick. 1989. *Cultures of Solidarity: Consciousness, Action, and Contemporary American Workers.* Berkeley: University of California Press.

Fantasia, Rick, and Kim Voss. 2004. *Hard Work: Remaking the American Labor Movement.* Berkeley: University of California Press.

Farber, Henry S. 1999. "Union Success in Representation Elections: Why Does Unit Size Matter?" National Bureau of Economic Research Working Paper 7229, National Bureau of Economic Research, Cambridge, MA.

Farber, Henry S., and Helen Levy. 2000. "Recent Trends in Employer-Sponsored Health Insurance Coverage: Are Bad Jobs Getting Worse?" *Journal of Health Economics* 19:93–119.

Farber, Henry S., and Bruce Western. 2001. "Accounting for the Decline of Unions in the Private Sector, 1973–1998." *Journal of Labor Research* 22:459–485.

———. 2002. "Ronald Reagan and the Politics of Declining Union Organization." *British Journal of Industrial Relations* 40:385–401.

Fernandez, Roberto. 2001. "Skill-Biased Technological Change and Wage Inequality: Evidence from a Plant Retooling." *American Journal of Sociology* 107:273–320.

Fields, Reginald. 2011. "Ohio Voters Overwhelmingly Reject Issue 2, Dealing a Blow to Gov. John Kasich." *Cleveland Plain Dealer.* November 8.

Fisk, Catherine L., Daniel J. B. Mitchell, and Christopher L. Erickson. 2000. "Union Representation of Immigrant Janitors in Southern California: Economic and Legal Challenges." In *Organizing Immigrants: The Challenge for Unions in Contemporary California,* edited by Ruth Milkman, 199–224. Ithaca, NY: Cornell University Press.

Fletcher, Michael A. 2008. "Labor Seeks Election Rewards; Union Organizing Rights Could Be Early Obama Test." *Washington Post.* November 6.

Fones-Wolf, Elizabeth A. 1995. *Selling Free Enterprise: The Business Assault on Labor and Liberalism, 1945–1960.* Champaign: University of Illinois Press.

Foulkes, Fred K. 1980. *Personnel Policies in Large Nonunion Companies.* Englewood Cliffs, NJ: Prentice-Hall.

Frank, Thomas. 2008. "It's Time to Give Voters the Liberalism They Want." *Wall Street Journal.* November 19.

Franklin, Stephen. 2005. "Indiana to Be Battleground—Unions Fight Back after Governor Strips Them of Recognition." *Chicago Tribune.* June 17.

Fraser, Steven. 1991. *Labor Will Rule: Sidney Hillman and the Rise of American Labor.* New York: Free Press.

Freeman, Richard B. 1981. "The Effect of Unionism on Fringe Benefits." *Industrial and Labor Relations Review* 34:489–509.

———. 1984. "Longitudinal Analyses of the Effects of Trade Unions." *Journal of Labor Economics* 2:1–26.

———. 1988. "Contraction and Expansion: The Divergence of Private Sector and Public Sector Unionism in the United States." *Journal of Economic Perspectives* 2:63–88.

———. 2003. "What Do Unions Do to Voting?" National Bureau of Economic Research Working Paper 9992, National Bureau of Economic Research, Cambridge, MA.

———. 2007. "Do Workers Still Want Unions? *More Than Ever.*" EPI Briefing Paper 182, Economic Policy Institute, Washington, DC.

Freeman, Richard B., and Morris M. Kleiner. 1990. "Employer Behavior in the Face of Union Organizing Drives." *Industrial and Labor Relations Review* 43:351–365.

Freeman, Richard B., and James L. Medoff. 1984. *What Do Unions Do?* New York: Basic Books.

Freeman, Richard B., and Joel Rogers. 1999. *What Workers Want*. Ithaca, NY: Cornell University Press.

Frymer, Paul. 2008. *Black and Blue: African Americans, the Labor Movement, and the Decline of the Democratic Party*. Princeton, NJ: Princeton University Press.

Gage, Beverly. 2007. "The Rockefellers and the Angry Commoners." *Slate*. October 19.

———. 2009. *The Day Wall Street Exploded: A Story of America in Its First Age of Terror*. New York: Oxford University Press.

Galloway, Jim. 2004. "Religious Vote Fuels Victory for GOP." *Atlanta Journal-Constitution*. November 4.

Garand, James C., Catherine T. Parkhurst, and Rusanne Jourdan Seoud. 1991. "Bureaucrats, Policy Attitudes, and Political Behavior: Extension of the Bureau Voting Model of Government Growth." *Journal of Public Administration Research and Theory* 1:177–212.

Genoways, Ted. 2011. "The Spam Factory's Dirty Secret." *Mother Jones*. July/August.

Geoghegan, Thomas. 1991. *Which Side Are You On? Trying to Be for Labor When It's Flat on Its Back*. New York: Plume.

Gerber, Alan, Jonathan Gruber, and Daniel M. Hungerman. 2008. "Does Church Attendance Cause People to Vote? Using Blue Laws' Repeal to Estimate the Effect of Religiosity on Voter Turnout." National Bureau of Economic Research Working Paper 14303, National Bureau of Economic Research, Cambridge, MA.

Gittleman, Maury, and Brooks Pierce. 2007. "New Estimates of Union Wage Effects in the U.S." *Economics Letters* 95:198–202.

Glenn, Evelyn Nakano. 1985. "Racial Ethnic Women's Labor: The Intersection of Race, Gender and Class Oppression." *Review of Radical Political Economics* 17:86–108.

Godard, John. 2009. "The Exceptional Decline of the American Labor Movement." *Industrial and Labor Relations Review* 63:82–108.

Goldfield, Michael. 1987. *The Decline of Organized Labor in the United States*. Chicago: University of Chicago Press.

———. 1993. "Race and the CIO: The Possibilities for Racial Egalitarianism during the 1930s and 1940s." *International Labor and Working Class History* 44:1–32.

Goldin, Claudia, and Lawrence F. Katz. 2008. *The Race between Education and Technology*. Cambridge, MA: Harvard University Press.

Greenhouse, Steven. 1999. "In Biggest Drive since 1937, Union Gains a Victory." *New York Times.* February 26.

———. 2000. "Immigrants Flock to Union Banner at a Forum." *New York Times.* April 2.

———. 2003. "Two Sides Seem Entrenched in Supermarket Dispute." *New York Times.* November 10.

———. 2008. "After Push for Obama, Unions Seek New Rules." *New York Times.* November 8.

———. 2011. "Strained States Turning to Laws to Curb Labor Unions." *New York Times.* January 3.

———. 2012. "At Caterpillar, Pressing Labor while Business Booms." *New York Times.* July 22.

Greenhouse, Steven, and Reed Abelson. 2011. "Wal-Mart Cuts Some Health Care Benefits." *New York Times.* October 20.

Grodsky, Eric, and Devah Pager. 2001. "The Structure of Disadvantage: Individual and Occupational Determinants of the Black-White Wage Gap." *American Sociological Review* 66:542–567.

Hacker, Jacob S., and Paul Pierson. 2010. *Winner-Take-All Politics: How Washington Made the Rich Richer—and Turned Its Back on the Middle Class.* New York: Simon & Schuster.

Hall, Peter A., and David Soskice. 2001. *Varieties of Capitalism: The Institutional Foundations of Comparative Advantage.* New York: Oxford University Press.

Herbst, Moira. 2010. "Obama's 'Race to the Top' Education Fund Draws Fewer States amid Criticism." *Business Week.* June 2.

Hibbs, Douglas A., Jr. 1978. "On the Political Economy of Long-Run Trends in Strike Activity." *British Journal of Political Science* 8:153–175.

Hill, Herbert. 1996. "The Problem of Race in American Labor History." *Reviews in American History* 24:189–208.

Hirsch, Barry T. 2004. "Reconsidering Union Wage Effects: Surveying New Evidence on an Old Topic." *Journal of Labor Research* 25:233–266.

———. 2007. "What Do Unions Do for Economic Performance?" In *What Do Unions Do? A Twenty Year Perspective,* edited by James T. Bennett and Bruce E. Kaufman, 193–237. New Brunswick, NJ: Transaction Publishers.

———. 2008. "Sluggish Institutions in a Dynamic World: Can Unions and Industrial Competition Coexist?" *Journal of Economic Perspectives* 22:153–176.

Hirsch, Barry T., and John T. Addison. 1986. *The Economic Analysis of Unions: New Approaches and Evidence.* Boston: Allen & Unwin.

Hirsch, Barry T., and David A. Macpherson. 2003. "Union Membership and Coverage Database from the Current Population Survey: Note." *Industrial and Labor Relations Review* 56:349–354.

Hirsch, Barry T., and Edward J. Schumacher. 1998. "Unions, Wages, and Skills." *Journal of Human Resources* 33:201–219.

———. 2004. "Match Bias in Wage Gap Estimates Due to Earnings Imputation." *Journal of Labor Economics* 22:689–722.

Hollister, Matissa N. 2004. "Does Firm Size Matter Anymore? The New Economy and Firm Size Wage Effects." *American Sociological Review* 69:659–676.

Honey, Michael Keith. 1999. *Black Workers Remember: An Oral History of Segregation, Unionism, and the Freedom Struggle.* Berkeley: University of California Press.

Hourwich, Isaac A. 1912. *Immigration and Labor: The Economic Aspects of European Immigration to the United States.* New York: G. P. Putnam's Sons.

Jacobs, James B. 2006. *Mobsters, Unions, and Feds: The Mafia and the American Labor Movement.* New York: NYU Press.

Jones, Tim. 2011. "Taking a Page from the Republican Playbook: Illinois State Democrats Rumble with the Unions over Benefits." *Bloomberg Businessweek.* May 12.

Kalleberg, Arne L., Michael Wallace, and Lawrence E. Raffalovich. 1984. "Accounting for Labor's Share: Class and Income Distribution in the Printing Industry." *Industrial and Labor Relations Review* 37:386–402.

Katznelson, Ira, Kim Geiger, and Daniel Kryder. 1993. "Limiting Liberalism: The Southern Veto in Congress, 1933–1950." *Political Science Quarterly* 108:283–306.

Kaufman, Bruce E. 1982. "The Determinants of Strikes in the United States, 1900–1977." *Industrial and Labor Relations Review* 35:473–490.

———. 1992. "Research on Strike Models and Outcomes in the 1980s: Accomplishments and Shortcomings." In *Research Frontiers in Industrial Relations and Human Resources,* edited by David Lewin, Olivia S. Mitchell, and Peter D. Sherer, 77–130. Ithaca, NY: Cornell University Press.

Kearney, Richard C. 2001. *Labor Relations in the Public Sector.* New York: Marcel Dekker Inc.

Kelleher, James. 2011. "Wisconsin Passes Anti-Union Law in Labor Rebuke." Reuters. March 10.

Kennedy, Howard. 1960. "Film Work to Resume as Strike Ends." *Los Angeles Times.* April 9.

Kinnard, Meg. 2012. "Gov. Nikki Haley Wins Appeal in a Lawsuit over Anti-Union Remarks." Associated Press. May 4.

Kleiner, Morris M. 2001. "Intensity of Management Resistance: Understanding the Decline of Unionization in the Private Sector." *Journal of Labor Research* 22:519–540.

Knowledge@Wharton. 2012a. "Declining Employee Loyalty: A Casualty of the New Workplace." May 9.

———. 2012b. "State of the Unions: What it Means for Workers—and Everyone Else." May 9.

Korpi, Walter, and Michael Shalev. 1979. "Strikes, Industrial Relations, and Class Conflict in Capitalist Societies." *British Journal of Sociology* 30:164–187.

———. 1980. "Strikes, Power, and Politics in the Western Nations, 1900–1976." *Political Power and Social Theory* 1:301–334.

Korstad, Robert. 1993. "The Possibilities for Racial Egalitarianism: Context Matters." *International Labor and Working-Class History* 44:41–44.

Korstad, Robert, and Nelson Lichtenstein. 1988. "Opportunities Found and Lost: Labor, Radicals, and the Early Civil Rights Movement." *Journal of American History* 75:786–811.

Kotz, Nick. 1977. "Can Labor's Tired Leaders Deal with a Troubled Movement?" *New York Times Magazine*. September 4.

Kuhnhenn, Jim. 2011. "Tax the Rich, Obama Says; Class Warfare, Says GOP." Associated Press. September 19.

Lambert, Josiah Bartlett. 2005. *"If the Workers Took a Notion": The Right to Strike and American Political Development*. Ithaca, NY: Cornell University Press.

Lee, Cheol-Sung. 2005. "International Migration, Deindustrialization and Union Decline in 16 Affluent OECD Countries, 1962–1997." *Social Forces* 84:71–88.

Lee, David, and Alexandre Mas. 2009. "Long-Run Impacts of Unions on Firms: New Evidence from Financial Markets, 1961–1999." National Bureau of Economic Research Working Paper 14709, National Bureau of Economic Research, Cambridge, MA.

Leicht, Kevin T. 1989. "On the Estimation of Union Threat Effects." *American Sociological Review* 54:1035–1057.

Leighley, Jan E., and Jonathan Nagler. 2007. "Unions, Voter Turnout, and Class Bias in the U.S. Electorate, 1964–2004." *Journal of Politics* 69:430–441.

Lemieux, Thomas. 2006. "Increasing Residual Wage Inequality: Composition Effects, Noisy Data, or Rising Demand for Skill?" *American Economic Review* 96:461–498.

Lemieux, Thomas, W. Bentley MacLeod, and Daniel Parent. 2009. "Performance Pay and Wage Inequality." *Quarterly Journal of Economics* 124:1–49.

LeRoy, Michael H. 1995. "The Changing Character of Strikes Involving Permanent Striker Replacements, 1935–1990." *Journal of Labor Research* 16:423–437.

Levenstein, Harvey A. 1968. "The AFL and Mexican Immigration in the 1920s: An Experiment in Labor Diplomacy." *Hispanic American Historical Review* 48:206–219.

Levine, Richard J. 1969. "Nixon's Union Man: Usery Moves Smoothly from Machinists Post to Role as Labor Aide." *Wall Street Journal*. December 2.

Lichtenstein, Nelson. 1995. *Walter Reuther: The Most Dangerous Man in Detroit*. New York: Basic Books.

———. 2002. *State of the Union: A Century of American Labor.* Princeton, NJ: Princeton University Press.

———. 2005. "Wal-Mart and the New World Order: A Template for Twenty-First Century Capitalism?" *New Labor Forum* 14:21–30.

Lieberson, Stanley. 1980. *A Piece of the Pie: Blacks and White Immigrants since 1880.* Berkeley: University of California Press.

Lofaso, Anne Marie. 2011. "Promises, Promises: Assessing the Obama Administration's Record on Labor Reform." *New Labor Forum* 20:65–72.

Logan, John. 2008. "Permanent Replacements and the End of Labor's 'Only True Weapon.'" *International Labor and Working-Class History* 74:171–192.

Los Angeles Times. 1946. "Sidney Hillman Dies in New York: Humble Immigrant Rose to World Renown as Militant Union Leader." July 11.

———. 1976. "Usery Nominated Labor Secretary; Meany Approves." January 22.

Mak, Tim. 2011. "Poll: Union Divide Hits Record." *Politico.* September 1.

Martin, Philip, and Elizabeth Midgley. 2006. "Immigration: Shaping and Reshaping America: 2nd Edition." *Population Bulletin* 61:1–28.

Masters, Marick F. 2004. "Unions in the 2000 Election: A Strategic Choice Perspective." *Journal of Labor Research* 25:139–182.

Matusow, Allen J. 1998. *Nixon's Economy: Boom, Busts, Dollars, and Votes.* Lawrence: University Press of Kansas.

Mayer, Gerald. 2004. "Union Membership Trends in the United States." Federal Publications Paper 174, Cornell University ILR School, Ithaca, NY.

Maynard, Micheline. 2008. "U.A.W. at Center of Dispute over Bailout." *New York Times.* December 12.

McCall, Leslie. 2001. "Sources of Racial Wage Inequality in Metropolitan Labor Markets: Racial, Ethnic, and Gender Differences." *American Sociological Review* 66:520–541.

McCammon, Holly J. 2001. "Labor's Legal Mobilization: Why and When Do Workers File Unfair Labor Practices?" *Work and Occupations* 28:143–175.

McCartin, Joseph A. 2011. *Collision Course: Ronald Reagan, the Air Traffic Controllers, and the Strike That Changed America.* New York: Oxford University Press.

McKenzie, Brian D. 2001. "Self-Selection, Church Attendance, and Local Civic Participation." *Journal for the Scientific Study of Religion* 40:479–488.

Meany, George. 1955. "Meany Looks into Labor's Future: As the American Federation of Labor and the Congress of Industrial Organizations Become the United A.F.L.-C.I.O, Its Leader Defines What Its Role Should and Can Be." *New York Times Magazine.* December 4.

Meyerson, Harold. 2011. "Corporate America's Chokehold on Wages." *Washington Post.* July 19.

Milbank, Dana. 2004. "For the President, a Vote of Full Faith and Credit: Evangelical Christians Shed Their Reluctance to Mix Religion and Politics on Election Day." *Washington Post*. November 7.

Milkman, Ruth. 2000. *Organizing Immigrants: The Challenge for Unions in Contemporary California*. Ithaca, NY: Cornell University Press.

———. 2006. *L.A. Story: Immigrant Workers and the Future of the U.S. Labor Movement*. New York: Russell Sage Foundation.

Milkman, Ruth, and Kim Voss. 2004. *Rebuilding Labor: Organizing and Organizers in the New Union Movement*. Ithaca, NY: Cornell University Press.

Mills, C. Wright, and Mildred Atkinson. 1945. "The Trade Union Leader: A Collective Portrait." *Public Opinion Quarterly* 9:158–175.

Minchin, Timothy J. 1999. *Hiring the Black Worker: The Racial Integration of the Southern Textile Industry, 1960–1980*. Chapel Hill: University of North Carolina Press.

Mink, Gwendolyn. 1986. *Old Labor and New Immigrants in American Political Development: Union, Party, and State, 1875–1920*. Ithaca, NY: Cornell University Press.

Mishel, Lawrence. 2011. "The Overselling of Education." *American Prospect*. February 7.

Montgomery, David. 1984. "Immigrants, Industrial Unions, and Social Reconstruction in the United States, 1916–1923." *Labour / Le Travail* 13:101–113.

———. 1987. *The Fall of the House of Labor: The Workplace, the State, and American Labor Activism, 1865–1925*. Cambridge, UK: Cambridge University Press.

Moody, Kim. 1988. *An Injury to All: The Decline of American Unionism*. New York: Verso Press.

Morawska, Ewa. 1985. *For Bread with Butter: Life-Worlds of East Central Europeans in Johnstown, Pennsylvania, 1890–1940*. Cambridge, UK: Cambridge University Press.

Mouw, Ted, and Arne Kalleberg. 2010. "Occupations and the Structure of Wage Inequality in the United States, 1980s to 2000s." *American Sociological Review* 75:402–431.

Mullins, Brody, and Kris Maher. 2008. "Labor Woos Whites for Obama: Labor's Election Year Push." *Wall Street Journal*. October 7.

Neumark, David, and Michael L. Wachter. 1995. "Union Effects on Nonunion Wages: Evidence from Panel Data on Industries and Cities." *Industrial and Labor Relations Review* 49:20–38.

Newburger, Eric, and Thomas Gryn. 2009. "The Foreign-Born Labor Force in the United States: 2007." *American Community Survey Reports*, U.S. Census Bureau, Washington DC.

Newton-Small, Jay. 2008. "Will Obama Deliver for Organized Labor?" *Time*. December 22.

New York Times. 1907. "All-Day Riots End Longshore Strike." June 15.
———. 1908. "Strikers Stone a Mayor." November 25.
———. 1912. "Ugly Temper from Start in Utah Copper Strike." September 19.
———. 1919. "Wyoming Foreigners Threaten Americans." November 19.
———. 1964. "Text of Goldwater's Speech Formally Opening Presidential Campaign." September 4.
———. 1965. "Senate Unit Vote Backs Union Shop." August 13.
———. 1966. "House Roll-Call on Minimum Wage Bill." September 8.
———. 1976. "Excerpts from the Address by Dole to the Convention." August 20.
———. 1981. "Text of Reagan Talk on Strike." August 4.
Northrup, Herbert R., and John A. Larson. 1979. *The Impact of the AT&T-EEO Consent Decree.* University of Pennsylvania Industrial Research Unit.
OECD. 2009. *Government at a Glance 2009.* Organisation for Economic Co-operation and Development Publications.
Olsen, Marvin E. 1972. "Social Participation and Voting Turnout: A Multivariate Analysis." *American Sociological Review* 37:317–333.
Olzak, Susan. 1989. "Labor Unrest, Immigration, and Ethnic Conflict in Urban America, 1880–1914." *American Journal of Sociology* 94:1303–1333.
Paldam, Martin. 1983. "Industrial Conflicts and Economic Conditions: A Comparative Empirical Investigation." *European Economic Review* 20:231–256.
Pawel, Miriam. 2006. "Former Chavez Ally Took His Own Path." *Los Angeles Times.* January 11.
———. 2009. *The Union of Their Dreams: Power, Hope, and Struggle in Cesar Chavez's Farm Worker Movement.* New York: Bloomsbury Press.
Pencavel, John. 2005. "Unionism Viewed Internationally." *Journal of Labor Research* 26:65–97.
Perlman, Selig. 1928. *A Theory of the Labor Movement.* New York: Macmillan.
Pettit, Becky, and Stephanie Ewert. 2009. "Employment Gains and Wage Declines: The Erosion of Black Women's Relative Wages since 1980." *Demography* 46:469–492.
Pfeffer, Jeffrey. 2007. "Human Resources from an Organizational Behavior Perspective: Some Paradoxes Explained." *Journal of Economic Perspectives* 21:115–34.
Piketty, Thomas, and Emmanuel Saez. 2003. "Income Inequality in the United States, 1913–1998." *Quarterly Journal of Economics* 118:1–39.
Piore, Michael J. 1979. Cambridge, UK: *Birds of Passage: Migrant Labor and Industrial Societies.* Cambridge University Press.
Preston, Darrell. 2011. "Christie Says 'Sue Me' as Pensioners Challenge Cuts." *Bloomberg News.* February 2.
Ramsey, Mike. 2011. "VW Chops Labor Costs in U.S." *Wall Street Journal.* May 23.
Raynor, Bruce. 2006. "Losing by Winning." *American Prospect Online.* December 21.

Rees, Albert. 1952. "Industrial Conflict and Business Fluctuations." *Journal of Political Economy* 60:371–82.

Renshaw, Patrick. 1986. "Organized Labour and the United States War Economy, 1939–1945." *Journal of Contemporary History* 21:3–22.

Reuters. 1992. "The 1992 Campaign; Excerpts from Bush's Speech on Clinton's Record." September 23.

Romer, Christina. 1986. "Spurious Volatility in Historical Unemployment Data." *Journal of Political Economy* 94:1–37.

Rosenblum, Jonathan D. 1995. *Copper Crucible: How the Arizona Miners' Strike of 1983 Recast Labor-Management Relations in America.* 2nd ed. Ithaca, NY: ILR Press.

Rosenfeld, Jake. 2006a. "Desperate Measures: Strikes and Wages in Post-Accord America." *Social Forces* 85:235–265.

———. 2006b. "Widening the Gap: The Effect of Declining Unionization on Managerial and Worker Pay, 1983–2000." *Research in Social Stratification and Mobility* 24:223–238.

———. 2010a. "Economic Determinants of Voting in an Era of Union Decline." *Social Science Quarterly* 91:379–395.

———. 2010b. "Little Labor: How Union Decline Is Changing the American Landscape." *Pathways.* Summer.

Rosenfeld, Jake, and Meredith Kleykamp. 2009. "Hispanics and Organized Labor in the United States, 1973–2007." *American Sociological Review* 74:916–937.

———. 2012. "Organized Labor and Racial Wage Inequality in the United States." *American Journal of Sociology* 117:1460–1502.

Rubin, Beth A. 1986. "Class Struggle American Style: Unions, Strikes, and Wages." *American Sociological Review* 51:618–633.

Sands, David R. 2008. "Labor's 'Priority' on Back Burner; Hill to Defer on 'Card Check.'" *Washington Times.* December 29.

Saxton, Alexander. 1975. *The Indispensable Enemy: Labor and the Anti-Chinese Movement in California.* Berkeley: University of California Press.

Schaper, David. 2011. "Wisconsin Budget-Repair Bill Exempts Public Safety Unions." *NPR.org.* February 22.

Schmitt, John. 2008. "Unions and Upward Mobility for Young Workers." Center for Economic and Policy Research Report, Washington, DC.

Seelye, Katharine Q. 2000. "The 2000 Campaign: The Vice President; Gore Accuses Bush of Waging 'Class Warfare.'" *New York Times.* November 1.

Serrin, William. 1983. "Auto Union Shares the Industry's Woes." *New York Times.* May 15.

Shaw, Randy. 2007. "SF Weekly Reaches New Low in Hit Piece on SEIU." *BeyondChron.com.* April 16.

———. 2008. *Beyond the Fields: Cesar Chavez, the UFW, and the Struggle for Justice in the 21st Century.* Berkeley: University of California Press.

Shore-Sheppard, Lara. 1996. "Medicaid and Health Insurance for Children: Essays in Empirical Economics." PhD dissertation, Princeton University.

Shostak, Arthur B., and David Skocik. 1986. *The Air Controllers' Controversy: Lessons from the PATCO Strike.* New York: Human Sciences Press.

Sites, William, and Virginia Parks. 2011. "What Do We Really Know about Racial Inequality? Labor Markets, Politics, and the Historical Basis of Black Economic Fortunes." *Politics & Society* 39:40–73.

Skeels, Jack W., Paul McGrath, and Gangadha Arshanapalli. 1988. "The Importance of Strike Size in Strike Research." *Industrial and Labor Relations Review* 41:582–591.

Smith, Ben, and Maggie Haberman. 2010. "Pols Turn on Labor Unions." *Politico.* June 6.

Smith, James P., and Michael P. Ward. 1985. "Times-Series Growth in the Female Labor Force." *Journal of Labor Economics* 3:S59–S90.

Smith, Ryan A. 1999. "Racial Differences in Access to Hierarchical Authority: An Analysis of Change over Time, 1972–1994." *Sociological Quarterly* 40:367–395.

Stein, Judith. 1998. *Running Steel, Running America: Race, Economic Policy, and the Decline of Liberalism.* Chapel Hill: University of North Carolina Press.

Stepan-Norris, Judith, and Maurice Zeitlin. 2003. *Left Out: Reds and America's Industrial Unions.* Cambridge, UK: Cambridge University Press.

Stetson, Damon. 1958. "Ford and U.A.W. Set 3-Year Pact; Brief Strike Ends." *New York Times.* September 18.

Sugrue, Thomas J. 2005. *The Origins of the Urban Crisis: Race and Inequality in Postwar Detroit.* Princeton, NJ: Princeton University Press.

Surowiecki, James. 2011. "State of the Unions." *New Yorker.* January 17.

Swenson, Peter A. 2002. *Capitalists against Markets: The Making of Labor Markets and Welfare States in the United States and Sweden.* New York: Oxford University Press.

Telles, Edward E., and Vilma Ortiz. 2008. *Generations of Exclusion: Mexican Americans, Assimilation, and Race.* New York: Russell Sage Foundation.

Thurston, Scott. 2000. "Delta Air Lines Union Drive on Final Approach This Week." *Atlanta Journal and Constitution.* February 27.

Time. 1944. "The Election: The Side Issues." November 13.

Tomlins, Christopher L. 1979. "AFL Unions in the 1930s: Their Performance in Historical Perspective." *Journal of American History* 65:1021–1042.

Towers, Brian. 1989. "Running the Gauntlet: British Trade Unions under Thatcher, 1979–1988." *Industrial and Labor Relations Review* 42:163–188.

Trottman, Melanie. 2008. "Showdown Looms over 'Card Check' Union Drives." *Wall Street Journal.* November 29.

Troy, Leo. 1965. *Trade Union Membership, 1897–1962.* New York: National Bureau of Economic Research Books.

Tuttle, William M., Jr. 1969. "Labor Conflict and Racial Violence: The Black Worker in Chicago, 1894–1919." *Labor History* 10:408–432.

U.S. Council of Economic Advisers. 2010. "Economic Report of the President." Technical report, U.S. Government Printing Office, Washington, DC.

U.S. News & World Report. 1972. "U.S. Needs 30,000 New Jobs a Week Just to Break Even." February 21.

VanGiezen, Robert, and Albert E. Schwenk. 2001. "Compensation from before World War I through the Great Depression." *Compensation and Working Conditions.* Fall.

Visser, Jelle. 2006. "Union Membership Statistics in 24 Countries." *Monthly Labor Review* 129:38–49.

Visser, Jelle. 2009. *The ICTWSS database: Database on Institutional Characteristics of Trade Unions, Wage Setting, State Intervention and Social Pacts in 34 Countries between 1960 and 2007, Version 2.* Amsterdam: Amsterdam Institute for Advanced Labour Studies, University of Amsterdam.

Waddoups, C. Jeffrey. 1999. "Union Wage Effects in Nevada's Hotel and Casino Industry." *Industrial Relations* 38:577–583.

Waldinger, Roger, and Claudia Der-Martirosian. 2000. "Immigrant Workers and American Labor: Challenge . . . or Disaster?" In *Organizing Immigrants: The Challenge for Unions in Contemporary California,* edited by Ruth Milkman, 49–80. Ithaca, NY: Cornell University Press.

Waldinger, Roger, Chris Erickson, Ruth Milkman, Daniel J.B. Mitchell, Abel Valenzuela, Kent Wong, and Maurice Zeitlin. 1998. "Helots No More: A Case Study of the Justice for Janitors Campaign in Los Angeles." In *Organizing to Win: New Research on Union Strategies,* edited by Kate Bronfenbrenner, Sheldon Friedman, Richard W. Hurd, Rudolph A. Oswald, and Ronald L. Seeber, 102–120. Ithaca, NY: Cornell University Press.

Wallace, Michael. 1989. "Aggressive Economism, Defensive Control: Contours of American Labour Militancy, 1947–81." *Economic and Industrial Democracy* 10:7–34.

Wallace, Michael, Kevin T. Leicht, and Don Sherman Grant II. 1993. "Positional Power, Class, and Individual Earnings Inequality: Advancing New Structuralist Explanations." *Sociological Quarterly* 34:85–109.

Wall Street Journal. 1967. "Rubber Firms' Output Climbs as Last Strike of 'Big Five' Is Settled." July 28.

———. 2010. "The Public-Union Ascendancy." February 3.

Walsh, Mary Williams. 2011. "A Path Is Sought for States to Escape Their Debt Burdens." *New York Times.* January 20.

Weber, Max. 1947. *The Theory of Economic and Social Organization.* New York: Oxford University Press.

Western, Bruce. 1993. "Postwar Unionization in Eighteen Advanced Capitalist Countries." *American Sociological Review* 58:266–282.

———. 1994. "Institutional Mechanisms for Unionization in Sixteen OECD Countries: An Analysis of Social Survey Data." *Social Forces* 73:497–519.

———. 1995. "A Comparative Study of Working-Class Disorganization: Union Decline in Eighteen Advanced Capitalist Countries." *American Sociological Review* 60:179–201.

Western, Bruce, and Jake Rosenfeld. 2011. "Unions, Norms, and the Rise in U.S. Wage Inequality." *American Sociological Review* 76:513–537.

———. 2012. "Workers of the World Divide." *Foreign Affairs* 91:88–99.

Wilson, William Julius. 1987. *The Truly Disadvantaged: The Inner City, the Underclass, and Public Policy.* Chicago: University of Chicago Press.

Wolman, Leo. 1936. *Ebb and Flow in Trade Unionism*. New York: National Bureau of Economic Research Books.

Wozniacka, Gosia. 2011. "United Farm Workers Fight Dwindling Membership." Associated Press. April 20.

Wyatt, Edward, and Steven Greenhouse. 2011. "Worry Grows over Delays in F.A.A. Pay." *New York Times.* August 3.

Yellowitz, Irwin. 1977. *Industrialization and the American Labor Movement, 1850–1900.* Port Washington, NY: Kennikat Press.

Yeselson, Richard. 2012. "Not with a Bang, but a Whimper: The Long, Slow Death Spiral of America's Labor Movement." *New Republic.* June 6.

Zimmerman, Ann. 2004. "Costco's Dilemma: Be Kind to Its Workers, or Wall Street?" *Wall Street Journal.* March 26.

Zipp, John F. 1994. "Government Employment and Black-White Earnings Inequality, 1980–1990." *Social Problems* 41:363–382.

Acknowledgments

The inspiration for this project came a decade ago during a conversation with Bruce Western about organized labor's relevance in the contemporary United States. He insisted that inside and outside of the academy attention would soon turn to the decline of the labor movement and what labor's demise portended for wage stagnation and widening inequality. It took a while, but subsequent events—ranging from the turmoil in Wisconsin over collective bargaining in the public sector, to the Occupy Wall Street protests that helped prod the nation's press to focus on growing economic inequity—proved him right. At the time I didn't believe him, but nevertheless did what I had learned was always the best course of action: I took his advice, and embarked on a project investigating the major consequences of labor's collapse in the United States. This book is the cornerstone of the project.

Since that talk, Bruce has provided invaluable guidance and training in the various dimensions of our craft. Above all, he has served as a model intellectual, one whose own work provides a constant reminder of the promise of what social science can be when done well. Meredith Kleykamp's imprint on all of my work is substantial; this book is no exception. Her combination of a critical eye and methodological sophistication made this a much better book. Finally, there would be no book were it not for the excellent assistance of Jennifer Laird. More than anyone else, Jennifer was a partner in this effort, developing most of the visuals and offering advice on all aspects of the project.

I am indebted to numerous other individuals for their contributions to this book. My colleagues at the University of Washington gave me the freedom to see the project through to fruition. Becky Pettit, Bob Crutchfield, and Stewart Tolnay provided the encouragement to develop the book, offering helpful advice on structuring the project. I thank Michael Aronson at Harvard University Press for his initial interest in the book and for his guidance along the way. Two anonymous reviewers gave the original manuscript a thorough read; the final version is substantially improved thanks to their efforts.

My occupation is a family affair, and this book bears my family's influence. Sam Rosenfeld, resident historian, provided a constant reminder of the importance of historically grounded social science. Our conversations opened up new lines of inquiry while steering me clear of dead ends. No detail was too minor to escape his critical eye, and his final read of the manuscript helped clean away unnecessary debris. Soon I hope to repay the favor by providing whatever assistance I can to his own work. Richard Rosenfeld's constant confidence in my research propelled the project when my own energy was flagging. I've cherished all his advice and support. The thanking of a spouse for putting up with the author is a well-worn trope in academic books, and one that I had promised myself I would avoid. Alas, when the time came the temptation proved too great, the truth of the sentiment too powerful. Erin McGaughey absorbed much of the author's frustrations and obsessions with this project with her usual cheer, grace, and faith. In return, I can only offer my undying love.

While all the analyses in the book are new, parts of a few chapters are based on previously published journal articles. The analyses in Chapter 5 draw on my 2012 article with Meredith Kleykamp, "Organized Labor and Racial Wage Inequality in the United States," *American Journal of Sociology* 117: 1460–1502. Chapter 6 incorporates a brief excerpt from my 2009 article with Meredith Kleykamp, "Hispanics and Organized Labor in the United States, 1973–2007," *American Sociological Review* 74: 916–937. For the union and voter turnout analyses in the first half of Chapter 7 I adapt parts of my 2010 article, "Economic Determinants of Voting in an Era of Union Decline," *Social Science Quarterly* 91: 379–395. Finally, two brief portions of the Introduction were first published in 2010 as "Little Labor: How Union Decline Is Changing the American Landscape," *Pathways*, Summer: 3–6.

Index